NELLA LAST'S PEACE

W9-BNR-300

Robert Malcolmson is Professor Emeritus of history at Queen's University, Kingston, Canada. **Patricia Malcolmson** is a historian and a former executive in the Ontario public service. They live in Cobourg, Ontario.

The Mass Observation Archive at the University of Sussex holds the papers of the British social research organisation Mass Observation. The papers from the original phase cover the years 1937 until the early 1950s and provide an especially rich historical resource on civilian life during the Second World War. New collections relating to everyday life in the UK in the 20th and 21st century have been added to the original collection since the Archive was established at Sussex in 1970.

PRAISE FOR *Nella Last's Peace*

'Anyone who imagines there couldn't be any drama in Nella's diaries because the war was over would be gravely mistaken. I found myself captivated – whether smiling or holding my breath in anticipation. What a treat.' Margaret Forster

'A vivid, intimate account of austerity Britain. Superb.' David Kynaston

'Compassionate, gossipy and observant ... She is brave, lovable and a born writer.' Virginia Nicholson

'Nella's eye for detail and penetrating interest in the people around her make her diary a social document of extraordinary interest and value.' D. J. Taylor

ALSO AVAILABLE

Nella Last's War
The Second World War diaries of Housewife, 49

'I relished it ... her personality is so powerful ... There are so many things to admire about her' Margaret Forster

'A classic of wartime literature ... highly engaging, very moving. All Home Front life is here, especially the kitchen sink' Simon Garfield

NELLA LAST'S PEACE

The post-war diaries of *Housewife, 49*

Edited by
PATRICIA AND ROBERT MALCOLMSON

PROFILE BOOKS

Published in Great Britain in 2008 by
PROFILE BOOKS LTD
3A Exmouth House
Pine Street
Exmouth Market
London ECIR OJH
www.profilebooks.com

Mass Observation material © Trustees of the Mass Observation Archive
Nella Last's Peace, selections and editorial matter © Patricia and Robert Malcolmson, 2008

10 9 8 7 6 5 4 3 2

Typeset in Garamond 3 by MacGuru Ltd
info@macguru.org.uk
Printed and bound in Great Britain by
CPI Group (UK) Ltd, Croydon, CRO 4YY

The moral right of the authors has been asserted.

All rights reserved. Without limiting the rights under copyright reserved above, no part
of this publication may be reproduced, stored or introduced into a retrieval system, or
transmitted, in any form or by any means (electronic, mechanical, photocopying, recording
or otherwise), without the prior written permission of both the copyright owner and the
publisher of this book.

A CIP catalogue record for this book is available from the British Library.

ISBN 978 1 84668 074 8

This book is printed on FSC certified paper

The editors and publishers would like to thank the following for their kind permission to
reproduce the photographs: 1,2, 7, 13, courtesy of Margaret Procter and Norah Redhead;
3, 4, 5, 6, courtesy of Peter Last; 8 courtesy of Cumbria Record Office and Local Studies
Library Barrow; 9, courtesy of the National Archives (INF9/193); 10, 11, 12 with
permission of the *North West Evening Mail*.

CONTENTS

Maps   vi

Introduction   ix

The Setting: Barrow-in-Furness   xi

Nella Last's Family, Friends, Neighbours and Associates   xiii

CHAPTER ONE Endings: *August–October 1945*   1

CHAPTER TWO A Sort of Peace: *October 1945–January 1946*   32

CHAPTER THREE 'Nice to be Loved': *January–May 1946*   65

CHAPTER FOUR Post-war Summer: *June–September 1946*   96

CHAPTER FIVE Stresses and Storms: *October 1946–April 1947*   124

CHAPTER SIX 'Sunshine is Life to Me': *April–October 1947*   154

CHAPTER SEVEN 'I Can be Real Bitchy': *October–December 1947*   185

CHAPTER EIGHT Babies: *January–June 1948*   216

CHAPTER NINE Close-Ups: *June–December 1948*   251

Afterword   287

Glossary and Abbreviations   293

Money and Its Value   295

Chronology   296

Editing Nella Last's Diary   299

Mass Observation   302

Acknowledgements   305

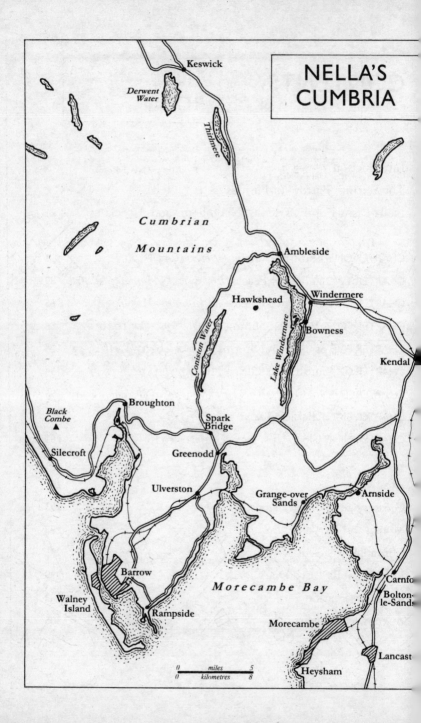

THE RESIDENTS ON ILKLEY ROAD

A - George and Jessie Holme
B - Charles, Winifred and Margaret Atkinson
C - Will and Nella Last
D - Frank and Fanny Helm
E - Steve and Evelyn Howson
F - Dick and Norah Redhead

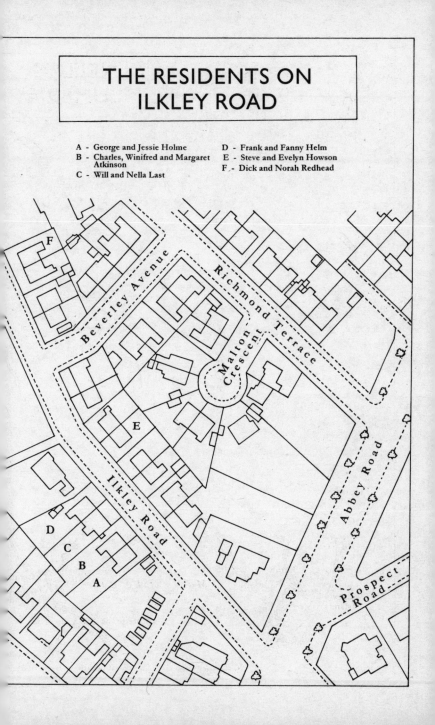

INTRODUCTION

'Supposing I'd been clever, there could have been a few books.'

Nella Last, 17 September, 1947

Nella Last was a dedicated writer whom few knew to be a writer. Her immediate family knew, though they had little if any knowledge of what she wrote about, except in the letters she sent. Her next-door neighbours, the Atkinsons, were also aware that she liked to write, partly because every Friday morning, on his way to work, Mr Atkinson often dropped off at the post office a package containing the diary she wrote for Mass Observation, the social research organisation set up in 1937 to foster a 'science of ourselves'. Mass Observation encouraged its hundreds of volunteers to write in detail about everyday life (this was then a novelty), and about how these incidents, routines and even intimacies were experienced by the Observer.

Almost nothing Nella Last wrote was published in her lifetime. Aside from a handful of people associated with Mass Observation, no one read her diary until the 1980s. And yet it is a remarkable piece of work. Not only is it, almost certainly, one of the longest diaries in the English language – so vast that no one has read it all from start to finish – it is also a diary of quality, for Nella was sensitive, observant, imaginative and often acutely introspective, and she poured herself into her daily writing with a disciplined persistence, over close to thirty years, that few diarists have matched.

Nella Last started to write for Mass Observation in late August 1939. Her wartime diary, *Nella Last's War*, edited by Richard

Broad and Suzie Fleming, was published first in 1981 and republished in 2006, and the book has been the inspiration for an acclaimed television drama, *Housewife, 49* (the '49' referring to her age when the diary began). But the war did not see the end of her writing for Mass Observation – commonly known as MO. She continued to write for the organisation, and during the three and a half years between the middle of 1945 and the end of 1948 she wrote perhaps a million and a quarter words. Her post-war writing as presented in this book is a little less than a tenth of her original handwritten diary, which is held in the Mass Observation Archive at the University of Sussex and is open to the public. So, like *Nella Last's War*, this post-war volume is highly selective. Nella also responded to most of MO's questionnaires, known as Directives, which were sent out monthly to its volunteer Observers from 1939 to 1945 and less regularly thereafter.

We have chosen to highlight, broadly, four features of Nella's diary: passages where she revealed something of her private outlooks, opinions and emotions; where she wrote about personal relations, notably those with her husband, who had his own joinery business, and with her two adult sons; where she ruminated on her own life and family history; and occasions when she described matters of public life – action in the streets, conversations overheard and participated in, commercial transactions, transportation and travel, rumours and gossip and scandal. It is our desire to allow a life story to unfold – a story played out in those unheroic post-war years of soul-searching and privation, but of hope and satisfaction as well. 'If the historians could see clearly enough,' Nella wrote on 30 July 1947, 'this could well be called the age of frustration. People seem to have such unnecessary worries and setbacks, and after all, for ordinary people, it's the little things that count, whether for good or ill.'

THE SETTING: BARROW-IN-FURNESS

Barrow-in-Furness was, as Nella and others remarked, 'a young town'. From virtual non-existence (only a few dozen families lived there before the 1840s), it grew dramatically in the second half of the nineteenth and early twentieth centuries. Its population peaked at almost 75,000 in the early 1920s; in the later 1940s Barrovians numbered around 67,000. It was very much a centre of heavy industry – 'Barrow is a working class town, with no "society" really,' Nella observed in late 1948.

Barrow had sprung to life in the mid nineteenth century with the construction of the railways. Iron and steel led the way; later shipbuilding predominated – this was very much the town's leading industry in the 1940s. Barrow 'is late enough to be well planned,' observed one writer in 1940, 'and its cleanliness shows a high degree of civic pride on the part of the inhabitants'. The town offered little in the way of antiquities or scenery, and 'most of the town's visitors must come for the sake of the famous ship-yards'.* When Nella wrote of the 'Yard', this is what she was referring to. Geographically Barrow was decidedly isolated and detached from the rest of the county – it was then in Lancashire rather than in Cumbria – and surrounded by sea except to the north, where the Lake District was close and reasonably acces-sible, especially for those who had a car, as the Lasts did.

Nella's modern semi-detached house, built in 1936, was on an estate towards the then northern outskirts of Barrow, much of

* Doreen Wallace, *English Lakeland* (London: Batsford, 1940), p. 47.

which had been constructed in the 1930s. Ilkley Road, where she lived, runs north-west off Abbey Road, the main artery that led and still leads from the north in Barrow southward to the centre of town. When Nella spoke of going down town, a little over a mile from her home, she meant she had travelled or planned to travel, usually by bus, south-west on Abbey Road to the town's centre, where most of the main shops and services were located. The houses on Ilkley Road and nearby are mainly two-storeyed and semi-detached, with a sitting room at the front and dining room and kitchen at the back, three bedrooms above and usually an ample garden. 'This is an exceptionally nice neighbourhood to live in,' Nella wrote in response to MO's September 1947 Directive. 'I've been here eleven years and it was a few years old and our four houses the last to be built. We came in September and I was surprised to have strangers coming with flowers and roots and rockery plants they had split and which they thought would help establish my garden.' The Lasts' house was exceptional in having an attached garage, which could be entered from the house as well as from outside; and theirs was one of the few homes on Ilkley Road with a telephone.

NELLA LAST'S FAMILY, FRIENDS, NEIGHBOURS AND ASSOCIATES

Arthur	*Elder son*
Arthur (Procter)	*Margaret's boyfriend, later fiancé*
Atkinson, Mrs	*Next-door neighbour*
Brown, Mrs	*Companion to her mother-in-law (from 1948)*
Cliff	*Younger son*
Cooper, Mrs	*Cleaning helper*
Dearie	*Nella herself*
Dick (Redhead)	*Norah's husband*
Diss, Mrs	*Head of the local WVS*
Doug	*Family friend*
Edith	*Arthur's wife*
Eliza, Aunt	*Sister of her late mother*
Elsie	*Sister of her husband*
Ena	*A daughter of Mrs Whittam*
Flo	*Sister of her husband*
George (Holme)	*Neighbour; husband of Jessie*
Gran	*Deceased maternal grandmother; a Rawlinson*
Harrisson, Tom	*A founder of Mass Observation*
Harry	*Brother of her husband*
Helm, Mr and Mrs	*Neighbours in the house attached*
Higham, Mrs	*Friend*
Howson, Mrs	*Friend and neighbour*
Hunter, Isa	*Ex-friend*

Jessie	*Neighbour; wife of George*
Jim	*Edith's brother*
Joe	*Cousin of Aunt Sarah; lives with her*
Linda	*Friend of Margaret*
Margaret	*Atkinsons' younger daughter*
Murphy	*Cat*
Nellie	*Wife of Harry*
Newall, Mrs	*Co-worker at the WVS*
Norah	*Atkinsons' elder daughter*
Olga	*A daughter of Mrs Whittam*
Pattison, Mrs	*Cleaning helper*
Picken, Mrs	*Edith's mother*
Salisbury, Mrs	*Cleaning helper*
Sarah, Aunt	*Sister of her late mother*
Shan We	*Siamese cat*
Steve	*Husband of Mrs Howson*
Waite, Mrs	*Head of Hospital Supply*
Whittam, Mrs	*Friend; farms in Walney*
Will	*Husband*
Woods, Mrs	*A leader in the WVS*

CHAPTER ONE

ENDINGS

August–October 1945

With war winding down in the spring and summer of 1945, Nella Last often reflected on the changes, many of them dramatic and troubling, that the world was undergoing – the devastation on the Continent, the plight of refugees, the dislocations of so many lives, the dropping of two atomic bombs – and the changes that she and others might expect with the arrival of peace. She was anxious about the challenges of adapting to a post-war existence. She worried about her sons, Arthur and Cliff, the latter still in the Army, the former employed as a civil servant and living with his wife, Edith, in Belfast. She wondered what roles and purposes she would find for herself when those that the war had provided (notably the Women's Voluntary Services and other volunteer commitments) were terminated. Nella had felt 'useful'; but would she be able to find ways to continue to feel useful – beyond affording household services to her husband? How would she, now in her mid fifties, consume her time?

Nella had doubts, too, about her diary, which had absorbed so much of her time and energy since 1939. 'The thought struck me as I began my diary,' she wrote on 4 May, 'how much longer will they want them?' 'They' were the people at Mass Observation to whom she regularly dispatched her writings – 'miles' of them, as she remarked on 30 August.

On 15 August, the day that the Japanese Emperor announced the surrender of his country, Nella Last wrote twice for Mass Observation, first around 1 a.m. (parts of which are reproduced at the very end of her published wartime diary), and later, in the evening, when she and her husband were talking.

Monday, 15 August. We talked of things when we were small, and our early married days. He only sees the good bits. He has a calm mind which accepts. He has never known rebellion of heart and mind – or any struggle to keep his head above water. I've never let him know the rough side of 'managing' for he had poor health and it made him worse to be worried. He talks of the 'good days' only and makes me feel a bit sick. I see the struggles, the worries about the two boys, the frustration of spirit when I could not do all I would have liked for them …

I wonder what work there will be for me. It always worried me because in a clever family I seemed 'the odd one out' – my lameness when a child coming at the time when I needed most for learning, and in those days little notice was taken of girls and their education. I've learned my little gifts of cooking and managing. My love of peace and fun, and seeing folks happy, are real gifts, more useful at times than clever things, like knowing figures and book-keeping. I've learned to keep people together by a laugh, when to take notice of tempers could have meant a split. I've learned the beauty and worth of sustained service with and for others. I'll never go back into the cage of household duties alone, much as my home means and will always mean to me.

Tuesday, 21 August. I wonder how long before it looks like peace in Japan – and is it really peace or will it all break out again, or linger like a festering corroding sore for years, like the war in China? Vast countries like that are not like we are in Europe. Little things grow dearer and dearer to me. Sometimes I feel I run the danger of clinging too closely to things and by experience I know how foolish that can be. The little wood fire I made for my husband to have his supper by (for I know he always feels chilly after perspiring and working outdoors), the gleaming bits

of brass I'd found time to polish tonight, even my bread and gingerbread, seemed 'real' in a world of shadows and doubts. I feel
the everyday jobs and my little household gods are more real and
convincing than 'big news', which my tired head doesn't seem
to grasp. I said once at the WVS*† Centre, 'I feel like a piece of
elastic that has been stretched and stretched and now has no more
stretch – and cannot spring back.' They laughed, but several said
it was a pretty good description of their own post-war feelings
and I can tell Arthur has somewhat the same reaction. More and
more do I feel I must take each day as it comes, do the best I can
and lay my day aside, taking up the next. Sometimes I feel so
dead tired, like a burnt-out shell, craving only to relax and rest.
Then my mind rises and rebukes my tired body – says, 'So much
to be done, so little time.' The stars shine brightly tonight. I love
stars. They make me feel trivial and unimportant – and are so
stable. I don't wonder the old ones thought Heaven was above
the bright blue sky.

Wednesday, 22 August. The dusk fell quickly tonight and there
were no stars in the overcast sky. It's grand to think that this
winter will have no blackout, that bright lights will be in streets
and from lightly curtained windows. How remote the last six
years are becoming. It's odd to realise how Cliff has lost such a
slice from his life, turned from a charming if headstrong boy to
a man who shows his apprehension of life and having as yet no
stability of a settled place in the community, by moods, and a
general look of strain. He has all his limbs. I think of the poor
ones who came back handicapped so badly. I pray so deeply for

---

* The symbol † indicates that a word or words, or an acronym, are explained in
the Glossary.

real peace – for ordinary people who ask so little of life beyond simple needs, food and shelter for their families and a little for small enjoyments. I search for details of factories 'turning over' or opening, contracts received, but it's not very often I feel satisfied when I've read the papers. I read today an article written by an American armaments man, who urged America to 'go underground'. I recalled an article of Naylor the astrologist written when big underground shelters were being made in the beginning of the war. He said a time was coming when we would put all works and factories – and people would live in huge blocks of buildings – built deep down and air-conditioned. It made me feel terrified at the time. I so love the freedom of fresh winds and air.

Tonight I thought of the dreadful new bomb – we will always live in the shadow of fear now. With the dawn of new and comparatively easily made and handled weapons, no country will ever be safe, however big their armies and navies. Only by change of thought and heart can civilisation be saved. Old sayings are real truths – 'Put not your trust in Princes, or any sons of man' – more vitally real then ever. And what change of heart can be expected today? Bitter hatred, chaos, broken faith, lost ideals are poor foundations. I feel again this world of ours has blundered into a beam of wickedness and unrest. Call it Uranus the 'dark Planet' or what you will, it's some evil force that affects all. I've a deep sadness over my mind and heart like a shadow, instead of joy the war is ended. I tell myself impatiently that I'm tired out, that I'm run down, and I rest as much as I can, coming to bed early, but it does not lessen the shadow. I go and work in the garden and leave a little of it there and when the bright sun shines I feel I lift up my hands to it in delight, but cannot stir the heavy dead-weight shadow off my heart for long.

Wednesday, 29 August. I used to think how happy people would be when the war was over, but beyond thankfulness that it's over, I see few signs of the brave new world. People are beginning to have that fear they will be paid off. Women are not settling down very well after being at work. I hear many cases where they have lost touch with little children who have learned to do without Mam and turned to a granny or older sister, of wives and returned soldier husbands feeling the strain after living apart. After the last slump a lot of people in Barrow who had considered their job secure in Vickers got a nasty shake-up when they were sacked. I hear odd remarks or parts of them which show how women's thoughts are on 'whether Dad will get the sack', if this or that department is busy or likely to be. The stocks lie stark and empty – no big keels laid to make Barrow people feel secure. Only Sir Charles Craven's [*Chairman of Vickers-Armstrong 1936–1944*] keenness and foresight kept Barrow being like Jarrow or similar dead shipbuilding towns. He is dead now and things are different altogether. Little sleeping worries have risen after six years when work was assured for all-comers. People ask the prices in shops lately. There's none of their 'Give me a couple of pounds of those' but rather it's 'How much a pound?' and a consideration before saying how much is required, and flowers are not quickly bought regardless of price. The moneyed folk are beginning to see that war jobs don't last for ever …

When things went wrong with Gran – and so little in her overworked life seemed to do for long – she had a funny little way of rising on her toes and drawing a deep breath as she said, 'Ah well, we must do the best we can and pass on.' At times I feel her simple creed is my standard of life and living. I feel like a grain of sand on a seashore, feeling and knowing my utter, utter limitations; that however I try, I can do so little; feeling a strange loss when I cannot work directly as we did in the Red Cross shop; wondering what I will do when the Centre closes with its purpose and Canteen[†] with its service, making me feel I'm keeping things moving in the right direction, however small.

Sunday, 2 September. If I had pleased myself today, I'd not have got up at all, for after my usual Sunday rest I felt I'd forego even a drink of tea – never mind lunch – to just lie in bed. I had a bath and felt a bit better, and lunch was soon ready, and the good mutton soup reviving. The mutton was nice and tender, and I made a shredded cabbage salad with sliced tomatoes and a shred of grated onion, and chopped mint for a wee difference. As I drank a cup of tea afterwards I realised what a tea dope I've got since the war, rarely drinking coffee and never cocoa. I could drink many more cups a day than I do. My husband feels as out of sorts as I do – not ill, merely not well.

He said, 'Would you like a run to Ambleside?' I'd only expected to go on the Coast Road and felt a trip up the length of Windermere was a treat. I packed tea, taking a little loaf, butter, jam, tomatoes and cake, and we set off. Everywhere now there is a little hint of autumn, a golden tassel of one turned branch of beech, curled fading plane-tree leaves, vivid red of hawthorn berries, and blue-black elderberry, and far up in the woods on the slopes of the hills, cherry trees gleam like a torch in the dull green. The last of the corn sheaves were being carted and they looked as if they had only been waiting for transport. The shorn grain fields have already tufts of green grass springing up.

We stared in amazement at the Bowness car and chara[†] parks. Never did we see so many before war, for an adjoining field had had to be used and was full of private cars. The odd part was that most of the charas were from Blackpool and Preston and from the other direction from Cleator Moor and Cockermouth – twice the distance allowed for travel in coaches – but no one bothered and everyone looked happy in spite of there being no accommodation for tea as there once would have been. As there were no signs of picnic meals we wondered if they had had tea on the way. The big motor launches were packed and the small ones were doing a good trade. It's made Bowness very busy with the petrol allowance. My husband said, 'What will it be like when the rationing goes and cars can be bought again?' I said, 'Perhaps no more crowded. It's exceptional just now – VJ trips and little outings so long denied.'

We went on to quiet Ambleside – too far for Blackpool coaches to go. Yet it too was full of parked motors, wherever they could be squeezed along the lake front. But we found one unused spot – had just room for us to edge in. I'm always attracted by the carriers with one child in and the fearless way they handle them, shooting cleverly about, never bothering about big motor launches or rowing boats with the two elders moving strongly. I'd taken a bit of sewing and a book, but I just sat quietly watching the boats and sailing ships, till I dozed off to sleep for over an hour. We had tea and a little walk along the shore and were home by 8.30.

Mr and Mrs Atkinson were very cool when we spoke over the fence, although we did not say we had been to Ambleside. I know they think it odd when we don't fill the back of the car whenever we go out. They cannot be happy unless someone is with them. I feel my husband's moods are best if he is quiet, and somehow lately I've felt more than ever the need, the real necessity, to relax. Perhaps it's with being at Centre and Canteen, and the shop when it was open, and having to study so many, keeping them happy, joking little squabbles away. But whatever it is, lately I've felt glad to escape into the quiet of the countryside, or to sit by the sea. Mrs Atkinson likes to know exactly what each day brings. Three evenings she goes to a whist drive, and two afternoons as well. On Saturday evenings they visit relatives, also for cards, and she has tried to persuade me to 'make a date' every week for cards or to go to the pictures, as she thinks I need a 'bit of a life'. I feel I gain more life by relaxing with a book after my busy days, that an evening which is good for her after a day's housework and shopping is not suitable for me; and anyway, beyond a pleasant neighbourliness there is no friendship, nor could ever be, for we have no tastes in common.

Margaret is different. We have so much in common, both in ideals and views. Her mother said one day, 'Our Margaret is more like you than me.' I thought of the lonely evenings little Margaret always had till she began to come in our house, bringing her little problems, reading my books and discussing them, picking up little cooking and sewing ways. It grieves me sorely when I feel Margaret cheapens herself with her many light friendships, tearing away a bit of her affections each time and giving it away, feeling sure it's the right one every time. She came in tonight looking a bit dim. Her latest friend is an Australian airman, son of a very prosperous farmer who gave all his children a good college education (agriculture) and sets them up when they marry. While he is in England waiting to go home, he has been given leave to go to a farm somewhere in the Midlands where he can study artificial semination and then he will take it up in a big way on his return, as 'the old man will be highly delighted'. Margaret said dolefully, 'I'll never see him again I suppose, and if he had asked me, I'd have gone out to Australia. I would make a good wife for a busy man you know, Mrs Last!' I hugged her and gave her a kiss, feeling so sorry for her. I said, 'Perhaps, ducks, you are too adaptable. You know men like a girl to be a little aloof.' She said a bit surprisingly, 'Oh, things are so different nowadays to what they were when you were a girl.' I agreed in my mind. I remember the tidal shock I got when one moonlight night when I was drawing the bedroom curtains, I saw a young airman kissing Margaret with a fervour generally only seen on the screen, and later found out she had only met him that evening, and was told 'Don't be silly – a boy *always* expects to kiss you if he brings you home.'

I felt so shaky and ill. I was glad to come to bed. This little epidemic going round seems to follow its course – sick and bad pains, followed by about two days of intense weariness and aching bones, and then a cold comes on with sneezing and nose running.

Wednesday, 5 September. We ought to have gone down this morning to the WVS really but it was no use. It was beyond me, and Mrs Howson called in and did not know the ones working, putting up the stalls, and she is too shy to work with anyone she doesn't know. We were to have the ice cream and jelly, but the scoop was very stiff and my small hand soon tired – arthritis has sapped the strength from my knotting fingers. A friend offered – she said laughingly as she spread her hand, 'My fist won't tire' – and because I went on to refreshments, Mrs Higham wouldn't stay on the ice-cream stall. Not that I minded. We work well together and the ones in the kitchen, while well-known WVS, were unknown to me by working together. We had the little buffet where people who did not want the sit-down tea of 1s 6d could buy what they wanted. All passed off well, except that we were so held up at the Mayor's non-arrival. We let the Matron open the proceedings, and then the fat ill-bred woman who is our Mayor waddled in beaming, saying she was sorry to be late but she had been listening in to the big race. Shades of Labour mayors of the old school – and women – ugh. I detest women in power unless they are something out of the ordinary.

We gave Matron a big teddy bear instead of a bouquet after she spoke, and we have decided that the Children's Ward badly needs decorating and refurnishing and our £500 target will be used for that, and the WVS always takes an interest in their ward. The Mayor got a lovely little begonia in a pot – such a jewel bright thing, covered with buds, which would have lasted for weeks. It did not endear her to us when she swept it off and broke the pot, and after breaking off two bright flowers for her buttonhole, left the rest lying. Perhaps she thought we would have put it down to her having greenhouses full of plants, forgetting that we who were Barrovians remembered her upbringing in a back street and knew her *very* well. When I saw the giver's face as the little plant was trodden and swept aside, I felt I'd have enjoyed stuffing it down the Mayor's too-elaborate silk dress! When she came to office she applied for more coupons, to 'dress the part', and got the answer that 'in her position, it was up to her to set a good example'! It's very easy to spot people who buy things without coupons in Barrow. They have the 'Jewish' stamp – over-decorated and doll-eyed† bits and pieces of fur and tucks. How the authorities have failed to find out about Davidson's racket I don't know – a dress without coupons is £1 more. Quite openly a girl will say, 'I had to go for my wedding dress to Davidson's as I'd no coupons to spare, but I got my going away costume at Ireland's. After all, you only wear a wedding dress once and you can always sell it and if you've not given coupons it's no loss at all.'

Friday, 7 September. Such a lovely nostalgic September morning. At this time of the year I've always such a craving to be off and away over the hills and far away, an urge that when I was younger used to tear and weary me with its intensity. The smell of chrys-anths, smudge fires, sun scorched grass, the long shadows on the grass, and the autumn colouring in hedges and woods was a delight and a torment to me. I knew I'd be too tired to cut the lawn when I came in from Canteen, so went out as soon as I'd washed up, to do it before I vacced and dusted. I seemed to find weeds and twitch grass to take up more of my time, but I made a real good job of it, in spite of the fact that the shears were red rust and I had to clean them up, sharpen and oil them before I could trim the edges. For a man who has to use tools, my husband is careless over any for the garden. Everything is let get rusty and dilapidated and I always tell him it takes more time with bad tools. I brushed all the fallen apple tree leaves off and I did feel so suited with my job and thought how glad my husband would be when I'd done it, and he never ever noticed I'd done it all! I had soup and cornflour for a sweet from yesterday and I made a really tasty casserole out of the kidney, onions, carrots and sliced pota-toes, and boiled a little cauliflower, vacced and dusted, packed Cliff's clean laundry and just managed to get washed and changed for Canteen before lunch.

Mrs Howson and I stared when we went into the greengro-cer's. There were such heaps of things, onions, tomatoes, pears (not so good and too ripe), eating and baking apples, cucumbers, runner beans, celery, carrots – quite like a pre-war shop – and the flowers were a glory. It's not a shop I'll patronise. I hate their furtive passing of bags of indifferent fruit – third-rate at top-rate prices – and their 'biggest in the window' way. It had rather that name before the war but lately everyone complains. Yet at present, unless you are a regular customer, there is little chance of getting even furtively handled goods, kept for 'customers' so they don't have to queue. Today I refused to take three pounds of apples the girl had weighed with two half bad ones and calmly insisted she replace them with sound ones, and when she had got her breath back she did so. I was always a keen shopper. I'd always a little more to do with my housekeeping money than most, with so many doctors' bills and illness. And then again, I love managing a house and the best of everything as far as freshness and quality go. To go round the market with a big basket was a real delight to me. No shopkeeper gets my custom who sells inferior food.

Mrs Howson laughed when we came out. She said, 'Don't you feel in a good mood today?' and I said, 'Perhaps not', but it suddenly struck me how darn sick I was of controls and shortages of little ordinary things – 'Do you know, I've only one comb and that has two teeth out.' She said, 'We have one between the four of us!' There is not a scrap of soap in town, no matches or cigarettes; even regular customers are not able to get any, and I've only had sweets off one book[†] yet. When Cliff was here for ten days I let him take one emergency ticket back to London, in case he had to stay with friends, but said to send any remaining coupons back. He had not used any, had stayed two and then three days at a hotel. So I had his full rations. I thought I'd get the sugar, tea and points[†] (five) and put it away for another time he came unexpectedly, use the fats and swap the meat for fresh eggs off Mrs Whittam, who has plenty of eggs but prefers meat. I let her go for her meat herself and she had to go into five shops before she could get any. I'd made out with my rations of meat when Cliff was here, and we were never fond of a lot of meat, so the eggs will do for tomorrow's lunch with chips – I got three.

We found Canteen in a real bustle – sailors booking beds who had just come into town and some nice Americans going. It's really amazing how small-town Americans come back all the way from Germany for a few days' leave – and recommend their friends. This lot had been somewhere in the Midlands, but heard so good a report of Barrow they came here and stayed at the tatty Canteen to sleep, going round the country in buses and swimming at Walney. I found some string for one who needed it and he said, 'It's sure a swell place. I'll come back if I ever come to England for a holiday. The folk here are just like home folk.' He gave me all his little tinned goods – jam, cheese and a wee tin of butter. I drew lots for us all to have one, but kept the wee tin of butter for myself as well as the jam I drew ... We were kept on the go all the time, but no big rushes, and we peeled a lot of potatoes for chips, for the evening squad, before we left. Mrs Howson came in for a cup of tea because her mother was out and we sat talking idly. She suddenly said, 'How lovely your lawn and garden look. Do you have to cut it often?' My husband shook his head and then took another look at the lawn and noticed it had been done, but never said anything. I thought, 'You tiresome ungrateful thing', but didn't comment on it, and neither did he. My back ached and I felt very tired, so beyond ironing my one and only cotton frock to go blackberrying if it's fine tomorrow, I rested till supper time, glad my busy day was done. I've often talked of the rest I'd get when the war was over, but as yet it hasn't come along.

Saturday, 8 September. I woke with a feeling of real terror – bells clanging and a steady stream of heavy traffic down the main road at the corner of the street. I recognised the clang of fire vehicles, and getting out of bed I went into the back room and looked over the town, lit up as bright as day. I thought it must be a big fire but could only tell it was over in the direction of the Shipyard. Later I learned it was a big liner, the *Empress of Russia*, ablaze in the dock.

It will be a very great loss. She was due out next month after a refit and had stocks of oil and food, wines and spirits aboard. Mrs Atkinson wanted me to go and see it but I had to go to the hairdresser's for nine o'clock, and anyway I am not a sightseer. I'd have hated to see that proud ship in distress. I thought anxiously of the crew and hoped they would get off safely.

This vessel of almost 17,000 tons, a former Canadian Pacific liner, had been used recently for war service. The fire, in which two men died, was reported to be the first major disaster of its kind in the Barrow shipyard for over thirty years.

Many stayed at Canteen when they first came. Several shops have had no cakes all week, claiming they had no sugar left, and a cafe is advertised in the *Mail*[†] as being shut for a week as they have no foodstuffs. With 'Closed' on pubs and hotels, it makes me wonder if VJ celebrations are to blame! Such nice fish, but very long queues. As I passed the open window and saw they had big fish, I asked for a head for old Murphy, only 4d today. I jokingly apologised for going out of my turn, and showed the waiting women it was just a fish head, so escaped censure! Still a glut of tomatoes – it's rather spoilt the sale of the lovely home-grown ones – and flowers are in such profusion that our local gardeners are suffering. I'd changed my handbag at the last minute as I went out and found I'd left my ration books at home. I felt cross when I saw a tin of grapefruit. I hope they have not sold out by Monday. I wonder how much longer points will have to be given up for things, if shipping will increase. It's all right saving, but the eternal contriving and queuing is getting us all down a little. Aunt Sarah has a quaint saying which has always been a joke – 'As we get older, Dearie,* our heads won't stand it' – and she is not far wrong …

Yesterday I got a wee ham shank for a present from someone my husband knew. I simmered it till tender and minced and it did for my husband's tea with a little salad, and made a nice packet of sandwiches for Doug and us to take, and I packed two flasks of tea, cakes, tomatoes and apples. I had soup enough for lunch. The remains of yesterday's kidney casserole was the base, with shredded cabbage and tomatoes cooked in it to make out – very nice too. I scrambled two fresh eggs and served them on toasted wholemeal bread, and made custard to pour over a bit of stale cake and sultanas and bake under the grill for a little sweet.

My husband was so grumpy that Doug was coming. It emphasised in my mind the real need I'd have to look for outside contacts when my war activities are over and finished. He grows more mumpish and averse from company, and alas I'm much less patient, or perhaps more awake to the fact that my 'nervous breakdowns' were due to 'repressions' as Dr Miller said. I felt cross. I thought of all the women I knew who could please themselves more – go out alone to a whist drive or to pay a visit, invite people, not feel a criminal when not in for meals. He has got into the way of saying he never feels well on Saturday morning – wonders if it's with having to have his tea by himself on Fridays. I was a bit curt today. I said, 'Well, considering you had only to

---

* In reply to a question from Mass Observation about names, Nella reported that her parents had wanted to call her Deirdre but a clergyman objected to its Irish roots, so she was named Nellie, which she always hated (this is the name on her birth certificate). However, her mother called her Deirdre, 'which got shortened to Dearie and which the boys as well have always called me'. The name 'Nella' was once used in a school concert; she was delighted, and it stuck. (*Directive Response*, May 1946)

brew your tea and cut bread and butter, I don't think you were so badly treated.' It's no use. His idea of love is for a person to always do the things he thinks, to have no ideas of their own. I've noticed men are attracted by qualities they admire – gaiety and fun, an independent spirit, etc. – and then proceed to alter and change the very things they admired. Doug came early. He told us the fire was out on the *Empress of Russia* but he said he feared the hulk was a total loss.

It was such a lovesome autumn day and we went on the Tops above Morecambe Bay, behind Greenodd, past Gran's old farm. I wandered off and left them and sat perched on an old stone wall, feeling the years slip away, feeling Gran very near, when I saw a little old woman bringing in a horse off the high field where I'd often gone with a lump of sugar to bring in old Tedder. Far off the Coniston hills showed on my right hand, the placid sea of the bay on my left. There was no sound but the buzz of bees and insects, and the sound of wood pigeons in the coppice. When the high mournful 'hoy, hoya' of a lad calling the cows came echoing, it sounded more primitive and more a part of the quiet hills than ever, and the quiet gentle beasts padded past, with only a glance at me. I felt thoroughly lazy and detached. I didn't care whether I got any blackberries or not but my husband and Doug were energetic and got the biscuit tins we had taken full of lovely ripe fruit.

Sunday, 9 September. Going by the date of the month, it's just nine years since we came to this house. Time has certainly passed quickly and a great deal happened. I had a rest till lunch time, rose and had a bath and wished I hadn't – it was a bit too warm and made me feel sick. Lunch was soon prepared – soup, cold meat, lettuce and mint jelly, stewed blackberries and custard. My husband was in rather a mood. He didn't seem to care whether he went out or not, but I packed tea and partly to cheer him and partly for a little celebration we had been in the house nine years, I took a tin of fruit salad off the shelf and tomato sandwiches, cake, two flasks of tea and a little slab of chocolate, and we went as far as the lake side and sat by the foot of the lake. Charas from Leigh and Blackpool, Morecambe and Lancaster, began to roll by on their long journey back home. The people looked tired but happy; the country was very lovely in spite of the grey sunless day. We did not stay long. My husband had a few letters to write and 7.30 found us home. So I baked some bread. It only took a few minutes to knead and set to rise. I wrote out my grocery order and planned out next week's work – think I'll wash all the curtains next week, except the dining room. I've ordered the sweep. My husband seems to be unwilling to say whether he will do it or not and I must know. Sweeps are very busy people. I have to wait till 12 October, but it will be clean for the winter anyway. It's begun to puff down in spite of the fact I've burned two 6d patent chimney cleaners from Boots. I found a few tidying-up jobs to do and then made supper and came to bed. The neuralgic pains have left my head and face, but they have left a little twitch in a nerve over my left eye – in my eyelid really – and I feel I wink at times, unpleasant but not painful.

Tuesday, 11 September. It poured heavily at our usual closing time and everyone lingered till it was a dash to lock up and catch the last bus before the workmen's buses started. I can hear of many being paid off, some transferred to other towns to work, some just on the dole. The Australian sergeant pilots who were going to work in the Yard, and in office as accountants, etc. till they could be gradually taken home, are going off in a bunch after all.

I'm glad. It has not made things better to see other lads found jobs to occupy their time when complaints of our own townsmen of 'having nothing to do at all' come by every post to wives and parents. I fear there will be trouble if demobbing is not speeded up. If we have to let America have trade barriers reduced as return for help over Lend Lease, it will be a bad thing. The country will be all supplied before our lads get back into their jobs. Whatever plans were made in the past, I fear things have so changed. We are in a worse plight than after the last war, and with the discovery of the atomic bomb, every future preparation for industry as well as security will have to be taken with one eye on its possibilities. When I think of Europe's demobbing problems, my head reels, and I wonder will we ever get straightened out? America again has emerged unscathed, her people at home unaware there has been a war, except for a little rationing and of course those who have had men in the Forces.

I fried bacon and sweet apples cut in thick slices and there was wholemeal bread and butter, raspberry jam and plain cake. I got out Cliff's shirts and settled to unpick and tack new neck bands on, and repairing them where necessary, ready for machining. There is no real hurry to do them, but I like to finish off one job before I start another and put it away. I'll be able to settle down to my dollies† without having to feel that guilty feeling of a more important job. I'll be glad when a few 'features' come back on the wireless – *Monday Night at Eight O'clock*, for one. I don't know what I'd do without the wireless when I'm sitting sewing, when my husband has his moods, and conversations on my part peter out after vainly trying to interest him or rouse him. If I was sitting alone, my thoughts would be free to roam and wander, but it's different when manners alone make me want to interest a person sitting and glumping.

Thursday, 13 September. I rose early. I had to make a special trip to town to pay the Canteen bills, with it being early closing and not opening the Centre till 1.30. If things get any worse in the food line, I cannot see it being worthwhile to open the Canteen. There seems absolutely nothing to buy when there is no fish but tinned pilchards, no meats for sandwiches, and lettuce and tomatoes 'passing'. I could not get one tin of biscuits or potato crisps, no tinned beans in tomatoes, and short supplies of dried eggs and dried milk. It was such a heavy grey day, but oranges were in the shops in plenty and the string shopping bags full, and open baskets lit up the grey streets like little golden lamps. I'd not time to go to my greengrocer's, but there are plenty. I'll get them tomorrow. I hear grapefruit too are to be in next week, so I'll make some real good marmalade.

I got really beautiful fish – lemon sole filleted – and the shop-keeper, a bitch of a woman who has insulted people terribly in the war, was so polite I felt embarrassed! I'd never have gone in her hateful shop again, but there was no queue when I passed, and my husband dearly loves filleted sole or plaice and I can so seldom get it for him. I asked for 3d of the heads I saw, thinking they were at least a pick for my little cat. She wrapped up half a dozen – in her own paper!!! – and didn't charge me, said it was a PLEASURE!!! By Gad, I hoped when I came out feeling dazed that I'd looked it!! Nasty wretch. When things are plentiful I bet she doesn't get much custom. I know I'll never spend a penny in her shop. I spent the sweet coupon out of my book. I could not get any till now beyond peppermints, and I can make good ones myself out of dried milk, etc., better than any bought ones. No cigarettes on the shop shelves, and by what I made out, few under the counter. Soldiers stopped me several times, hopefully thinking I might know a shop where they could get them. It's high time this barter business stopped on the Continent. I know people who have sent hundreds of cigarettes to soldiers, sons and husbands and got cameras and cheap jewellery – I've yet to see anything worthwhile.

I saw an amazing sight – a tall overblown rose of a woman, that sallow complexion that seems to follow a lifetime of coffee drinking, a heavy greasy Veronica Lake style of hairdressing; and her clothes – a jaunty smartness and perky hat, but never have I seen such shoddy material, and on her fat calves she had a pair of knitted red turnover socks, gartered below her huge dimpled knees, from which her full skirt swung. Her costume was black, and her black hat had an upstanding red quill, and she carried an awful-looking bag made of the same red string as her socks. Her shoes were of a heavy cloth with wooden soles. She seemed to be asking the way and when I appeared the two women seemed to make her understand I would help her – WVS seem universal aunts. Then I saw her dog, a dirty woolly French poodle, clipped like a boulevard doggie, and his bright clown eyes sparkled from under his dirty top knot. He was a pet. I'm stupid with any language, but oddly enough can always get by, and I somehow understood she wanted the railway station, and off we went. The dog liked me and came quite happily and we did attract attention! I think she must have been Dutch or Belgian, for when the train came in two heavily built Merchant Navy men got off the train. One spoke English and thanked me for 'looking after Therese' – and I was not sure whether it was the girl's or the dog's name. He seemed the most pleased to see the latter! He was very sad. I gathered he had been somewhere to identify a body washed off his ship and swept ashore by the tide …

My husband does worry me. He grows more and more detached and really I often feel I'm not a good influence for him. When he is tired out I always feel so sorry for him and do every little thing to comfort him, but at times I wonder if it would have been better if I had nagged and stormed him out of his moods. I looked at him tonight as he sat – he surprised me by a remark he passed, and I thought I knew them all. I've been looking forward to going into the aerodrome on Saturday when it's open for inspection when our big Savings push opens. A bus runs up to within a mile and a half. We could take the car and go nearer. Granted it's a cold windswept spot, and it would be tiring walking round, but it's a chance we will not get again to see anything like it. He spoke of a bad cold he had coming on, the need to go to Ulverston, how tiring it would be, and all the people who would be there, and we would have to stop and talk to them. I had that irritable feeling at myself for my weak streak when I heard myself say, 'All right, if you don't feel like going, we will go to Ulverston and then on to Spark Bridge to see Aunt Sarah.' I felt angry with myself when I saw the look of relief open over his face. I thought, 'Now why couldn't you have said, "All right, you go to Ulverston and I'll go with the Atkinsons and see the aerodrome"?'...

The first chill of autumn makes me think of winter, and of winter in Europe, making me wish that America had had more of a share in war than she has. She shows very plain signs of her old grab and brag. The word 'peace' will have little meaning for them who have no shelter or warmth. The jaunty smartness, the fat unwholeness of the woman in the red stockings I met today, came back to me. She was one of the lucky ones. Diet and right food will bring down her puppy fat. Her courage showed in her eyes, her attempt to look fashionable and her shaven poodle. I thought of the old ones, the little children, the displaced people who may be suffering for others' sins and do not deserve that they should be turned adrift, back into a homeland that does not want them. I see so little signs of the brotherhood that seemed as if, when it flowered in wartime, it would come to fruit when peace was signed. Arthur's words come back to me. He said he would 'like to retire to a desert island with a handful of congenial souls'. I feel at some time, in some former life, I've been a nun – sought the cloistered life – or maybe I'm the type who seeks it. I feel as if I withdraw within myself more and more in my mind. I feel so useless and little, my efforts so futile and feeble. Nothing I can do or think or say can really help the poor ones. My heart's ease and feeling of being worthwhile in the scheme of things passed when our dear tatty Red Cross shop closed its doors. When I could gloat over the week's taking, thinking, 'So many poor men made happy for a little while', it was always like oil in the lamp.

Maybe I'm war weary and a bit debilitated. Certainly things have rather got me down lately, try as I may. People seem to come too close to me, bruising my mind, tiring me inside. Little things annoy me. My worries go to bed with me, sleep lightly, wake at a touch and are ready when I rise to keep pace with me all day. In spite of all my gay chatter and nonsense, I have no one with whom to talk things over. Come to think of it, the only one I can let me back hair down with is Arthur. We grew up together, poor kid. He helped share burdens from a very early age. Letters are not satisfactory. Beside, it's not fair to worry him with formless little worries and fears. He has his own. My husband's health, little half-formed worries about Cliff, a vague mist of fright and fear, a feeling of chaos all round, fret me when I sit quiet. I feel a feeble lifting up of my hands rather than words when I pray, a feeling that God just knows how I feel and any help would be received with gratitude by me – renewed faith, a chance to help, serenity of mind that seems to have fled me for the present.

One great feeling though – I can read a book, taking interest and losing myself. The Herries books to me are always a delight, beyond their style, bringing alive the places I love in the Lakes, peopling them with what could be the family of Rawlinsons instead of Herries, tracing resemblance and thinking of our old ones lying quiet in Hawkshead churchyard, who lived when the Herries folk lived, feeling akin.* It is a blessing when I can read. I do my duty writing and then read on into the night, when I don't sleep, and if I wake restless, put on the light and read awhile, blessing my room to myself, the fact I've not to lie staring into the darkness, afraid of disturbing my husband, who needs his sleep when he has to work so hard.

Friday, 14 September. I felt exhausted when we were going home, but it was my own fault. I'd only had a very little lunch and nothing but cups of tea. The flies seemed to be over the food and the sink smelled till I went out and got some disinfectant. I felt annoyed when I had to pay 1s 6d again – really mad. I thought, 'I bought this and I'll use it', so poured nearly half down the sink, some down the staff lavatory, and gave a sailor the rest to use in the men's lav – then found out the pong came from the pig tub rather than the sink! I rested and ate some bread and butter when I got in, thinking of the announcement that the WVS will go on for another two years. When we have got through all the material, and Matron's work at Hospital Supply, we will close down, but there remains still the clothing to bale and pack and dispatch to the Red Cross Headquarters – garments sent from the

---

* Hugh Walpole's regional fiction, the 'Herries Chronicle' (1930–33), which comprised four historical novels, featuring narratives of violence and romance, was set in the Lake District in the eighteenth and nineteenth centuries. Nella was a great admirer of these novels. Her mother's family were Rawlinsons.†

American Red Cross. Then there is Canteen, and when Hospital
Supply closes I will do more there if necessary, but none of us will
agree to be exploited in any way. We have worked constantly and
uncomplainingly all the war years, but we will not blackleg or do
work someone else would be paid for doing.

Tonight as I sat I thought of six years ago when Cliff went
off in the second lot of Militia – such a lifetime ago it seems; so
many who went about then will never return. I had a sadness at
the utter stupidity of war, and the blindness and complacency
which allowed us to look on while Hitler armed and prepared,
chuckling at his antics as we would at those of a clown's, telling
ourselves silly things like 'the rolling stock of Germany is so
outworn it could never stand any big strains', shutting our eyes
to the huge strategical arterial roads being made. My dad was an
ardent admirer and disciple of Lord Roberts, never trusted the
Germans, and after the last war worried over the muddled peace.
It's a terrible thought that so much can hang on the way things
are handled now, what dreadful results could and may come in
another twenty-five years.*

Thursday, 20 September. The years slipped back to six years ago,
when war had only started and we were sewing cloth rugs, in very
spare moments. When our minds were half crazed with fear for
the future I loved talk. Men were being called up. Now it's over,
the fighting and killing part, but it's dreadful to read of the food
and fuel shortage and the winter coming on. Poor gay Vienna
again facing famine, and all the Balkan states, which are only a

---

* Field Marshal Earl Roberts (1832–1914) had advocated a robust British
rearmament to defend against (as he saw it) an understandably expansionist
Germany. A street in Barrow is named after him.

name in the paper to us. Greeks, French, Dutch – all the same, hungry and cold. I've had to pinch and scrape at times, economise the rest, to make things go round, but have always managed to serve a tempting meal if it had only been baked potatoes and herrings, when the boys rushed in 'simply starving, Dearie' from school. There has been always a fire to welcome them home, a door to shut out the worries and hurts of the day, a bed for tired heads to sleep and wake refreshed.

When I think of those poor women who suffer twice – once for their families and then for themselves – my heart aches. I'm rather glad that Mrs Woods has not been with us all these last weeks. Today she jarred on us badly when she said that half of Europe *should* die out including the treacherous French who had 'let us down and didn't deserve help in any way'. I thought as I looked at her, 'Well, after all, if we all got our deserts you might be in prison for bribing shop girls to give you extra rations and buying everything you could in the black market.' She thought Mrs Higham and I had 'no sense of proportion' when, in answer to some girl about sending the baby bundles which might be used for a traitor French baby, I said there was no such thing as a traitor baby and Mrs Higham said if there were a thousand bundles and she knew they were going for German babies it would be all the same! I felt a row was very near. We don't think alike on a lot of subjects and Mrs Woods has that hateful air which many teachers have – that 'Be quiet, silly ignorant child, don't you hear me speak?'

Margaret brought some magazines back. There is a decided coolness now between us. I think my remarks about the Australian pilot have offended her out of all proportion – several times she has got in a dig about such a girl 'seeming to be good enough for so and so'. Useless to say anything. The cap has been crammed down over her ears and not just fitted. I wonder in my heart if I started a train of thought that night, if Margaret suddenly sees how many 'friends' she has had, how many heartbreaks. Her friend Linda is married and very sedate, rather snobbishly and slavishly so! She pauses to think how her husband – now left town – would like every little action. Margaret asked her to go to a show the other night and Linda said, 'Oh NO, Margaret. Eddie would not like it, for I know you would be sure to meet some of your boy friends and they would string along.' I looked at Margaret's gay vital face tonight, suddenly seeing why Cliff and she didn't draw any nearer as I'd hoped. They have both that lack of stability, that snatching at life, always wanting the next thing. They are too much alike. I hope Margaret doesn't keep up her offence with me. She is a sweet girl and never takes notice of my husband's moods and silences. I came to bed early, glad my mind is settled enough to read and enjoy a book. It's a great blessing when one can lose all sense of time, all worries, if only for a short time, in a book.

Friday, 21 September. I rose feeling tired but had a strong cup of tea and a bit of toast. The butter does go off nowadays. I thought as I tasted it this morning, 'It's just as well we don't get more than we do – that there is marg.' I baked a little ginger and date cake to share with my mother-in-law, who sent up sugar and her lard ration; made a little hot pot from my scrag of mutton, baked apples and dried egg custard. I had some bits of fat to render and thought I'd clarify my fat in the chip pan. When I took off the lid I felt so annoyed. Mrs Atkinson has borrowed it three times since last Saturday; it was so burnt I feared it would not be any more use – in fact, at one time I'd just have thrown it away. There were bits of blackened fish as well as potatoes and she knows very well that if I do fish in it I always clean it by pouring the fat when boiling into a large dish half filled with water, and letting the fat set before scraping off any scraps from the bottom. I had to boil up and set twice and will do it tomorrow – and keep my chip pan in a different place and not in the garage where she can pop in and get it when she wants without asking.

Tuesday, 25 September. I feel I've never had such a sour attitude on life in general. I thought of the fun and laughter there used to be at Centre, even in the darkest days of war. Sometimes they say in the office, 'You are quiet' – say it in wonder – and I just smile, but think, 'I feel quiet, I'm tired out', and wonder if that is why others feel dim. There was such an eager looking forward to the end of the war. When I used to talk of still lean times till all got reorganised, I was looked on as a real dismal Jimmy. Now it's over. We look forward to a winter which promises to be short of coal and food. Women who thought their husbands would be released if their job was waiting are feeling disappointed. Husbands are coming home so changed and with such altered outlooks they seem strangers. Women are leaving their wartime jobs and finding it's not as easy to pick up threads as lay them down. Clothes coupons are beginning to seem inadequate lately when big things are needed. Meat is scarcer and nothing to replace it in the menus of harried landladies and mothers of families. Milk is down to two pints a head per week. There is so little brightness in life, and people's heads are so tired. Speaking for myself, I feel as if anyone said, 'Tell me what you would really like to do', I could not tell them. I could say I'd like to go somewhere where there were no bitter winds and damp to make me dread winter, somewhere where I could lie in the sun and feel warm, but I feel too indifferent to think of anything I'd really like to buy, or do, and what I do seems only like another job – all except when I come to bed and lie reading. It's my chief joy today. I think of this tiredness magnified to the highest degree amongst the homeless ones. Sometimes I wonder if we get wavelengths of their despair and depression. I wonder what would happen if anything like the Spanish influenza swept over the world like it did after the last war – people would die in greater numbers than even in the war.

Thursday, 4 October. My 55th birthday – and Centre finally finished except for a little whist drive next Tuesday and our trip to Blackpool on Wednesday. I feel a bit dim tonight. We were down early and worked like niggers. Mrs Woods came down soon after Mrs Higham and I did and helped us sort out six years' accumulation of junk in the way of old cardboard boxes, old letters – Mrs Waite has a Chinaman's aversion to destroying any written or printed matter! Carters trailed in and out for various lent things. The place got emptier. We were glad of our hot lunches – really hot with junk we had burnt and got the oven hot. Mrs Waite came in, and Mrs Lord and Mrs Ledgerwood would not have anything at all to do with her and kept out of the Committee room. I got into trouble with the organisers of the trip to Blackpool for having asked Mrs Woods to go with us. I said impatiently, 'Oh, don't be daft – you invited Mrs Higham and I, and Mrs Woods is on the Committee', and got the answer 'Well, we like you'! They knew it was my birthday and teased me to tell them how old I was, one woman saying, 'Well, *I* know you are nearer fifty than forty', and made those who knew my age laugh …

I was home at 4.15 and before I changed or washed I relaxed on the settee and read Cliff's letter – quite an ordinary and newsy one. I need not have worried so with visions of him being ill.

He is so happy just now in his work, he says. He would make the Army his career if he had a small private income! I've been astonished to hear many remarks which show the same trend – married men too who speak of living in occupied countries with their families later on ...

Aunt Eliza came in with some pears and a wee buttonhole of two flat clover-coloured daisies, which will be the making of my clover flannel frock. She has such an eye for colour as form – surprisingly so for an old country woman. We sat and talked. She will be eighty this December but her mind is as keen and clear as Aunt Sarah's and her memory like a book whose pages can be turned back for reference. Surprisingly enough, tonight she talked of Mother, who died at fifty-two – poor Mother whose heart broke at twenty-one and for the rest of her life had little to give her second husband or her three children; who, looking back, seemed to live in a world entirely her own and preferred shadows and might-have-beens to real people. My husband said, 'If Nell doesn't stop losing weight she is going to grow very like her mother in figure and general looks.' Aunt Eliza was shocked. She said, 'Oh no, Will – why, Nell's mother was a beauty. I'm sure Nell takes after Grandma Lord', which, considering I've heard Aunt Eliza discuss the short stature and the all-round worthlessness of a family who had lived for generations in Woolwich – 'which they tell me is London' – I thought it a bit comic. She looks well for her change of air and speaks of trying to get a cottage in the country next summer. I thought of the way Mother and her sisters had squandered money, just lately letting it drain away. I thought in that respect I was like the Lord's family, and of course I never had any to squander. My shillings have always had to go as far as eighteen pence.

I made some little felt shoes and got them on seven dollies.

They are coming on very nicely. I've a pile of odd bits of material from Centre, too, I can piece up for very wee ones' nighties and I'll make some little dressing gowns of crazy patchwork from my good scraps of pastel-coloured crêpe de Chine and silk. I'll find plenty to do all right, but I would like to find something where we could work in company. It's no use worrying. I had a job to break into the war but I did it.

Bed seems pretty good to my aching back and wretched bones and I'll read when I've written two letters.

Saturday, 6 October. It was such a queer foggy morning and when I went to the hairdresser's for nine o'clock the cars and buses all had lights on full. I cannot be in a good mood with myself. For the first time, getting my hair permed irked and fidgeted me, but it's a very good one and will last. It was my husband's birthday gift so cost me nothing either. When I came home at twelve o'clock, the sun was shining brightly and people thronged the streets. The sun, the heaps of celery, pears and apples, tomatoes and boiled peeled beetroots, and meeting so many children and young people happily munching apples or pears as they walked in the sun, seemed to give such an air of happy prosperity, quite like the pre-war days.

It always seems odd to me to see queues for shoes, but an incident I heard the other day made me wonder if it was people's greed that was partly to blame for the shortage. Favoured customers get a ring when Joyce or good branded shoes come in, and one woman who, before the war, would never have had more than three pair of shoes was heard to boast she had fifteen pairs of shoes that had never yet been mended and were as good as new. My husband, who never in his life owned more than one fountain pen, now has three. He had one from Arthur as a present and passed on the one

I bought to Clifford and was heard to say he could have done with a spare one and was offered two at different times and took them. I said, 'You cannot use more than one pen at once' but he seems to like to see them! I've noticed many little incidents like it at different times and feel it's one of the chief sources of everyday things being scarce. I had enough soup to heat and we had potted meat, celery and tomatoes, wholemeal bread and butter.

We decided to go to Kendal for our last little outing before the clocks were put back, and have our tea out. It was a glorious day for motoring, bright and clear and golden brown leaves softly falling like snow and drifting along the roads into heaps. I dearly love Kendal, its old hotels and buildings and its general air of peacefulness, only marred by the heavy North Road traffic thundering through. I think it should be by-passed from the narrow streets. I could have bought fat hares and rabbits, trout or mackerel, and the shops were so well stocked. I saw china and crockery I never thought to see again, and the antique shops had things of beauty and usefulness, not ugly museum pieces. I looked at chairs and presses, gay china and lovely glass, thinking 'Judith Paris† may have owned things like that', and laughed at my whimsy when I realised they would have come from every corner of England. I saw my first television set but was not very thrilled. The screen was so tiny any performers would have looked like dolls …

Mrs Howson came in for a chat. She got home last night and looks a bit down. She has had a nice time in Portsmouth. She says she doesn't know what she will do when the clothing job finishes at the WVS. She is a very lonely and somewhat aloof woman, and at times gets notions that everyone and everything is against her. I feel concern at times when she is in that mood, recalling how her father with no real cares felt the same – and one day was found hanging from a beam in his paint shop.

CHAPTER TWO

A SORT OF PEACE

October 1945–January 1946

Tuesday, 16 October. Sometimes I've a cold fear on me when I look at my husband. He never had a very firm hold on realities. Now he has an interest in nothing. At one time I grew frettish if I was not 'bright and amusing'. Often now he never speaks for the whole evening unless it's a grunt or 'Yes' or 'Oh'. I think of his parents and shudder. Beyond breathing and eating, they have not been alive for years, say quite frankly they 'don't want bothering' when their sons or daughters call. No memory, no interest in themselves or the outside world. I'm heart thankful the boys are not like that. I'd rather never have their company than they should grow so afraid and indifferent to life. All my wild rebellion seems over. Strong people don't dominate like weak ones. In a strong person there is something to fight, a chink in their armour somewhere. Everyone has something. I count my blessings and find I've a good many, and most of us walk alone. I often envy women with a big family. I look at Margaret often and wish she was my girl, though lately we seem very apart. I think my words about the Australian were a cap that fitted and for the first time she began to think.

Saturday, 20 October. I've a great sadness on me. Perhaps the grey day and the thought of winter contributed to my mood, but somehow the dockers' strike, the worldwide unrest, the widespread misery made me wonder how long it will be before we can say, 'Peace in our time, oh Lord.' The only peace is that there are no active hostilities, but the corrosion of the war years is eating deeper into civilisation. People have time to think, and their thoughts make them afraid. In the chaos that follows war there seems so little to grip. Things alter and move so quickly. Sometimes I feel I'm on a slide – and a greased one at that. In the simple code in which my generation were reared there was right and wrong, good and bad, things which were just not done, examples we strove to follow. All gone. Freud pointed out that behaviourism could be excused on the count of inhibitions and repressions. In a world where mass murder by bombing was looked on as necessary, where life was as little valued in the Western as the Eastern world, when young men went off on suicide expeditions by air and glider, where clergy had ceased to hold people by doctrine or natural dignity, where no hero lasted for long and where home ties were broken, and 'Mother' or 'Dad', as always handy to turn to, impossible, there seems none of the stability so necessary for each and all, if we have to have peace of mind at all.

I often feel as if the whole world had been a heap of compact bundles of sticks, and all the strings binding them were going and sticks lying round or floating downstream, blown in high winds, breaking each other or pressing the ones underneath into the ground to rot. I wish I could find some work which had to be done – a job to do outside my home, working with and for others. As I sat tonight I visualised all the piles of mending, my hospital dollies and garments, books I'd planned to read – and found them wanting. I don't want leisure to feel creeping tides of worry and unrest come nearer. I want to feel I am helping, in however small a way. I want the laughter and fellowship of the war years.

Tuesday, 23 October. My husband rang up and suggested going to the pictures tonight as he could not get home early tomorrow night. I scrambled an egg for him and I had cheese and tomato and there was loganberry jam and wholemeal bread and butter, and plain cake and gingerbread. I enjoyed the picture, *Roughly Speaking*, though it bordered somewhat on fantasy to English people, in its opportunities and ups and downs, but I thought it would be grand to be married to a man who hit back at life without whining and complaining.

I had a letter from Cliff today. It looks as if he has made up his mind to go with the Glider Pilot Regiment if he has a chance when they go to Palestine, although he says they may have one of their own flyers as adjutant. Things may work out for the best if he does. I've always said he needed discipline, and up to now he has kicked against everything, seeing authority as only to be flouted. Another year in the Army may make him more sure of his own capabilities. He is not lazy and if he can concentrate on a job where he will be happy it will be all for the good. I do miss Arthur sometimes, and long to talk things over and over. I sit and turn things over in my mind as my fingers fly over my sewing. The humour I've been in lately recalls six years ago, when I honestly think my rag dollies helped me to hold on. There's a great satisfaction in seeing a thing take shape and form under one's hands, especially if they are made from oddments into something worthwhile. I often have a sneaking wish I was strong minded like Mrs Atkinson and could say I was going to a whist drive a few nights a week. She tells her husband quite frankly, if he's too dull to talk or play cards, she will go where she *can* be amused. Yet cards never interest me for very long. It would be more of a penance than amusement if I went to play so often. In spite of my busy day I got two more dollies finished, little black girl dollies in gay dresses and a big bow in their mop of hair.

Saturday, 27 October. I've only one dollie to finish now, and their name labels to tie on. They look such a happy bright lot of little rag people. I always have a queer feeling when I look at them, feeling in some way they have life in their strangely different expressions. Perhaps the different textures of the scraps I use are responsible, but all seem individual. Matron likes peasant girls with plaits and bonnets with turnbacks – she is of Dutch extraction – so I've managed to make her ten girls and three gollywogs … I'll start on cot quilts and dressing gowns next week, though I've two cushion covers I'd like to make for the settee in the dining room. I'd planned to make them for Xmas and the new curtains too – such nice golden orange material I'd bought just before the war and never made when blackout curtains made out for so long, when faced with shabby darned ones.

I thought I'd have all nice for Xmas when Cliff came, but if as he expects he will be in Palestine by then, I think I'll make all gay for his leave – that is, if he comes. Surely he will come for a few days, dull as he finds home. I often wonder what queer kinks he has deep down, when he finds so much fault with all at home, with its size and set out, my decorations and 'old-fashioned ways'. I look round and think it's a very nice house really, and kept as well as anyone else's. Sometimes I tell myself it's a kind of twisted love of both home and me that makes him lash out. When he was younger he used to get cross at my weak streak and say I gave in too much for peace sake, but by Gad I've had to give in as much to him as anyone. I've known the impulse to strike him flat, to speak cuttingly and to the point, to strip him of some of his conceits and silly values – and that streak in me that made me always insist that home was a place where you came to recover from the knocks and pricks of life and not receive them laid a hand on my lips. Then again, I have a feeling hard to define that, in spite of all, I stand for some anchorage in Cliff's life. If Cliff knew how clearly I saw things, his way of thinking and acting, the worthlessness of so many of his 'friendships', I feel something would go. It's better I should let him think I'm sweet and dumb, seeing and understanding only what he thinks fit, knowing nothing but what he thinks fit to tell me. He forgets – or ignores – that talk and gossip filters through.

Tuesday, 30 October. It was a fine morning and I decided to go shopping and get rid of my heavy headache in the fresh air, and I wanted to see if my dress had come into a shop where a consignment was expected. I got a really beautiful one, a real 'dream dress', and by Gad my diary and I will be the only ones to know what I paid – eight guineas. I told my husband it was over £5 and he nearly had a fit. I felt peeved when I thought how little I'd ever spent on clothes, always making them myself till I got my two last coats tailored. He never realises the days of cheap remnants have gone, and he is so unobservant he never sees changing prices and supplies. It's a soft turquoise blue that blends perfectly with the russet of my coat. I thought at first it was too young but the shop girl said, 'It's exactly your dress in style and colours are never considered "young".' Silly old thing – I don't remember feeling so excited over a dress since I was a girl. Cliff will understand. Maybe I'll whisper my sin to him when he comes!

Wednesday, 31 October. Hallowe'en. I wonder if anyone remembers the jolly parties and 'duck apples' of pre-war days. Somehow my mind went back – it might have been sixty and not six years. I had rather an amazing letter from Cliff saying he had proposed to a WAAF† officer he had mentioned, but did not know yet if she had accepted. When I had recovered from my surprise I felt such a wild hope that she would accept him. I felt it would be an answer to prayer, that I'd never ask for anything for myself as long as I lived if Cliff could find steady happiness with someone he loved.

Poor little Mrs Cooper was in great distress. Neither of us put into words the fear we have about her husband. I fear it's malignant. She seemed as if she didn't want to be alone so I kept with her and when there was not actually anything to do alongside her. I intended talking cheerfully on any subject that came into my mind, and felt rewarded when I got her to laugh a little.

Friday, 2 November. It was such a fair, sweet morning – hard to realise it was so near Xmas. I had a pile of best tablecloths and napkins, doilies, and overalls, and I decided I'd take advantage of the fine morning. I had such hindrance – phone calls and people paying bills who lingered to chat and I felt I didn't get near done I'd planned. I had good soup to heat and enough meat roll, and I boiled potatoes and carrots and made a good steamed raisin pudding and a little marmalade jam. I felt tired and it was such a nice pleasure to be shut up in Canteen. A ring just before I went told me the result of the specially convened meeting last night. We cannot get a night porter – the one who applied last week only stayed one night – and it's been decided to close the bedrooms this week, or until we get a porter. If the beds are not let I only give the Canteen till Xmas to stay open, for it's an expensive place to run now we don't have as many for meals and snacks. I'd a little shopping to do and Mrs Higham picked me up at the corner and we managed to get all done before going into Canteen. I was glad to see 6 lb of sausage I'd had promised and we had the breakfast bacon but no potatoes for chips, after me getting the fat.

We felt vexed when we had to refuse nice lads a bed, but Mrs Goode, the bed-maker, was talking to us and she said it's not only that we don't pay well, but she says that since VE Day the Canadian behaviour worsened and since VJ Day it's been growing worse. Quite decent fellows come in dead drunk and wet the beds through and are sick on the floor – often all over their bed – without the least trace of shame. In wartime there was nothing of that, but now it's as if, she says, they don't fear reporting or have any decency when they have drink. She says that two night porters left for that, saying there was more decency in a common doss house. It will be a pity if that element is the cause of the Canteen closing, for we get older and more stable men and fellows on leave or who cannot get train connections. We were very busy all afternoon, for with it being cold we made toast and put cheese or scrambled egg on top.

We came home in the Highams' car, and I had a cup of tea and did some mending as I sat by the fire. Margaret came in to show me the material she had bought with the coupons I let her have. She has got black for she says it's such a good standby when she can use different accessories. She is going to make a long dress after all. She says they are coming back very quickly and she will have it long till after Xmas if not for after March. She looks very thin. She says she has no time for Barrow boys – 'They are all dull after RAF and Americans.' I held my tongue this time. I could have repeated remarks Cliff had passed about girls who liked Americans better than our own lads! I'm anxiously waiting now for letters from both Arthur and Cliff, to see if Arthur has been nominated for the exam for promotion, and to see if Cliff has been accepted by the WAAF girl! I felt dead tired tonight. I feel I've a cold hanging on me.

Saturday, 3 November. My husband had an appointment for 1.30, so I decided to do my ironing while waiting for him. We went to Spark Bridge at three o'clock. It was a pearl-grey day, dull but luminous, with the hills fairly clear. A lot of leaves still cling to the trees ... The still hazy air kept the wood smoke down, making all fragrant and homely, especially when the smell of baking bread came from cottage door. Aunt Sarah had been baking and her stock pot smelled very good. The cottage was warm all through; the canary's chirp and the little cat's purr seemed to add to the welcome we got. Nowadays it's so difficult to take a little present of food. In my 'lucky bag' today was gingerbread, parkin,† cheese, a wee bit of potted meat and two tomatoes, a bit of dripping and some sweet apples, and there was Joe's ounce of tobacco. We chatted about the different boys of the village, who had come on leave and who was married. Aunt Sarah takes a great interest in all around her even though she's so deaf. We were home by 5.15 and I boiled eggs – fresh ones I'd got off Mrs Whittam yesterday.

Sunday, 4 November. Last night I was kept awake by fireworks going off, as if those kiddies who had been lucky enough to get any had not the patience to wait till Monday. I had my usual rest and before I had my bath I slipped down in my dressing gown and popped a little dish I'd prepared last night in the oven. I put my soup on to heat on a low heat. I had sausage in a flat dish and stewed apples and made apple sauce and put it on the sausage and added a layer of mashed potatoes and it made a very tasty lunch. It was tinned soup – with not cooking my meat – but I added a little Bovril for flavour and extra goodness. We had a cup of tea and piece of cake for a sweet, and having washed up we were out by 1.45, for it was such a lovely day we planned to go to Ambleside, feeling there would not be many more fine days. The beech trees are still a golden glory and the sun turns the bracken-clad moss and hillsides to russet. As we passed under beech or oak trees their leaves fluttered down through the open top of the car, bringing in their scent, like withered apples. At Bowness they had little motor launches and sailing boats out, and even rowing boats for hire, and each big chara park had a good number in – and I counted them in one by the lake: twenty-seven. I've never known so long a season and the Lakes, and cafés and sweet and ice-cream shops were doing a good trade. It would be dark for the charas going home. It was dusk when we got in at five o'clock. There was bottled pears and unsweetened milk for cream, wholemeal bread and butter, parkin and plain cakes, and a leaping wood and coal fire. When I'd washed up I put a rather damp piece of oak log at the back of the fire and it lasted all right as we sat, and the wood smoke seemed to go through the whole house.

My husband was writing for a while so I sat quiet and stitched busily at one of the little cot quilts and got one finished. It's a really worthwhile little thing – both sides very good silk and neatly and strongly sewn on to a pad of cotton wool. It will do fine for the two tiny cots when they have poor babes of a few days old who need warmth of cotton wool. We listened to *Lorna Doone* and then the news. My husband has been very moody and quiet lately. I sat wrapped in my own thoughts and surmises – a montage of speculation about Cliff and if Arthur has got his nomination and if I'll see them this Xmas skimmed through my mind. I'd like to see the girl Cliff speaks of. He has spoken so often of never marrying that I think she must be exceptional! I went into the garden just before I came to bed. The stars were bright as if it were going to be frosty. All round fireworks popped and in one garden they even had a bonfire. Children of today have little restraint. They want what they want right now without that careful preparation for a given festa. It's part of the 'take the cash and let the credit go' of today which creeps in everywhere. 'Fish is in Jones,' you think rapidly. Will the sausage I had got keep till tomorrow? Better get fish while I've got a chance. You see cold cream in a shop, and although you have quite half a pot you buy another while it's there.

Unconsciously we are all changing in little ways. I thought tonight as I sat how hard I'd grown these last six years. No one would fret me into a nervous breakdown now. When my husband gets his moods, beyond seeing he has nothing to annoy him further, then a tasty meal, and warm fire waiting if it's cold, I let him alone with an 'Ah, the back of my hand to you' feeling. No coaxing and worrying – and he doesn't get the black moods he used to do. When he does, I don't even notice them. Somehow I've learned – or gained – serenity. I've come at long last to that place where Gran walked, and know what she meant when she talked of 'laying her burden down before God after she had done what she could to bear it'. Knowing too the Rhythm and Strength she spoke of – all there if we reach out. She had big worries and came through. My little worries fade before hers, but they are ever present. I feel too that now I don't go out two days a week I don't throw things off the same.

Monday, 5 November. My husband is off on a black horse of a mood because Cliff has proposed to a girl who, by what I make out, has money of her own and a certain amount of position. He says, 'Cliff wants nothing with a girl above him in position. She will look down on us.' I said, 'That won't matter, as long as she doesn't look down on Cliff.' Then I had to listen to a lot of half-baked grumbling and nattering till I felt I could have screamed, 'Ah, hold your tongue – *do*.' I said, 'If you begin to talk of what your parents said, by Gad I'll tell you a few mine said. Any "inferiority" you speak of between us was in your mind. I'd no better education than you had. Any learning came from reading or listening to people talk and if it came to that my "fine lady" ways of which you complain has kept your house and home on little money, has put up with your moods, plus your family's interference and intolerance, till I woke up to the fact I had no need to take notice of them. And mark you this – I've wakened to a full realisation of you too.' I shook with rage. I felt one of my rare storms of temper surge over me. I bit my lip hard to stem the spate of words I longed to utter, and went and ran cold water over my hands and wrists till they ached and burned with pain from the chill.

Saturday, 10 November. Lunch was quite tasty, but I am so tired of casseroles and stews. I long sometimes for a grilled steak or chop, a slice of prime roasted meat, rabbit or chicken pie. I feel tired of dodged-up† meals. I have to plan and scheme to get fresh flavours and always to make a tempting meal from scraps, seeing no prospects of anything different for a long time. Underneath my grouse, though, is a very thankful feeling that we have rations, when I look at the queues lined up for other short supplies.

Saturday, 17 November. My mind went back to a year ago – although by the calendar it's not till a year ago tomorrow – since I had the cable to say Cliff was dangerously wounded. Somehow I feel as if nothing will ever hurt me again, and that I could face anything that came. I plumbed the depths of my faith and endurance, taking each day as it came – and now he is off again.

Sunday, 18 November. We went to Spark Bridge. It was such a lovely bright day, like we get at the end of December when we have 'crossed the line'. Aunt Sarah was baking bread and they had chops done in the oven for a treat. The stock pot bubbled and, adding to the smell of baking bread and wood smoke, made a smell of home and comfort. They are as bright and cheerful as can be, happy in all their little blessings as if they had money and every of their hearts' best wishes – maybe happier! It grew dark rapidly and we came home, giving a lift to a very odd couple. He was a very young RAF officer; she was a pretty, very silent girl of perhaps eighteen–nineteen. They were walking along with heavy suitcases and I know they had a very long way before they could catch a bus to take them to Ulverston station. They didn't speak one word to each other, and he had a very pettish manner when he spoke of 'hanging round Ulverston till the six o'clock train'. I suggested spending an hour in an ice-cream café over a cup of tea and said, 'Perhaps they will have fires in the waiting room.' He gave me a look as if I'd suggested he pass the time singing in the streets. A more haughty spoilt infant I've not seen for a while, in spite of his RAF uniform. I tried to talk pleasantly to the girl but she was either very shy or afraid of him.

My husband said when they had got out, 'Perhaps a honeymoon couple.' I said, 'I hope it's only an unofficial one. That girl looked too nice to make a mistake and be punished all the rest of her life. She could live down a stolen weekend.' I could often giggle wildly when I see the effect of a lawless remark of mine on my husband. Poor lamb. He is really unique. His mind clings to the catechism and prayer book in general. He thinks marriage means utter possession of body and soul, thoughts and interest, of a wife by a husband. That I should say such things of a lord of creation shocked him to his soul case.[†] He would get a bigger shock if he realised my whole impression of men in general sometimes!

Wednesday, 21 November. I feel utterly bewildered by a letter from Cliff. He is not going to Palestine after all and it looks as if he will not sign for another twelve months, merely to stay in the Army, and not go off with this crowd he likes so much. I can tell he felt very unsettled, wishing his father's business had been anything else, or had been something he could have organised. After Mrs Howson went, I felt I remembered so clearly the chaos and heartbreak after 1918 of the demobbed officers and the ways of the untrained who had had three or four of the most important years of their lives in the Army or Navy. We lived in a street running from the centre of the town. The Town Hall seemed a starting place, and our street got every canvasser and hawker. I'd had a major operation and was very slow to recover and was rarely out in the day. The anxious, desperate young faces at my door worried me to distraction, the newspaper canvassers especially as I saw their jaunty smartness rapidly go shabby, their shoes broken under the polish, their linen frayed. I used to change my paper and place orders for *John Bull*, etc., offer cups of hot tea I had just made, and which were never refused, nor soup on cold days. Tired faces, old-young, dispirited ones seemed to flicker before my mind's eyes.

I heard my husband say suddenly, 'Whatever is to do, Dearie?' and realised my face was wet with tears running down and dripping on my little cat's black fur. I tried to tell him. I felt myself shake with deep sobs that choked me as I could only say, 'It's the *waste* of it all and the folly and the shame.' I so rarely cry that when I do I make up for it. I thought of broken lives, and homes, of bright lives cut short, the courage and endeavour which had gone for war and kept back a lot of the meanness of human frailty like a dam. I felt I wept for the children who would never be born, and for some who had been, as the face of a child I saw in town rose before me, pallid and blind, who had been born to a really charming girl after her husband had been in the East for two years and who had 'neglected an illness', as his innocent mother put it.

I've finished my book of Canada, with its short references to the state of the world in general just before and just after Napoleon's defeat. The world seemed pretty hopeless then. I wonder if it will settle and grow stable again after all this. 'Britain is dispersing her aircraft factories.' 'America is making atomic bombs still.' I once read somewhere that 'in the next war there is a strong possibility the British seat of Government will be moved to Canada'. That was years ago, before the last war – maybe the astrologer who wrote it had missed a war.

I felt my wits had been shaken loose in my head. I had two aspirin and a cup of tea for my supper, reflecting that my fit of the blues started when the afternoon post brought a letter from Edith to say Arthur had been given word he had missed nomination. I did so hope he got his chance. I felt a wild terror that he was going to be like me through life – always seeming to be on the outside looking in; that however he strived and planned, he would just miss things. I don't want Arthur to feel the gnaw and corrosion of frustration – as if it mattered one scrap what *I* wanted! 'There's an end that shapes our destiny', etc.

Christmas was approaching, and Nella decided to put austerity aside. 'I'm not going to save and scratch ever again,' she declared on 5 December.

The immediate beneficiary of this resolution was her husband, for whom she bought an extravagant Christmas gift – a lovely oak-framed electric clock (costing almost £3), which she thought would go nicely with the oak trim in their dining room. The hard times had gone on long enough, she thought, and in her view the restrictive policies of the new Labour government were decidedly objectionable. 'This government is going to rob us of all individuality,' she wrote on 5 December. 'I'll not live to see the reaping of the whirlwind, but I'm not going to help them. For the rest of my life I will spend any little surplus I get.' As if to underline this determination, later that day, when her husband asked what she would like for Christmas, she suggested a fur coat and a diamond ring.

Monday, 10 December. It's been a really evil day of icy fog, and maybe it was partly the cause of a really nervy day all day. I felt depressed and sad. I pictured homeless cold people, little children and old ones without fire and warmth. My snug little home and glowing fire seemed both lonesome things – and a reproach. I baked bread and some plain biscuits to put in a tin for when Cliff comes. He loves biscuits for supper and I've still half a tin of parkins so he will not have to worry about eating out. I had a bit of pastry in a bowl from last baking day, and I made a nice damson tart with a jar of bottled damsons. I made a very good suet pudding and there was some to send down to the old ones, with a little new cob† of bread and a few biscuits …

As I grow older I grow more convinced in, if not reincarnation exactly, that our life here is incomplete, is only a tiny paragraph of a long book, which will have to be taken as a whole. I feel the truth of so much of my old gran's sayings and teachings, wondering where she learned them. Her 'do the best you can and pass on, leaving the rest to God' might well be a teaching for today's problems. As I sat tonight I had the feeling of frustration I had before I got into war work proper – so much to do and no one wanted my services! Europe and its terrible sufferings might be on the moon and out of reach of our help, for all the aids it gets in Barrow. Perhaps when Xmas, our first peacetime Xmas, gets over, it will be different. Mrs Diss said, 'Trouble of it is, you know, if we do start a "make and mend" as you suggest, we might only be helping black-market crooks.' I think the Red Cross could give us a lead, for everyone could do a little and it would help as the shilling-a-week fund helped. So many people take the view that 'Germany has brought it all on herself.' I said to Mrs Woods, 'Well, there is France, and little French children.' Her big blue eyes rolled and flashed as she said, 'And for what are we to thank France, pray?' I feel we should leave punishment to the clever ones. The ordinary simple folk should hold out a hand to anyone in trouble or want – we are not God – and little children feel cold and frightened whatever their country or colour. It's a very remarkable thing that amongst the people who think Germany has brought it all on herself France is considered a traitor and should be punished for giving up – Belgium too in some people's opinion. These are the best church people I know. I shocked Mrs Woods terribly by saying, 'The kindly pitiful Christ you sing about would have been in the Belsen camp and in all the worst bombed places. He wouldn't recognise his churches as holy places.'

My husband said, 'You look very sad. Are you worrying about anything?' I said, 'I've got a real attack of the blues. I think I'm worrying more than I know about Cliff, and Arthur and Edith having to move, and it's opened the door to a whole battalion of worries and sad thoughts.' I'm glad I'm going to the little reunion whist drive tomorrow and meeting all the Hospital Supply lot. Mrs Caddy the caretaker died very suddenly. She was in the best of health and spirits when we had our last drive, and disappointed because we planned to have this one in the ARP† Club. She was upset a few weeks ago when her black cat Dear Dinkes was run over. She cried to me as she said, 'You know, I'll miss that cat this winter when the door is shut and the evenings are so long. When you live alone you grow so attached to your cat.' It's as well now he went before her. He followed her like a dog and his excited rush to greet her when she had been shopping made me hope he was waiting for her. He was a very nice cat.

Tuesday, 11 December. It's been a day of surprises, not the least being that I've slipped up somewhere and am fifty-six and not fifty-five! My husband is fifty-seven today. I went down town for my groceries and got some lovely sweet oranges, and when I said how glad I was to have them as I expected three of my family home for Xmas, my greengrocer let me have a pound each for them as well – he said they would not keep but I don't see why, they are not too ripe. I went into Canteen for the bills to pay and Mrs Goode the cleaner said what a poor Xmas it was for kiddies. She spoke of past Xmases when there had been apples, and a few tins of fruit. I said, 'Well, you would have to give points for fruit.' She said she never spent all her points – did I want any? I offered to swap bottled fruit for enough points to get a pound of chocolate biscuits, so I'll give her a 2 lb jar of unsweetened blackberries and a 1 lb jar of apples and 1 lb jar of damsons in syrup. She was delighted, and so was I …

I sat and planned my decorations. I'll get them out tomorrow. I've not much scope for anything different with my carefully saved streamers of red and green crinkled paper, but suddenly remembered they would be new to the boys and Edith. I keep prowling around trying to see anything which needs seeing to, renewing every little thing like my stock of condiments, soap flakes in the jar in the bathroom and ammonia in the bottle there, longing for the days of bath salts I loved – lovely eau de cologne or pine or verbena.

Wednesday, 12 December. When Mrs Cooper went I finished off the shirt I had tacked and then hunted out all my Xmas bits and bobs, carefully packed in boxes. Cliff's little tree carries its age very well – twenty-five! Perhaps the great love he had for it and the fact it would not be Xmas without it has helped preserve it! I put all the little glass ornaments on and the big star and two strands of tinsel I bought out of Mrs Waite's little hoard she gave us to sell at the Hospital Supply last Xmas. I bought a box of tiny crackers only thumb length for our last party, seven years ago. I caught my breath at the thought that only my own two and three of the girls were left. One girl died of TB – that was the outcome of going in the WAAFs and sleeping in a damp bed. One died when her baby was born – poor dear, she was the wife of one of the Boots' crowd. And one was killed in our raids. The other two we lost sight of completely when their family moved to Australia. I'd forgotten Jack Gorst, though – he was there, for it was the crackers he brought in, made like little dinner rolls, that made me forget to pull the wee ones off the tree. I had said, 'Never mind. I'll save them for the next party' – and 1939 brought something else but parties and I said to myself, 'I'll keep them till the next party as I said.' They look a bit tired and dusty, but then, aren't we all? I think they have little whistles or jewellery in – something hard. Mrs Atkinson said with a little sniff, 'Trust you to have something that no one else has, or can buy.' I was glad really that no one came in as I unpacked my little oddments, of paper rolled up from, I think, three other Xmases – two anyway.

I trimmed the little tree with the feeling that every little tawdry chipped bauble was alive and was glad to be on the tree again, for when I'd finished I felt myself musing and gently laughing over a remembered incident, and the tree twinkled and winked in the firelight as if to say, 'Go on remembering. Memory is the one thing that no one can break or tarnish, soil or destroy. It's your very own.'

Under my well-thought preparations and my plans I've a sadness which takes keeping down. Perhaps it's because of Cliff and his future. Perhaps thinking of Arthur and Edith flat-hunting. They talk of young folks having families. I see no chance as yet of Arthur starting a family in any reasonable comfort, and he is thirty-two and life passes so swiftly. Just as a clock often begins to go fast as it nears the end of its spring, and needs complete winding or it will stop, I feel we all are going faster.

I'd like to talk over, or rather listen to clever competent people talking about, this loan from America. I feel America has not acted like a good neighbour at all. My husband says that when travellers come round so much is written off their catalogues and they tell him all is for export. The New Year is going to be a shock for people. Things will be very tight and on the whole more difficult than in the war years, for there will be so many more civilians and so many less things to buy. I feel America is laying the foundations of resentment which will recoil on her, whereas she could have laid those of real comradeship, and in life there are no rewards and no revenge – only consequences. I feel it's the fact we have a Labour Government, that if Churchill had still led, things would have been a lot different. Rightly or wrongly, the USA Government fear Attlee and despise Harold Laski [*Chairman of the Labour Party*]. It would have been better if he had been in the hotel in Barrow when a bomb demolished it. He is that most unfortunate of men – one who does not know when to speak and when to hold his tongue, and in a public figure it's the unforgivable sin. The fact too that he is a Jew is unfortunate. I've often been astonished at the mistrust and real hatred of Jews in quite ordinary men in the street.

Friday, 14 December. I got a letter, or rather a note, to say Cliff would be coming Saturday or perhaps Friday. He was in London and doing a little shopping. I had to hurry and bake, for in any case I would not do so on Saturday morning as I had to go to the hairdresser's ...

I was talking to such a nice lad in Canteen today, well spoken and with that indefinable air of 'background'. We spoke of demob-ilisation. He hopes to be out by next June. He's twenty-four. He joined up at seventeen and a half because he was out of joint with the jarring course he had embarked upon, and the Army offered a grand escape. His uncle has since died – his father died when he was small – and he has absolutely no idea what he will do. He thought he might go in the building trade for he will have to help his mother. A boy in a nearby street was a ticket collector on the railway. Now he is demobbed a major – acting colonel when he came out – with a dainty, expensive-looking wife he married when a captain, and they have a little girl of two and another expected any time. I thought of housing problems as well as work and adjustments. I felt the Saturnalian 'Lord of misrule' was in charge of this lovely earth and its misused treasures. The dire feeling that lies like a bank of heavy snow clouds in my mind seemed to deepen. When Big Ben tolls I feel my heartfelt prayer urging, 'Please God, bless the young ones' more sincere than that for hopeless frightened ones or the cold and hungry. We older ones have had our day, have made or marred our lives, but we did have chances. Any courage we possess was rooted in security of some kind – home, Church, or faith in the clever ones who seemed omnipotent.

Till I die I'll remember the morning after our worst raid, when roofs and windows all went aground – tiled roofs. I felt I walked about in a daze. With a curious lack of any noise or talking or movement, except a persistent tinkling sound, like the little temple wind bells we once would buy, it was falling shovelfuls of glass as everyone swept it up and put it in heaps. Sometimes in my mind I feel and hear that tinkling noise, when I think of the shattered lives of so many, of the senselessness and the utter folly of war, when no one wins. America has won this war, but in a short time she will have a bigger depression than ever before. She has no soul and is too young a country to understand the problems of the old world. And there's a thing people tend to forget. One of the strongest cornerstones in American society as a whole is bitter resentment, either to their own country or another, which compelled them to seek a fuller life overseas. There is a deep hidden fear in Americans. That is why so many of them bluster and brag. They are not used to things. Prosperity hurts them as much as the poverty and hardship which sent their fathers wandering, but shows in their love of being top dog.

· I rave. It's after 12.30 and time I slept!

Cliff was now at home.

Saturday, 15 December. I had to hurry out for nine o'clock and I cooked enough bacon and sausage for two mornings for Cliff and put half in the pantry so that I can rest in the morning. I rose tired and have had a busy day, and I want to be well and gay for Xmas. Although it was still early, people were coming home with holly, holly wreaths, lovely chrysanths and mistletoe, which they had bought from the carts and lorries as soon as they came to market. A few lucky ones had little fir trees, and I hear they are very scarce this year in these days of deforestation. They will not want to cut trees that have survived a few years and begun to grow apace. No fish shops had even the shutters down, so supplies could not have been expected till the midday train at the earliest. There were piles of lovely big branches of mistletoe, but all the berries had come off most. Oranges were still about but still on ration books, and there was not a nut of any kind. I pictured the stacks and stacks of nuts – we must have been a nut-eating town, for every possible nut, including salted or puffed nuts, always had a ready sale. I wonder why at least some are not about. They are good food value.

I felt really annoyed in the hairdresser's and spoke my mind, telling them I would not come in the New Year if circumstances did not alter. They have two driers, one a very old type, but the proprietor was in the National Fire Service and was moved to Totnes, where he decided to open a shop when he was freed. He bought new gear to take and stripped this shop of anything he fancied, put in his sister-in-law as manager over two girls, sacked the better-paid hand, and generally rack-rented[†] the business, which is a very good little one. Today there was a perm in the next cubicle and it needed the dryer, before they could begin, after shampooing. The old one just refused to go on and the old one they were using for me had to be borrowed. I felt the wetness of my thick hair strike a chill, and as I pointed out, arthritic people could not afford to take risks. The manageress said, 'Such a deplorable accident', but as I pointed out, it was not an accident, it was carelessness and inefficiency on the owner's part. He wants his money but will not lay any out.

I went into the WVS office for a drink of hot tea and Mrs Diss said, 'Don't be surprised if a detective looks you up. There has been a hold-up at Gleaston and the postmistress could give a very good description of the soldier who did it.' I felt I didn't want to be bothered with a detective calling so I trotted round to the police station, but could give no help. The description could have fitted so many, though at the back of my mind I'd a vague feeling it fitted one soldier rather well, one who ate at the counter and talked of 'never bothering about tomorrow till it came' ...

I've been very lucky all round this Xmas. People seem to think the Red Cross shop was pretty good work, and with me being in most I seem to have got the credit for it! When I got the bottle of gin – and the port – I was diffident about asking for them, and the bottle of rum was offered and the manager said, 'If you don't deserve it, who does?' (!!) Again, Mr Truss, the manager at Diss's jewellery shop who was amazingly kind to me in valuing things when we had the shop, really likes me and said he was 'glad to be of service' when I was so grateful for getting Cliff's darling wee alarm clock – only the size of a man's watch but a good timekeeper and reliable Swiss make – and just what Cliff wanted for Xmas. Not to speak of the really beautiful electric clock I've got my husband. Oddly enough I'm never offered black-market goodies. Mrs Woods seems to get anything that way.

The fish was really delicious. I do so love nice food to cook and serve – and eat too if I feel picky and tired of simple same food. I said to Cliff, 'Ah, for the days of mixed grills and good ham and fish, and lots of fruit of every kind.' My husband said, 'Well, I'm quite content. Any grumbling comes from you. I never know there is a war or shortages', which, considering my dodging for different flavours, was really gratifying! Cliff went out. My husband did a bit at his book-keeping, but we both felt very tired and came to bed early. The phone rang at intervals – all for Cliff and two long-distance calls at that, one Manchester, one Lancaster. That one is certainly popular, and candidly speaking I'm often slightly puzzled.

On Monday, 17 December – 'such a mad crazy day – I've laughed myself limp!' – Nella had a foreign visitor, Jacques, a French-Egyptian friend of Cliff.

I felt my laughter and the feeling of happiness in my little gay decked house had recharged me, making me more vital than I've felt for a while. I like bustle and happy people round me. I don't mind work, and dearly love to see people round my table enjoying the food I've cooked – much better than I enjoy eating any of the goodies – thriving on fun and laughter, and seeing happy faces, more than on what I eat extra. I felt the war years and worry had rolled back like a soiled curtain and let sunshine in to flood my little house. I felt as I walked upstairs there was a different atmosphere, not altogether the fragrance of Egyptian cigarettes. I didn't tell Jacques I didn't smoke – the packet he left me will go into Edith's stocking. She loves good Egyptians.

Tuesday, 18 December. Cliff looks a lot better. He had been working hard before he came and I feel he is worrying a little about getting a start when he is demobbed. I hope he gets into interior décor and likes it. He has a queer streak of instability that has stayed from childhood and not been outgrown with his somewhat artificial life in the Army. Seven years nearly out of his life by the time he is demobbed – six and a half at any rate – and at the most important time. Maybe he would have had somewhat muddled values if he had not gone in the Army. He is very like my father's family. I see it very plainly when he is talking – that under their circumstances he too would have roved the world, to ride the crest of the waves, or sink below them.

I told him a few things of my father's family as we sat yesterday, more as a hint of where his footloose fancy can lead than anything else. They were all East India men, sailors or traders, up to my great-grandfather's day, who 'saw these new-fangled engines being used freely – even put in ships, maybe!' – and advised his sons to learn all about them. Some made good. My grandfather was one, but never happy. He married early and got tied down with responsibility. I recall him as a darling old man who loved to read of foreign parts, and his collection of oddments bought off sailors were a joy to us children and a curse to his wife and daughters. One of my father's brothers 'rode the crest' and crashed, and spent twenty years on the Cape breakwater for illicit diamond-buying, a savage sentence only possible in those days of De Beers' monopoly in South Africa. I feel my Cliff has so much hidden conflict from his ancestors. I try to be patient when he gets difficult, praying always he will be true to the best in himself. Beyond that, there is little to be done. Any influencing has been done when he was growing up and any lessons learned then may be remembered.

On 20 December Arthur and Edith arrived from Belfast.

Friday, 21 December. There was a one o'clock dance at a nearby hotel and the Atkinson girls were going, so Cliff decided to go and my husband settled to his books and we three to read and later play solo, with two, three and four of each suit picked out and the five of diamonds. Arthur's back troubles him. It could have meant an attack of lumbago, but I got him some pills we find good and he is being rubbed with wintergreen and menthol and says he doesn't feel any worse. He doesn't strike me as being in very good health. I feel he works at too high pressure, and he worries about things in general. He has no personal worries to bother him. He said, 'I know what you mean, Dearie, when you say you felt at times as if you were "a skin less", and felt outside worries and troubles perch on your head and seep willy nilly into your tired head.' I thought to myself that when I've felt like that I've been in a pretty poor shape. He thinks things out to a degree, trying to find a solution, a way out of today's perplexities. I said, 'It's no use, love. It's much the best to take your eyes off the horizon and see the pot holes and stones of the road we tread, lifting them or trying to mend the road, leaving the rest to the clever ones – or God.' We have neither ability nor opportunity to do big things – yet I know how he feels at times.

Cliff finds life a problem too. I feel he is always trying to run away from himself. His pleasures are cheap and must at times leave the taste of ashes. He flares up and contradicts and argues blindly and vehemently, at times almost with a note of frenzy. He cannot talk things over and has a real phobia about relaxation or concentration. I feel life for him should be that of a dispatch rider, always rushing from place to place!

We all felt tired and I made supper early, leaving a flask of coffee and a banked fire for Cliff.

Sunday, 23 December. My husband had been writing invoices as usual on a Sunday morning, and as the sun shone, Cliff said, 'You all go out, I'll get the table ready', and knowing how he loved arranging things I went off gladly for I felt a bit whacked. We went round Coniston, always my choice if I'm asked. The lake lay remote and grey, but a strong sunset drew tearing red fingers of pinky red across it, as if trying to rouse it to friendly movement. Its light touched the hills to gold where the bracken dried so valiantly this year. Arthur said, 'The bracken must have been a glory this year. Even now it's more colourful than I remember it.' Somehow I felt it was the last touch to our happy Xmas, to take that little loved run out.

Everything was ready. I had only to brew tea and cut bread and butter and scones ... The little tree in the corner, the lights lit round the arch of the bay window and the plentiful spread would have all been pre-war, only my lads were men and only Edith's and Margaret's faces fresh and girlish. I had a bit of sweetened milk for cream, rum butter and loganberry jam, Xmas cake, chocolate biscuits, mince pies and shortbread. My cloth with the embroidered hollyhocks picking up the red of the little tinsel baubles on the tree. Happy laughter and gay voices. Even my little cat purred extra loudly and blinked happily from someone's knee. He is growing too heavy to nurse for long and gets passed round! We pulled the little crackers – and everyone who did not take sugar in their tea insisted on a sugar lump to suck, saying it was 'the next party'. I'd saved my crackers, as I said. Seven years old or not, the tiny things went off with quite a loud pop, and wee lead charms were in each – tiny horses and spinning wheels, squirrels and horseshoes. Everything was soon cleared away and we started to play pontoon for a while, but got so interested we played till 10.30, when I made supper, as Doug had ordered a taxi for 11.30 ... I love parties – best in my own home.

Monday, 24 December, Xmas Eve. Mrs Whittam was very upset. Her best friend's daughter had been cut to pieces on the railway line and she was going to her funeral. Such a bright clever girl who worked in our public library and whose fiancé shot himself a few weeks ago. He was in the RAF and badly injured but they 'repaired' his poor face and his other injuries mended, but later he found himself going blind. A letter, not published, was to her mother, begging forgiveness but saying she could not face things without Bob, saying she knew she was acting wickedly in killing herself but that she chose that way to be with him – that 'it would never be Heaven unless she was with him'. Another of war's tragedies – one amongst many that we will not hear anything about …

We all felt we would like a breath of good fresh air and went in the car over to Walney. I walked along the beach. The huge waves rolled and crashed. Suddenly I felt my old love of the sea return. I felt as I looked that in spite of mines yet around in some places it was sweet and free, that the fear and menace of death had passed, leaving the ordinary risks and turmoil natural to it. I had a few calls to make – two on old people who visit Aunt Eliza and are over eighty …

All the buses are stopped for Xmas. They refused flatly to even run a skeleton service to enable people to visit or go to church. It's odd how high handed public servants like dockers and bus people can be. They say NO and that's that.

The following days featured customary seasonal celebrations, exchanges of gifts (including a single banana for the whole family from Australia, 'which had ripened perfectly') and socialising with family and friends. The Lasts enjoyed a goose for Christmas dinner, and Nella got 'a really lovely diamond ring from my husband'. On Christmas afternoon she visited the hospital where she had volunteered during the war, and later had fourteen people for tea, with even more visitors in the house in the evening, many of them people of her sons' generation, and very much in a party mood. 'I felt I could have sat down and howled for sheer happiness,' she wrote on Boxing

Day morning, 'for joy that in spite of everything young things could laugh and be gay'. Later that day they had 'a little run in the car' and at five o'clock were entertained by the Atkinsons for tea. 'Not a single thing has spoiled or marred our Xmas,' she thought (written early the next morning); and during that day, the 27th, she prepared a hearty breakfast for Cliff (who was taking the morning train to London), saw *My Friend Flicka* at the cinema, and in the evening accompanied Arthur and Edith to the station, who were travelling from there to catch a boat to Belfast. Returning from the station, 'I felt as if my little house still vibrated with love and happiness, laughter and gaiety. I felt as if all my little worries had been sorted out tidily ... I feel I have got things a little more in focus. Perhaps I've laughed a few mully grits away!'

Sunday, 30 December. I felt really thankful it was Sunday. I could hardly bear to stand on my right leg [*twisted the previous day*]. After I'd had the tea and toast my husband brought up, I knelt in very hot water in the bath and bathed in it, afterwards rubbing it well with wintergreen, and it was a little better. I had a very busy morning with letters and rose at twelve to make lunch – good mutton soup in which too were some goose bones. There was cold mutton, as tender as chicken – a nice chunky bit of chilled mutton, and much better meat than I've had lately – chutney and wholemeal bread and butter, egg custard and bottled apples and then a cup of tea when I made some to put in the flask to take out. All was white with frost. It never lifted all day, and we went to Spark Bridge to wish Aunt Sarah and Uncle Joe a Happy New Year and take a jar of good dripping, a bit of marg, a glass of sherry each and a big slice of Xmas cake.

We went on for a little run to Coniston Lake, and I never saw my dear lake lovelier. The bracken-clad hills were mirrored on the silver surface till it was a fantasy of gold and grey, with patches of blue sky in the mosaic. My husband stopped the car to pump up the tyres as he thought the pressure too low, and I sat with the windows wide open with the sun on my face. Such utter peace and beauty. I felt it was enough for all the troubled world. No sound save the gentle murmur of a wee beck as it hurried to lose itself in the placid lake. I could have sat all afternoon just listening to the silence, caught in the Rhythm I always feel in that quiet spot, nearer to God than anywhere else I know. I sat so quiet and still, thinking of the New Year, longing for a job of some kind. There seems so little to do in Barrow and so many to do it. Women like myself who have been busy and useful, feeling they were helping, cannot find a way to help the peace as we did in wartime. With 2,000 women on the Labour Exchange, it would not be right to do anything they could do, yet I know many who, like myself, long to do something. I felt I put my name down as I sat – my New Year resolution formless but willing.

We were home by 4.30. All was white and lovely with frost. It looked as if the trees and bracken-clad slopes were sprinkled with a powdering of snow. I had left a good banked fire. I put slippers to warm and made tea while my husband covered up the car. We had been eating chocolate this afternoon and so did not feel very hungry. I had some good Kraft spreading cheese a friend had sent from Canada and passed on to me, and I made sandwiches and we had rum butter. My husband can always eat cake, particularly Xmas cake, but I felt I did not want any more sweet stuff. We settled down quietly by the fire. I had a good detective book I had started last week, and my husband had some bills to make out. The cat settled on my knee and all was quiet till 8.30 when we listened to *The Man of Property*.

I keep wondering how Arthur's back is, fearing he is letting himself drift into the rheumatic state which so tormented my husband and his father and really clouded their lives for years. When he was home he told me he didn't want the piano after all, that he wanted to sell it and spend the money on something he would need for the going into their new house. Secretly I felt vexed. I'd certainly given him it years ago and often wished when they left home and there was no one to play it that I could sell it and buy the china cabinet I needed but had no room for in this small house. I could have done with the money for many occasions, but would never have thought of selling it when I'd said Arthur could have it. He said, 'Cliff can have half the money' and I'll see he does. Sometimes I'm appalled to see that Arthur and Edith are waiting for their money every month. Arthur never had any financial sense at all. I feel Edith could budget better if he would let her.

Monday, 31 December, Hogmanay. Such a bitter morning. My leg ached but was quite a lot better, and I went down town early for my rations and to pay my bill at the wine merchant's, and was offered a bottle of whisky and one of rum, both of which I accepted, for whisky is my standby in either gastric attacks or flu colds while my husband prefers rum, and there's no telling what we will need before winter is over. I was so lucky. I got two big fresh Bay plaice; they were rather large – 2s 4d the two – but I gladly bought them for tea. It's not often I have to ponder how to spend my points. My problem is generally to get what I want, but today I had difficulty in spending my last nine. I got a tin of beans and one of peas, and carried the other one till Monday. I felt really ill with cold when I got in, and made a cup of hot strong tea and sat by the fire to drink it, reflecting gratefully that the war was over and our soldiers and airmen didn't have to rough it so much, thinking of the poor cold and hungry people of Europe where the weather might be colder still. I had good soup, Xmas pudding and cold meat and made gravy, and while my potatoes boiled put slices of cold meat on a plate as a lid in the gravy to heat through. I boiled cabbage and made pudding sauce – and a hot tasty lunch was waiting for my husband when he came in.

I took the bus and went up to wish Mrs Waite a Happy New Year – and got in this time! Poor old dear. She is so disagreeable and is worried about her husband who, the doctor thinks, has something rather malignant at eighty-two. I looked at them both. They are so difficult and aloof. No real love or friendship. No interests. I hope and pray I don't live till I'm eighty, unless I can be like Aunt Sarah or Aunt Eliza, whose mind seems to keep their body in check and who plan ahead as if they had years and years to live. I didn't stay long. I hurried home gladly to do my ironing and some mending with my machine.

Tuesday, 1 January, New Year's Day. I keep wondering and wondering what will be the effect if the loan to Britain doesn't materialise. Prospects didn't look too rosy with it. I always thought a few bombs should have fallen in America – real big ones! Last war the same. They lost men like all countries but as a percentage it was not proportionate, and again they seem to have all the money in the world. All the brave talk of a 'new world' seems to be dying slowly. People have not changed one bit. Many in fact have turned selfish and self-seeking, and grown hard and bitter. Me – I never put a lot of reliance on uplift talk. We could start something, plant a tiny acorn which we might not see beyond the seedling stage, but that is the best we can hope to do …

Nowadays many talk as if atomic energy was a kind of philosopher's stone to turn everything into something new and wonderful. It may well be so – in material things. But that prayer 'And renew a right spirit within us' is the real and only solution in human relationships. I'd hate to live in a world where I had only to press a button. If I had a job to do outside my home I'd be grateful for any help, but the world is largely made up of every-day folk like myself who have to weave their lives and jobs and efforts for home comfort into one whole pattern, and not only have bright tinselly bits all over but the solid yarn of service and the joy that comes from a job you have done in your own particular way. 'Beauty', 'the Arts' and 'appreciation of literature', etc. come after. They are the parts that show – the simple things the foundation.

CHAPTER THREE

'NICE TO BE LOVED'

January–May 1946

On 3 January there was a big party for the Women's Voluntary Services, held in the British Restaurant[†] next to Barrow's Town Hall, with nearly 300 women in attendance, and as the event ended Nella 'thought what a great pity it was that those of us who were so willing to help could not find something. The Regional WVS representative, who came from Manchester, said the same. She said in Manchester even, few as yet had found a niche in the peace as they had done in war, and she "regretted it deeply".' Still, Nella wanted to check any drift to discontent. That evening, back at home, 'As I sat feeling warmth steal through me, I felt again what a lot of blessings I had. I thought of others who had lost all, who had seen their lives crash in ruins.' Certainly, she had cause to be grateful. The next day, 4 January, after chatting with Mrs Whittam, 'I thought suddenly of my dear lads, as well as my husband's love, which, if at times is a bit "possessive" and demanding, is sincere. I realised how blessed I was. Edith loves me too. It's grand beyond words or price to be loved.'

Saturday, 5 January. I never recall anything which has caused such a stir in town as the Newalls' matrimonial troubles. Everyone takes sides who knows them. This morning Janet was all for Mr Newall. She said, 'It's all right talking of Mrs N.'s kindliness, good singing voice, being such a good mixer and so forth, but she was a fat careless lump wherever she went. My husband would never have taken me out if I'd looked like she did at several really good dinner dances. And her home was as happy go lucky as her appearance.' Now with fretting and not being able to eat, she has grown really slim and she seems to look nice in her clothes. I suppose a woman's general untidiness could start something.

Sunday, 6 January. I feel very grateful that, as yet, it's been a mild winter and I've not been as bad as previous winters. This evening as I sat warm and relaxed, I suddenly wondered how I'd kept on sometimes, feeling strength was given for war years to all who had to carry on. Now it's all past, the efforts and sacrifices and anguish and worry, bad and good alike. Now there are anxious spirit-awaking moments – me, I've always Cliff in my mind, wondering if he will get a start at interior decorating. There are so many already signing on at the Exchange – men from the Yard – and returning soldiers are finding it difficult. This next demob will be a big one in Barrow alone … Wives and mothers look so anxious when they talk of their men folk being demobbed. There are few who have jobs guaranteed unless it's teaching, Town Hall or Civil Service. I cannot help wondering, too, what will be the result of plenty of men in industry. Will it kill their dreadful go slow which so many trades suffer from, when men won't go to work to 'only pay income tax', or will the returning servicemen, with individuality stamped on till it's almost non-existent, fall in with the rest? I don't see much happiness in this new world. Problems are plainly increasing, without the white flame which carried us along in wartime. When war was on we all consciously or unconsciously looked forward to when peace came. Now it's come – with post-war problems of all kinds, few houses for newly weds, Bretton Woods,* and worry over

---

* A conference in July 1944, held at Bretton Woods, New Hampshire, was

nationalisation, atomic bomb, displaced persons, crime waves, and Europe's plight and America seeming as if she wants to be top dog and give orders, not doing anything unless she wants, reminding me more and more of Mrs Woods, who '*would* have' things regardless of whoever else went short.

Wednesday, 9 January. Such a wild stormy day, wild sleet and thunder. Mrs Cooper came, and the van men for the piano [*which she had just sold for £30*], so we got the cabinet moved out of the dining room into the front room. I watched the piano go with a strangely lost feeling. It was not a thing of wood and wires, but a large part of the 'youth' of the house. Dad bought it for me when I was eleven and could walk without my ugly high boot as a reward for my patience under massage and a wretched harness every night to pull my right leg after the effects of a broken hip and pelvis and its after-effects when I was only five. Perhaps if my teacher had had patience I could have learned. I've always loved music, and taught Arthur long enough for it only to cost me a few quarters' lessons at a good teacher. He had music in him. Cliff, whom I spent pounds on, would never practise. Yet Arthur and several music-loving friends made up for Cliff and I. I felt very dim when I saw it go, knowing that it would belong to strangers now ...

Mrs Cooper did not go till nearly three o'clock, for moving the cabinet hindered us, for I had to empty it to lift it and then put all back. Mrs Cooper is worried, poor dear. Her husband has crawled back to work but looks very ill and the doctor seems puzzled, though on his certificate they put 'gastric and duodenal

---

designed to plan for post-war, worldwide economic cooperation. It led to the formation of the International Monetary Fund and the World Bank.

ulcer'. Like the rest of us, she worries too about her daughter's future when she comes out of the ATS.[†] She is a very good tailor-ess, has been engaged twice and is only twenty-two and a half now, and announces she 'will never come back to a dump like Barrow' and talks of the big money and good opportunities to be had in London.

The wind howled and my head ached badly. I felt as strung up as the little cat, who raced up and down madly, and then the wild thunder crashed and it seemed to clear the air ... The storm wind had made the chimney smoke puff down in gusts, so I burnt wood. I thought, 'If I have to smell smoke, it shall at least be fragrant', and chose cherry and oak pieces from my shelf. With four hundredweight each month, I'm thankful I can get wood and firebricks, though I don't suppose we will get any more of the latter; the firm which supplies them – from Lancaster – has bought a coal business and as they are all eagerly bought I suppose they will go to his coal customers when he delivers coal. Mrs Atkinson is so cross, but as I point out, we have had the advantage all the war years. We should be content; and anyway all the angry things she says only upset her – it won't alter things.

Today when she was in, she was full of the talk of the German scientists brought to Barrow. The women of Barrow are very angry. They are housed like valued guests in Miss Heath's lovely big house, which, as she says, she is glad now she sold just before war finished to the Co-op for a Youth Centre. They say that the Germans have valuable secrets to disclose, but when it's to the Yard they come, we all feel they will be there for war and future destruction. If they had come to a dye works, plastic or anything like that, it would have been taken better. When they came it was said they would be housed by the Admiralty and it was understood they would be living at the Naval Depot away from people,

not in the centre of the best residential area.* We listened to the
wireless. Mrs Howson came in for an hour, then Margaret, who
seems very down in the dumps lately, and the evening passed
very quickly.

Thursday, January 10. I'm very tired tonight. I've had a busy day.
I had to go to the bank for my husband and to the library, so went
down town early, hoping the oranges had come off the books, but
they don't till Saturday morning. I cannot get wholemeal flour
at any shop. I wonder if last season's milling is due – meal has
been impossible to get lately. Last Saturday, shops had whiten-
ing[†] notices to say it was in. Not a scrap of fish, no meat pies or
sausage, and I could not hear of any prospects of the latter for
Canteen tomorrow, but I got a small case of Spam and I'll see
we have a tin left out for our shift. A neighbour gave me a big
bowl of dripping for chips for the Canteen, quite enough for the
afternoon, so I felt thankful. If we are as busy as we were last week
we will be glad of any help. It rather looks as if Mrs Howson will
keep to Clothing for the future and that means with Mrs Higham
being ill, at best we will only be three at Canteen. If we have no
rush we can manage, and it's difficult to get anyone interested
enough to start Canteen now.

I called in at the WVS office. Mrs Newall was in alone, but
just finishing a chat on the phone. She simpered, 'That was my
silly B—— of a husband.' I felt at a loss for an answer. I've never

---

* The arrival of these German scientists attracted the notice of three issues of the
Barrow News, which was published weekly on Saturdays. On 12 January it wrote
of 'the intense dislike Barrovian women felt towards men who had so recently
accomplished the destruction of their sons and husbands', especially when it
was thought that these foreigners would be housed more comfortably than most
citizens.

discussed her matrimonial troubles with her, but she went on. 'I'm *not* going to divorce him – not yet at any rate.' I told her of Flo and her problems, and how from threatening to sell her home over her head if she did not divorce him, he pleaded for her not to get one in view of the fact he would have to marry Connie then! Mrs Newall lit a cigarette and took a deep draw, blew it through her nose, and said, 'Well, I really wish he would go off and sleep with my successor to his affections. It might bring him to his senses. As it is he is all high faluting and chivalrous, promising me the earth, hating to leave his home, hoping we will still keep being friends – a kind of muddled mental adultery.' I looked at her good-humoured face. I never knew anyone with such a toler-ant and good-humoured approach to life, or imagined anyone who could manage to live at peace with all and sundry who drifted through the WVS office. I've never heard her speak unkindly or mischievously or do a mean thing, and know no one who has taken more strays from Canteen, often putting up wives who expected waiting on, and being totally different to the pleasant RAF or soldiers we knew in Canteen. The only thing I could say about her was that her happy-go-lucky nature made her untidy. Her hair so often looked like a bird's nest, her nose shiny, and lack of exercise and her love of starchy things, sweets and cocoa made her fat. I felt a little sadness for her. She should have had a brood of growing children. The girls would have bullied her into a semblance of smartness and the boys would have adored her.

It was such a lovely day. I was glad I was going to Mrs Higham's and walking through the Park. I fried bacon for lunch, heated soup and some beans left from yesterday, boiled sprouts and potatoes and made a dried egg custard sauce to eat with some dried apricots I'd soaked and stewed. I set out before two o'clock, for Mrs Higham had begged me to 'come early and let's have a nice long afternoon by the fire'. I met several people I knew, and stopped to chat. One had an adorable new spaniel, so gravely well behaved for he had been partly trained for the gun. I chuckled at the offhand way its owner said it had cost twelve guineas, recalling the days when twelve pence would have been a matter of consideration for both of us! We walked together through the Park, each looking in the gardens as we passed, amazed to find so many roses and chrysanths yet blooming, marigolds, snowdrops, polyanthus, almond blossom, jasmine and flowering shrubs. I never recall so many flowers in winter. The trees etched their bare boughs and branches against the clear sky. The birds twittered so happily it sounded like singing. And there was that feeling in the quiet trees that they were all ready and waiting, that all their preparations for spring were made – they only wanted the signal to burst into leafy beauty.

I felt shocked to see Mrs Higham. She looks so very ill and her cough is hacking and shakes her, but her back is quite a lot better. The doctor says she must stay indoors till he gives her permission to go out, however fine the weather may be. We sat and talked. The friend who is staying with her had gone out for the afternoon. I'd taken a bit of sewing but Mrs Higham's busy hands were idle on her lap. I said, 'You must be poorly sick', and she said, 'I don't feel I've the energy for anything.' I left before five and walked slowly back. I had to loosen my scarf and take my fur-backed gloves off. I felt it was brewing for a storm again.

My husband was already in, looking petulant and irritable because tea was not brewed and bread cut, although everything else was ready, including the curtains drawn and his slippers by the fire before I went out. He sulked over his tea and I just left him alone. Moods don't affect me nowadays beyond a point, and perhaps that point makes him indulge in them less.

Margaret came in for the evening and brought her knitting. She really wanted some scraps of gay wool for Fair Isle†, but Edith kept all the bits I had when she finished my jumper. I feel sorry for busy-fingered girls and women nowadays who cannot get wool, rug wool (decent worthwhile stuff at a reasonable price) or little cheap remnants of good material to make up into undies or blouses. Margaret is completely worked up. I went and looked through my drawers and box to see if I could find anything and found a green woollen jumper she could unravel and knit up into something. We listened to *The Count of Monte Cristo* and dined. I made some tea and Margaret had cheese. We didn't, for we had had it for tea, and I'd some nice wholemeal biscuits I got this week. Norah's job in the Yard finishes very soon. Margaret has a good one which could lead to a good secretary's job as she is a very good typist and shorthand writer, and has a pleasant almoner manner. Yet she's far from happy. I feel she is one of those simple homely girls at heart, the type who are ready for marriage and home making at twenty or twenty-one, all her too-vivid lipstick and nail varnish, her passion for dancing – and cocktails when she is at dances – a very thin veneer. Yet today, when nice ordinary people are wanted so badly, there seems to be everything against them. If they marry there is little chance of setting up a home of their own, of having babies and rearing them simply, pushing their prams out in their own garden or back yard while they do their work. Yet it's ordinary, simple people who will be the salvation of the world. I wished tonight as so often that Margaret was my girl – it would have been nice to have her bright gay personality around.

Friday, 11 January. Three of our Polish friends came into the Canteen to say goodbye. Such nice lads. They could not speak

very much English when they came and one had such a poor
smashed face, which has gradually been repaired and quite a good
matching eye put on. The first time I saw it I nearly fainted. I felt
a frantic prayer to keep smiling at him and I must have done for
he stayed to talk at the counter. It made Mrs Fletcher and Mrs
Howson ill so I always served him, poor dear. They brought in
each a bunch of violets and shook hands as they said goodbye. I
said to Georgy, the boy with the damaged face, 'My blessing and
good wishes go with you my dear and may you find your mother
and sister very soon.' He bent and kissed me and said, 'I thank
you, little mother' and suddenly I could have howled, thinking
that soon all our Canteen friends would go and not need us any
more ...

Wherever women are congregated, you hear snatches of argument and talk about the German scientists who have come to
work here. While a few have the 'wipe the lot out' way of talking,
most of the sensible women think as I do myself – if Germany
has anything to offer to help build the post-war world, let them
by all means do so, but to let men come to a place which only
deals in weapons of war, submarines particularly, is a dreadful
thing to think. Their help will make our subs more dangerous.
Already it looks as if in men's minds they begin to prepare for
another war ...

Arthur's letter made me lovingly amused. He had read the
Honours List and thought his Mom should have an OBE! As
others see us – bless his loving heart. He would 'like to see my
work recognised'. No one will ever know, except God Himself,
the glory I've had, how near I've been to 'hearing anything'
when that tatty little shop was going. To know every ten shillings meant hope and comfort for a POW, to gloat over good
weeks, be spurred on to beg (a detestable thing which, for myself,

I could NOT do), to get top price for all gifts, even if it meant doing them up, to see a mob of dirty, worn-out soldiers come into Canteen, give them lots of hot water to wash and a cup of scalding hot tea while we dodged up a tasty hot meal, laugh and jolly them and park them off upstairs for a nap by the fire in the old steamer chairs, meet tired women and cuddle little cold babies and change their nappies while their mothers found a spot in the Rest Centre and told you of London's terror – why, WVS women have been blessed beyond any recognition. It's like wearing the same old coat that has had a fur lining put in, a lining that is a comfort and joy, however little the wind blows. Still, it's nice when a loved son feels that way. I am a very blessed woman.

Friday, 18 January. Mrs Newall came in. She had nothing to come in for, but she likes sympathy and to know we all are sorry for her marriage break-up. She said an odd thing to me the other day – something about 'Dick should sleep with her – it would soon get over then.' I thought it a queer cynical remark, but Mrs Fletcher, who knows both Newalls, said, 'I'd have killed that wretch long ago. He has always been a skirt chaser and has gone back when he has tired. This is the first time he has wanted a divorce and that Dorothy Crosbie is clever enough to insist on marriage.' Mrs Fletcher said, 'I'd not divorce him either.' Mrs Howson was not sure – it would depend how old she was and if she had future prospects, etc. Mrs Whittam and I were 'nose bitten off'. We would not have clung to anyone who so badly wanted to get free …

The wind whistled and howled. My chilled toes were grateful for warm slippers. The fire leaped with wood logs piled on the little bed of glowing coal. I felt a great pity for fireless cold people, wondering as often why I should have so many blessings when poor mothers with little children, or old sick ones, had neither warmth or home. Many have no coal in Barrow, but it's because they have burnt their stock up and the ration doesn't go far – the Co-op only allow four hundredweight a month. I could not have such gorgeous fires in the evenings if I'd not hoarded in summer, and bought my £2 worth of little logs. I must have been a fire worshipper in the ancient days. Of all inanimate things, I love the sunshine and warm fires.

Saturday, 19 January. I said to my husband, 'Have you never thought of leaving me?' I said it jokingly, but he considered it very seriously and said, 'No – why should I? I would have everything to lose.' I said, 'Tell me then – what do you consider my greatest attraction for you?' I didn't expect him to say, 'Your beauty', but did think he would say, 'Because you are such a good cook' or at least something 'positive'. Instead he said, 'Because you are such a comfortable person to live with.' I felt all flat feet and red flannel – as others see us!

Sunday, 20 January. I've fussed more about food and its values and looks since war finished than I'm sure I did all the war years, and watched over my husband's health more. Perhaps it's because so many people I know have cracked up and, if they have not died, have seemed to go all to pieces. This morning when the sea birds came over in screaming clouds, he came upstairs and said, 'You should come and see your pitiful pensioners', and I said 'Tip those boiled scraps in the bucket, under the crab-apple tree. If you put it by the rockery the gulls gobble all and the rest don't get a chance.' He said, 'Well, I never thought to see birds fight over boiled potato peelings. They flapped round me head till I felt their wings brush me. I'm glad you don't like to see things hungry' – and he smiled at me. I said, 'Ah well, you said I was "comfortable to live with". I suppose you referred to me feeding you.' He said, 'I don't know why you feel so snippy about me saying that. I meant to say there was comfort and peace wherever you were, and I think it's the best compliment that could be paid a woman.' I suppose it is, but it's the demanding women who get most fun!

Friday, 25 January. Mrs Whittam caught the 5.30 bus to her home. She said the smell of gas had given her such a splitting headache. She really amazed me – she whispered, 'Don't tell them anything about me killing the pig. Don't say a word. We killed it ourselves.' I said, 'WHAT – and two policemen so near in the village?' She said, 'Ah, it's all right. Whenever a farmer wants to kill a pig he drops a hint and the policeman is sure to be out of the way – and he gets a nice piece always.' She added, 'After all, we are not really doing wrong. It's our pig. We raised it and we don't draw bacon rations when we have our own flitch.' I thought of the plenty of all the farmers I've ever known, many in lonely farm houses. I thought she would not be the only one to reason like that.

The next day, Saturday 26th, Nella started to feel 'queer and light headed', and by the 29th she was sick in bed, apparently with the flu. Her diary entries became shorter and (most unusually) she did not write at all on a couple of days. Only in the second week of February was her health improving, though still haltingly, and it was some time till she recovered her strength.

Saturday, 9 February. It was bright sunshine this morning, and when I looked out of the dining room window I saw a little flash of gold in the border and I put on my coat and went out to look at it — my first crocus — and beside it three frail snowdrops danced and nodded in the keen wind. The crab-apple tree plainly shows tiny buds, and the rambler roses have had leaf buds for a while. I felt as always the miracle of spring, of life from seeming death. All was quiet except for the crying gulls overhead. My little garden seemed a precious thing as I walked down the path, already in my mind's eye seeing the colour and beauty of what will soon be. The stirring life shows in little weeds and tufts of grass in the crazy paving, the bulbs pushing through and that uplift of bare branches before the buds break through ...

Inside me I'm growing very old, and it's as if I feel a wide vision, less tendency to worry and fret, to tell God all about things rather than to pray. There's a lot of truth in the old saying 'It's the happiest time of your life when your children are round your knees.' I feel I would have been a happier woman with a 'long' family, with young things still to love and cherish and not just a little mog of a cat, wise and kindly as he is. As I lay back in the chair tonight I felt a great sadness on me, not altogether flu after-effects. I don't like the blueish patches on my cheeks and lips if I have any exertion. I hope I am not going to have to step aside from any little I could do to help. There is so much to do and life slips so swiftly by.

I tried to talk to my husband and tell him what was in my mind, but he only looked blankly at me. He said, 'I cannot see what you are worrying about. You have done more than anyone else I know. You should be glad when you can take things easy.' I suppose he is right to a certain extent, but I feel torn in two sometimes when I think of the frightened, homeless people, of hopeless mothers with little hungry children, of homeless, cold, old ones. I feel I've a wailing wall in my heart. If I could only feel I was helping. I realise more and more the goodness of God when I was able to work steadily

through the war, through the worry of Cliff's illness, and the weary
weeks when he was so out of joint with life. My husband said, 'You
must start going to the pictures in an afternoon like other women',
but I feel when it's warmer weather I'd sooner work in the garden
than go to see pictures I'd no interest in. It's all right if it's a good
picture, but we do seem to have had poor ones lately on the whole.
Unless anyone was in the habit of going they would not have been
attracted.

Tuesday, 12 February. I had a little weep over Cliff's letter today
– a bright, somewhat impersonal letter with the sting in the last
when he signed himself 'Your wabbit'. The years rolled away and
I recalled the first time I'd called him that. He was an infuriating
baby, and my husband never had any patience with children. I
was ill after a major operation and Cliff had grown really beyond
them all, only good on the occasions he had been brought in
the hospital. That particular night the wild shrieks and my husband's loud, angry voice had distressed me terribly and I could
not rise and go downstairs. I'd only been home a few days. Suddenly the bedroom door opened with a crash and a wildly yelling
and kicking baby was hurled on my bed – poor lamb, he was
only nineteen months old – and my husband shouted, 'I can do
nothing with the little devil. I feel like killing him.' I reached
down and patted my angry baby and said gently, 'He is not
naughty, Daddy. He is only a tired little wabbit who wants to
cuddle up to Mammy wabbit.' He stopped roaring, looked a bit
surprised, and then nodded as he crawled, slippers and dirty play
overall, into my bed and cuddled up. Later I drew his clothes off
and he slept all night as he had first laid down, and somehow I'd
found the way to quieten his tantrums. I think he found things
too much for him at times. As he grew up there was always a

mood he had called 'wabbitish', and I always tried to plan a little outing or try and find his worry.

Wednesday, 13 February. My husband and I had a little laugh when we recalled the time Cliff was born and I was so ill for weeks, unable to get my strength back at all. I had a queer eccentric doctor, who relieved other doctors and lived in one of the loveliest old houses I've seen, with a charming wife quite twenty years younger than he was and two clever children, one at Eton and the girl at Girton. (He had tried to replace a doctor called up in the war before last.) He said, 'She should have champagne, oysters, beefsteak – tempting food. These nervous patients are the devil, you know. Give me a person who likes to eat, every time.' As I lived in the New Forest, had no pull with any tradesman or knew no one likely to be able to get any extras, we just dismissed the whole idea, but out of his own cellar he brought all kinds of wine beside champagne! – and all kind of little dainties, crisp red apples and grapes from his own growing. He said, 'I like North Country folk – they always put up a good fight' – and then used to sit and tell me of his years as an Army surgeon, and as the great uncle who took Mother to bring up when Grandfather died was also an Army doctor and I could remember yarns Mother told of life and conditions in the Crimean War, we always had an interest. He had everything in life, but looked back wistfully to, and clearly enjoyed, his war work – and I never got a bill. He said when Cliff was so tiny, 'Oh, he will grow; we'll make a soldier of him yet', never realising how true his words would be.

Norah's husband, who had served in the Navy, was about to return from Australia, and the couple were to move into a house at 24 Ilkley Road.

Friday, 15 February. Margaret came in for a while. She seems to have lost a lot of her gaiety somehow – like most of us lately! Norah and Mrs Atkinson are cleaning Norah's house up the street. They have got a shock to realise it might be months before Norah gets her furniture. She has not got her dockets yet and then there is often a wait of up to six months. None of us had realised that. Norah thought of being able to have all ready when Dick comes home at the end of March. My husband was busy book-keeping and all was quiet. I've got out a piece of Jacobean embroidery I started before the war and had forgotten about. Its gay wools are cheerful to work with, but there is a great deal of thread counts in it and my hands tire of close stitching and holding the frame. I wish it had been a tray. I could do with a new one.

Arthur and Edith are finding how tiresome it is to be waiting for builders to finish a house. They relied on their word it would be finished by the middle of February, and the roof tiles don't seem to be on yet and then there will be a lot to do inside. The prefabs at Barrow are a laughing stock. If they are all like these in the country, there's a deal of time being wasted. The plumbing arrangements which were supposed to be so simple that one man could assemble them and connect in eight hours have taken a man three weeks for the first one and he is still at it.

Tuesday, 19 February. Everything seems to have conspired to irritate or worry me. No letter from Cliff to say whether he had yet got his washing, gramophone or his watch he should have received yesterday morning. I'd one phone call after another, two tedious people to pay bills, and my milk boiled over – all over the stove – and then to put the cap on things I put some garden rubbish on the fire my husband had left to blow over the rockery, and set my chimney on fire! Luckily no policeman was about and the thick cloud of smoke blew away, but I got palpitations so bad I felt I'd choke and had to lie down. Luckily I'd got my casserole of mutton out of the weekend meat, leeks, celery and potatoes and had made the steamed date pudding yesterday so I'd only soup to heat and sauce to make. I sat and cleaned my bits of brass and silver so that tomorrow I could bake a cake and work with Mrs Cooper a little.

I was down town for 1.30. I left my lunch dishes in water so as to have plenty of time to walk slowly to the bus stop. My hairdresser has another girl and is booked up for weeks except for odd appointments. No more perms can be pushed in for three weeks. I said, 'It's odd, after Xmas and so long before Easter. You are generally slack, aren't you?' She said, 'Yes, but don't forget women are getting ready to meet demobbed husbands and many certainly need a perm. They have put off and put off, often if working, with not much time.' The heat of the cubicle made me realise how much better it was to be first customer in the morning. I booked my usual appointment for Saturday morning week but had to take it at ten o'clock instead of nine.

This time I have needed house slippers for months and the ones I made have got completely done with wearing them so much lately, so I bought a new pair today, deep blue leather ones with a bit of black fur round, and at one time I'd have got better ones at Marks & Spencer's for their ceiling price of 4s 11d – and paid 14s 9d and five coupons. The awful felt and cloth things for four coupons made me realise how valuable a coupon was when people would buy gay trash for 23s 9d if they could spare one wee coupon! All the fish had gone, but when I saw the huge cod heads and kipper boxes I felt I didn't want either herring or coarse fish. I'd have liked a bit of plaice or a Dover sole. There were lots of sweet biscuits about, but I didn't get any. I've only fourteen points left after getting raisins, for most of my points go in tinned milk, beans and peas, cornflakes – since I've had a little with my Bemax[†] for breakfast and supper   and dried fruit. I was lucky enough to get a box of Braggs charcoal biscuits. I used to always have them if I felt my tummy. Little things like charcoal biscuits and rest after meals did more good than anything.

I was glad to get back home, and I had a rest till teatime, glad indeed I had got in when I did, for a shrill wind sprang up and brought heavy rain showers. I did cheese on toast for tea and there was baked egg custard and bottled damsons, malt bread, wholemeal bread and butter, honey and plain cake. There seems a lot of misunderstanding about the clothes coupons – amazing the people who think they are extra, not having listened properly to the broadcast. Even Mrs Atkinson had it wrong, saying what a good help it would be, when underclothes are simply fading away. I wangled a few coupons off Cliff, thinking of Margaret, but before I could spend them – with being ill – he sent for his book back, but I told him I'd like a few later if he could spare them. I badly need a few new towels. Wartime ones have not the wear in them that the pre-war ones had, and perhaps the laundries don't use the soap they did, relying more on chemicals which would rot fabric. Giving our Lakehead Laundries every credit due though, they have been marvellous. They are a big firm, travelling the outlying districts, but the van men and shop (receiving) people never leave them. Several have been there all my married life and it's like the small business, which I prefer. I can tell there will be a pretty good changeover of grocers and butchers when rationing cards are issued again. Due to general unrest and memory of wartime unfairness – often no fault of the shopkeepers – women seem to have reached the end of their patience and feel any change will be better than going on.

Nella had lauded this laundry service several years before, in her Directive Response for May 1939. 'Here in this district', she said, 'we have the most wonderful laundry I've ever struck. It operates all over the Lake District from Carlisle to Ingleton in Yorkshire. Generally a monopoly makes for indifferent service, but not in this case. Clothes are beautifully and carefully washed and there are three services to pick from. I choose the middle … They are washed as well as the first class but only flat ironed. At that the shirts, etc. are better finished than high priced services in most laundries I've used in different parts of the country. By this service I find it cheaper to send the bulk of my wash rather than have a washerwoman.'

Norah Atkinson came in, looking utterly spent. She and her mother are cleaning out her house, which had been neglected, and they are distempering the pantry and one bedroom themselves and getting ready for the painter. I felt it was false economy to spare a few shillings and take it out of Norah – Mrs A. is as strong as a horse. The kettle was boiling and they had a cup of Bovril. I suggested it as a better pick-me-up than tea, and I made toast and they spread it with soft cheese – such nice cheese this week.

No letter from Cliff again. I don't know whether he has got his washing or gramophone, and he should have got his watch yesterday. He used to be mannerly if nothing else in his letters, answering them with detail. Now he often forgets to tell me whether he gets his laundry.

Thursday, 28 February. We settled by the radiator, I thought for a quiet evening, until my husband began to wonder what he could hang on the wall in place of the picture I would not have up again. Then the balloon went up. I felt something snap in my tired head. He got told a few things – not altogether connected with the picture! Yet through all my anger and annoyance I strove to control my tongue a little. With so many of his uncles and his father ageing so soon, he has always feared it. At fifty he had the worn-out physique and mentality of a man ten or fifteen years older and any energy of mind or body has gone in his day's work. I feel such a deep pity for him. It's made me give way so much, but I wonder if it's been altogether wise. I think of the real squalor of mind and body of his people's home. I see the writing on the wall as I strive to keep things together, try to interest him in outside things – in the boys and their affairs – making excuses for him always, that he is tired or worried or busy. Tonight I could have run out into the cold wintry night and ran and ran till I dropped. Boyishness, which is engaging at twenty, can be childishness at thirty, and each ten years grow more hard to put up with. I came to bed, feeling things work out. I felt lost and a little adrift when he decided he would like to sleep alone, but it's another oddity of the family and now I'm glad of it. I feel my bed is a peaceful haven where I can relax alone and read or write, try and sort out my values, and count my blessings.

Friday, 1 March. Mrs Howson called for me to go to Canteen and I posted a little parcel of bits for Aunt Sarah in case we couldn't get up this weekend – a tin of soup, a scrap of marg and dripping, a slice of bacon left from what I'm brought and a bit of cheese. There is so little to give nowadays. It often gives me a sadness. Somehow so much of the 'sweet' of life has passed. How can we teach children to be unselfish, to 'pass the sweeties', 'give a bite of their apple' or 'break a piece of cake off and give a bit to the poor doggie'? It used to be said of a greedy adolescent, 'Well, he was the only one and there was no one to share things with.' A generation is growing up who don't know what it is to have many little goodies themselves, and even tiny tots know the value of points and what is rationed.

Sometimes I think all the colour as well as sweetness is dormant, if not dead. I see Norah Atkinson borrowing oddments for her new home – and she is so grateful for my old curtains. When I reflect that I bought them in 1939, had them always up at my front windows, mended the glass cuts after the raids, turned them so that the faded side was inside and then altered them for the dining room where the remaining colour was almost bleached out by the sun – I feel they are no treasure. I wondered whether to cover two old thin blankets with them, and wondered if it would be worth the trouble. Little things annoy and, on the other hand, delight women. If bright gay curtain material could be coupon free – say four yards on each coupon book – it would mean such a lot. If it only meant one window bright – there doesn't seem much hope though, and everything grows shabbier and more down at heel.

Saturday, 2 March. It was a lovely bright morning, but cold enough to keep the snow wherever the sun did not melt it. I was not feeling too bad with myself, just going slow, when my husband came in. Then the fun and games started. He was determined that all pictures should go back on the walls. I was as determined they should NOT. Knowing my hatred of a scene, I felt he played up, thinking I'd give way when the painter and Mrs Cooper were about, but this time he was quite mistaken. I'd got to that pitch of nerves when jumping on them would have been the mildest thing I'd do. I've won, beyond my two good little oil paintings of Wartdale Lake and the tarn above Hawkshead, the mirror over the fireplace and the little carved garden mirror facing the window. My nice new wallpapered room is not cluttered. Of all outlooks to live with, the Victorian cum early Edwardian is the darndest – always to bring back mementos from a holiday and buy useless dust traps for presents, and never part with anything.

Sunday, 3 March. Norah and Dick came in for a few minutes. He is delighted with the house, but rather taken back at the thought of Norah having to work for two years. He will not be able to pay £2 out of his wages for a beginning, so there seems little to be done if they want a house of their own at first. It's so dreadfully hard on young people setting up a home. It strikes at the very root of happiness. He had brought a piece of coconut matting – from Woolworths at Gibraltar. It made me laugh when he spoke of shopping there, with all the shops in Sydney and the glamorous East. We went to Spark Bridge. I don't feel happy about them if I don't see them fairly often. They had not expected us with me sending the little parcel, so it was a nice surprise. Food seems scarcer than ever in the villages. It's only with shopping in town there are any little extras, and just now there is so little in the gardens. I wish people would not keep saying, 'Well, *you* have had no surprise when things worsened', as if I'd gone round like Cassandra! Joe said, 'You always said, lass, that things would be worse for a while after the war finished.' I said, 'Well, maybe, but I didn't see quite the shortages and muddle, or take into account the Allies themselves would start to fall apart' …

We were back early. I made up the fire and soon had tea ready. Toasted fruit bread – I put raisins and a little honey in one of my little loaves when I baked – bottled pears and unsweetened milk, lemon cheese and wholemeal bread and butter and fruit cake. The table looked so gay and inviting, and still I did not feel I cared whether I had any food or not, and what I ate soon satisfied me. I could have giggled wildly at my husband's attitude, barely speaking when spoken to, glancing at the changed walls pitifully like a ham actor. Odd how little his reactions affect me nowadays. I cannot believe at one time I worried and worried and let his monkey-shines drive me into a nervous breakdown. Now any breakdown would not be mine. I feel often I look at a rather tiresome stranger, wonder at my own weakness of attitude, which led me to be shut up like a dog, only taken out on a chain, called to heel, petted and patted but never let out of sight or off the chain. I must have been a fool. I feel it has fostered something in me that would have been better not. I was never dull or bored that I can ever remember. If I could not do one thing, I turned to another, while longing for friends who would not notice if they were snubbed or let see they were not welcome. My war work bridged that gap. I loved working with people, feeling 'I'll never be shut up again', and when I'm well enough I hope I can find something outside my home.

I sat and embroidered my cushion cover, feeling tonight I'd be well to start my blouses this week and then I'd have a bit of useful sewing on the go. I'll have to take my curtains down too and let the hem down. They have shrunk one and a half inches, and it fidgets me if a thing is not right and I have to keep looking at it.

I keep thinking of Cliff. He is always at the back of my mind. I wonder if he will get a start soon, feeling the real calamity it would be if he had to come back to work with his father, knowing how impossible it would be, feeling I could never stand the strain nowadays as I once did, when they were so totally different in every possible way, in every line of thought and action.

Monday, 18 March. The heavy rain and hailstones seem to have broken the back of winter. I woke to birds twittering and chirping, and the garden looked as if spring might be soon here. I felt tired when I rose, and my back was bad to start the day, but I thought fresh air would do me good and I went down town to get my rations. There was a real Monday look about the shops – no fish or meat, sausage or cakes. I met several women I knew well. All complained of the poverty of Barrow shops compared to Ulverston and the Lake towns. All but two were worried about returning sons and their jobs. One who has been so high hat about her son being a captain – she has been shunned a little – today was especially worried. I'd not known the son or his job before he joined up, but was surprised to learn he had only worked for a newsagent who had asthma badly and could not meet the early train for his newspapers or deliver on cold wet days. Somehow I had the idea her son had been in a bank. She is desperately wondering how he and his wife and baby will fit into life on their return. She seems in awe of her daughter-in-law, who seems a 'captain's lady'.

Cliff, who had just been demobilised, arrived on 20 March in Barrow for a brief visit. She found him in good spirits, though she admitted the next day that 'I sighed as I noticed how slow he was with his right hand – but checked myself when I thought it was only a finger gone after all.'

Friday, 22 March. I had to rise earlier to cook breakfast and pack sandwiches for Cliff. I made him a nice breakfast: half a grapefruit prepared overnight, a little rasher of bacon, two sausages and an egg. The potted meat I'd made from the sheep's head made nice sandwiches with chutney and cress, and I kept two slices for my husband's tea. I packed a slice of cake, two buttered slices of malt bread, an orange and a flask of tea in the Thermos I bought him at Xmas. The taxi came at 8.30 but I didn't go to the station. I felt a bit shaky with rushing about and laid on the settee for half an hour. I had to take Cliff's watch back to the watchmaker's. The repair I'd had done a few weeks back had gone wrong again.

Why *do* newspapers print things before they are official? Every knot of women I passed seemed to be talking of the marg and soap cut – then tonight on the wireless there was 'nothing sure', as if women haven't enough worries. There were no queues for fish, and plenty of variety, but I never can have fish for Fridays what with going to Canteen. The bus conductors are quickly replacing the clippies[†] and it's a real pleasure to be spoken to politely. So many of the girls gave one the feeling they were completely indifferent, whether you rode on the bus or fell off it ...

I had half an hour's rest after lunch, for we were going down in Mrs Higham's car so had no waiting or walking to the bus stop. I've felt so out of joint with Canteen since I had flu. Somehow the gaunt, nearly empty place, short supplies of food, cutlery and crocks, and the type of soldiers who come in, seemed to repel me. Gone are the friendly nice lads, and rather curt and sometimes insolent fellows come in now, as if instead of friendliness they work off annoyance on us. Today two of them did upset Mrs Fletcher. Poor Marjorie. She is so big and strong looking, but her thyroid makes her very nervy and frightened. We had such short supplies of cakes and could only eke them out with cheese sandwiches, buttered teacakes and hot dogs. I like to be fair to all the boys and said to the helper, 'We will only let each lad have one cake.' These two piled up four on one plate, six on the other, and gave Marjorie cheek. I'd been sitting down resting and she served for me. I went to the counter and one of them snarled at me and told me he would darn well please himself – they were for sale, weren't they? I tipped the cakes back on the dish and

I said – he was over six feet and soared over me – 'Little man, what a shock you are going to get in civvy street after your life of luxury in the Army.' If I'd been as nasty as I felt it would have done little good. I felt the roars of laughter of his friends were better than any sharp remarks. Mrs Whittam said, 'You can get under anyone's skin. That lout said "please" when he came for his cup refilled' ...

Mrs Whittam *is* an oddity. She has always a huge roll of notes in her bag from selling something – horse, cow, etc. – or looking for something worth buying, and we thought nothing could surprise us but she certainly did today when she fished out of her sleazy leather bag 100 clothing coupons for which she had paid £10! It was more of a bombshell than once when she had over £300 in her bag and I revolted and trotted her off to the bank with it, fearing at that time, when we were always so crowded, someone could hear her – she has a loud voice – and rob her as she went home. I saw Mrs Higham's mouth open and shut like a fish's and felt mine did the same! I said, 'Now what on earth are you possibly going to do with those? You naughty old thing. You know you have stacks of good clothes you say are too smart for you.' She beamed all over her very weather-beaten face and said, 'Well, I badly want a new hat', and joined in the burst of laughter. She has a very good velour hat that wind and weather has altered and which she puts on her head with the delicacy of a cow stamping in the mud and which we always call her 'creations'. I said, 'Silly, you don't need coupons for hats, and I know you have some nice ones. Pass that one for keeps to your cat. I know she must have had kittens in it several times.' Crude remarks like that are priceless wit to Mrs Whittam. She shook and rolled with mirth till she nearly fell off the chair. Dear knows what she will do with all those coupons if, as I pointed out, 'she kept out of jail'.

Saturday, 23 March. I've had a maddeningly tiresome day. I don't remember worse. I had a hair appointment for nine o'clock but missed two buses which were crowded and when I got down it was 9.10. I needn't have worried. I had to sit waiting till 9.30 and then the water was not as hot as it should have been, for something had gone wrong with the thermostat in the tank. I got fish for lunch – nice haddock fillets – and a nice piece of smoked cod for Aunt Sarah. It's such a problem nowadays to get a little tasty bit for them.

When I got back there were two real tinkers mending jute doormats and I said they could mend mine. I could have done it myself with a packing needle and coarse string, but they looked so lost and hungry, and they talked in such sing-song Welsh they were bad to understand. I made the mistake of not asking how much it would be, and I'm sure I look soft, for when they brought it back they demanded fifteen shillings. It's a very good 'has been', for I always believed in buying the best, or else I'd have said, 'You can have the mat.' They came in the garage and were half in the kitchenette before I realised they were there, and both neighbours were out. I don't remember being so frightened of anyone, but I stood firm. They would not let me have the mat, but on the pretext of examining the work – very badly and sloppily done – I seized my potato knife off the stove where I had laid it and said, 'NO – I'm going to give you your valuable jute back', and made to unpick it. They agreed to take five shillings – for about ten minutes' badly done work and six pence of jute string just caught round and not oversewn as usual, and I told them I was ringing up the police and laying a charge of trying to extort money. They believed me, for they gathered up their bass bag[†] and left the road hurriedly.

It upset me badly and I shook from head to foot and felt glad when I heard a ring – till I went to the door. A queer-eyed untidy woman who might have belonged to them stepped up on to the top step and began begging, for food, coppers and clothes. I felt it the last straw. I said, 'There is a telephone at my hand. If you don't go away I'll call the police.' She looked very surprised and stopped cursing me and began to whine. I said, 'The police of this town are very severe with beggars', and off she went. I'm sure they were all together. I cannot recall beggars at the door for years.

During the next several weeks Nella travelled much more than she had in the previous year – a day trip to Lancaster, Easter weekend in Morecambe, and a weekend in London to visit Cliff. In London she went shopping, and on 27 April 'went to Derry and Tom's lovely roof garden' and later to the theatre, and did lots of sightseeing, though not as much as she had hoped to do (her 27-year-old son didn't approve of his 56-year-old mother going out on her own). Cliff, she felt, put on some big-city airs 'I tried not to act country cousins and only slipped up a few times,' she wrote on the 29th, 'and was only reproved once, and anyway the little waitress did look tired and the aspirins I gave her and the sniff of my smelling salts did her good, for her head ached. She was a really nice little girl but annoyed Cliff when she stood talking and told me she had a baby of three and twins a year old and worked every Sunday in the Richmond café to help out while her husband minded the babies. Cliff said, "Londoners don't talk to people. You would be looked on as eccentric if you lived here, you know."'

On Saturday, 4 May Nella accompanied her husband on a business trip, as she sometimes did, this time to Kendal. 'Country people stood in groups waiting for their own particular bus, all so smart and neat,' she wrote, 'only their country dialect making them unlike townsfolk. Gone are the tasteless, clumsy ways of dressing, of heavy clod-hopping shoes, except for work.' She remembered 'the cotton bonnets and big white aprons of the cottage

women when I was a child, the heavy corduroys and blue shirts and red
kerchiefs round the necks of the men', and reflected on 'the real revolution
of thought and behaviour started before the last war'.

That this spring was an unsettling time for Nella was clear from how
often she remarked on the imminent closing of the canteen. On 1 April she
was with Mrs Howson. 'We used to feel such eagerness to help fellows who
might be going overseas and not come back, such happiness in making a
meal for sailors off to join their ships,' she recalled. 'Now all that seems to
have gone. They are just men folk with no desire for friendship unless it's to
confide their demob grievances.' The canteen no longer seemed to merit
the investment of time and effort. On 11 April she wrote that 'So many
women take the line "Service people get such better rations and are only
hanging round. I don't see why we should give up time now to let them have
cheap food. If they want refreshments, let them go to an ordinary café."'

On 24 April she and Mrs Howson were again talking of the canteen,
which was then expected to close by the end of May. 'We both feel sorry,
but more for the past than the present. We always tried to be friends to
the boys, and we laughed as we talked over little incidents, now so far off it
might be much longer.' She felt a sense of loss. 'I feel as if doors were slowly
closing me in … A dimness of "not being wanted to help" is hardening into
a film of not bothering.' (The canteen did indeed close at the end of May.
'Our happy life of service together was over,' she wrote on the evening it
happened. 'Today saw something pretty nice come to an end.')

Tuesday, 14 May. I cleared tea, did a bit of mending, had a little
chat with Mrs Waite and Mrs Higham on the phone and then
relaxed on the settee with a book. My husband was a bit lost.
He was tired and would have liked to go out in the car. He says
driving rests him. I thought of Mrs Waite's voice complaining
that no one went to see her, and in the next sentence admitting
callers were not let in if Mr Waite felt that way, or was rude to

them if he did let them in. I looked across at my husband and wondered what he would be like at eighty – perhaps like his father, who has never been interested in much since I've remembered and who is content if he has fire and food and doesn't notice anything else.

Saturday, 18 May. We gave a lift to a young fellow who had missed the bus. He interested me, poor dear. He was eager to talk and told me he was a porter at the Lakeside Hotel, but had no home nor people – that he had been a Barnardo boy. I could tell he had a deep sadness about having no background. He was essentially a family unit. I said, 'You must try and find a nice home-loving girl in the country and have a family of your own. You will value and appreciate a family lots more and there will be a great deal of happiness in it for you.' He had big wistful blue eyes. He would have been an adorable baby, and his ears and mouth and hands showed breeding. He was not a slum child. I wondered at his history. Such a topsy-turvy time. Some don't want homes and the tie of hometown life. Some wistfully long for them.

Monday, 20 May. My husband came in in great distress. He had a crate of lead lights taken up to some houses they were repairing and somehow it had overbalanced, due, as he admitted, to destroying the balance when he took small ones out of one side, and the larger ones tipped and over it went. Besides about £24 worth going, there is the delay of weeks. It worried me so as he talked about 'not having any head these days' and his 'wishing we won the Irish Sweep so that he needn't work any more'. One thing I was thankful for – he ate a good lunch ...

When I got in and thankfully put my feet up on the settee to rest them I felt worried, with that dread of not being able to get out and about feeling, that comes to arthritic people. I listened to *Justice*, the Saturday night play, and in the strung-up humour I was in I felt I could have put my head down and wept bitterly, thinking how much injustice there was. I felt as if I could feel it in the dark thunder clouds overhead. I thought of all the good earth, warm sunshine, enough folks to dig and delve, and yet people are suffering from fear of death by starvation. I felt wildly that if I was God I'd spin the world wildly to shake off all the foolish people on this lovely earth and start all over again …

My husband looked so nervy and worried. He ate his tea in silence. I left him quiet till he had half finished, and then talked on little subjects I thought might take his mind off that wretched glass. He sat back in his chair and said, 'Thank God for home.' I felt I could have burst into tears! He rarely pays any compliments and when he does they are so devastatingly sincere.

CHAPTER FOUR

POST-WAR SUMMER

June–September 1946

Saturday, 1 June. I looked round at the shoppers. A casual glance would have said 'so well fed', but the too-fat young and early middle-aged women, to a keen observer, would have confirmed too big a starch diet. If bread and potatoes are cut, women will be the hardest hit – those who just buy a pie or cake and who make do on that for themselves, especially. I'm always so thankful we like soup, odd savouries and vegetables. One confectioner had a great idea – little trifles set in paper cases, the prices ranging from 3d to 1s. Mrs Higham brought in four for tea at Canteen, saying they were quite good. Granted I've a picky, finicky appetite and prefer a very small portion of anything nice than double the quantity if it doesn't appeal to me, but I thought I'd never tasted such trash. It had synthetic jelly at the bottom, tasting and looking like red ink, and then a tasteless layer of yellow custard sweetened with saccharin and topped with a flavourless dab of something like soap suds. Politeness alone made me swallow the nauseous concoction and I managed to palm most of the jelly in the bottom and put the paper container in the pig bin. I felt more grateful than ever I could look after Cliff's food for him. I believe in good wholesome food well served as one of the chief essentials of life, from both a physical and mental standpoint.

I reflected how things work themselves out. I come of a clever family, whose girls dance, sing, roller skate or go in for sports effortlessly, and of whom many are really beautiful. I was lame when a child. Only somewhat crude methods of sleeping with a heavy weight on my right foot while lying on a hard mattress stretched my right leg out after a hip and pelvis fracture. I was never very active. My father scorned a good education for women as unnecessary. I always felt a sneaking envy for my clever cousins. Now I've no envy of any cleverness, not even for people who can add up well. I've a *superiority* complex instead!! I'm never at a loss for a meal. My husband says he has 'never known there has been a war' because he has always had tasty meals, has never been without some little tastie of bottled or preserves for a little treat, and my thrifty country ways of always a bit on the shelf rather than a feast and then a famine has been after all a gift that is better than a cleverness.

We went round by Ulverston and then sat all afternoon on the Coast Road, my husband writing and I had my books and dipped into them, mended some stockings and had a nap with the sun on my face. We were home for eight o'clock and made a wood fire and we listened to *Music Hall*. Mrs Howson came in with her husband who is home on leave, and they had a drink and a chat. I feel sorry for Steve. He will soon be forty and is a warrant officer whose time is up about February. His pension will not be enough to keep them – he has only been a warrant officer a short time – and he says he will be up against young, well-educated men in the wage market. There is a possibility of him staying on till he is fifty, but that means he would have to give up his dream of a real home of their own for over ten years. I feel Mrs Howson has not been as careful as she could have been. She could have had a well-paid job all the war – she is a very expert dressmaker – and saved money instead of spending all on non-utility materials and making lovely unnecessary things, always for herself. They haven't by any means enough to set up much of a home, and she whines about it a lot, blaming poor pay and treatment by the Navy for them not having more money saved. I wondered as I looked at her tonight what she would do if compelled by circumstances to live on Steve's pension.

Wednesday, 5 June. Down town I met several people I knew, and they and the women who hurried from shop to shop looked so harassed, all speaking of 'more difficult to get things than in the war when U-boats were sinking our ships'. Not one word about V celebrations. No one seems to be bothering in Barrow. My mind went back to last Peace celebrations. We were in Southampton. Cliff was only a few months old, Arthur five and a half years. I recall the happy feeling, the wonderful parade where Southampton history from prehistoric to 1918 was wonderfully portrayed, the lavish decorations, the fireworks, the fun and gaiety. We went out before lunch and came back about three in the morning, with Arthur curled up asleep in the big pram by Cliff. I'd taken flasks of tea, and Glaxo[†] for Cliff, lemonade and sandwiches and fruit. We bought ice cream and hot baked potatoes, and hot Horlicks as we trailed home to where we lodged. Such a wonderful day. I recall my happy heart as I looked at my sleeping boys, the feeling of deep thankfulness that the war was over, that we will never have another war. Now no one feels gay or happy about this one being over. People feel suspicious about 'war to end war' and no one talks like that now. Rather there is that feeling that discord is spreading, that given the opportunity, there would be an even bigger war, where 'nerves' and atomic bombs would wipe everyone out. We have so little to look forward to. As I came home I felt my little loved house more welcoming than ever. I closed my front door with the feeling that not even the raids ever took from me, as if I shut all discord out

and entered a little corner of peace. It's such a nice house somehow.
I feel it likes me.

Thursday, 6 June. Mrs Higham said, 'I hope I'll not begin to grow
old as well as fat.' I said, 'Steady on. What about me? I'm ten years
older than you and never had your good health.' Her answer gave
me a little sadness. She said, 'You will never be old. You have your
two sons and are too wrapped up in them to notice such trifles
as passing years.' She and her husband would have made such
good parents and could have done much for children, both with
their understanding and money. It's been a great grief to them.
We had buttered malt bread and shortbread and parkin biscuits
by the fire, and she went at five o'clock and I made my husband
tea, savoury sandwiches, lettuce, baked egg custard, honey and
wholemeal bread and butter, malt bread and shortbread. He said
he would cut the lawn in spite of it being rather too damp, and I
got a bit of ironing done and some mending.

Margaret sat down for a chat when she ran in to show me
some lovely Fair Isle gloves and berets she had knitted – at work,
of course! – and I took down our small suitcases and laid them
on the back-room bed ready to pack at leisure. I cannot think
that we will be in Ireland this time next week. I'm not looking
forward to the journey. I wonder how my wretched tummy will
stand the sea trip, and a week is not very long to get over any
upset and enjoy things, and my husband is NOT a good traveller. It seems to bring out the worst possible in him! He doesn't
like a change in any habits, hates strangers, especially if they
talk to me, gets excited about things left undone at home, and
is sure he left a light on or a door unfastened, etc! When he goes
anywhere in the car it's not so bad. But memories of holidays
by train come back – after weeks' battle to go at all. I'm glad

we are going to Arthur and Edith, though, for the boys never stand nonsense.

Whit weekend was approaching, and Nella and her husband had plans to enjoy themselves (drives to Morecambe, Ambleside and Kendal) – though on the Friday morning she had another reminder of the war when 'I woke in terror at a loud bang which shook the windows, wondering what it could possibly be. Later I learned it was a big sea mine that they had exploded, and as the crow flies we are not far off Walney beach on the Irish Sea side.' Then they were off to Northern Ireland.

Tuesday, 11 June. I've all packed except my costume jacket and my husband's sports coat. I'd put the two suitcases on the back-room bed and my poor little cat seems to realise he will be left on his own, to sleep in the garage at night and wander in the garden and into the Atkinsons in the day. Tonight when I came up to bed he had curled up between the two cases as if he had packed himself up to go! It's so long since we had a holiday and didn't go in the car. I feel strange packing all in two small cases, and thinking out carefully what will do rather than what we might need, and my husband has not the slightest idea of packing anything, for I've always seen to everything. When I'm not well I often feel pettish and think that next time I come on earth I hope I'm beautiful and dumb – someone always looks after them, and I'd like a turn! It's not looking promising. The wind is backing to west. I hope it's not a very wet journey to Heysham, but anyway rain would be better than a north wind storming the Irish Sea.

Thursday, 13 June. We had a smooth passage. No one seemed to be ill anywhere. When we docked we saw Arthur and Edith and we got a taxi and were soon at 'Lowick'. It's a beautifully planned house in lovely surroundings. A group of shops serves the little estate, and a bus stand for the city is handy. I never saw such a well-planned kitchenette, both for size and handiness of cupboards, shelves, etc., and for now nothing stands between the wide window and the rolling hillside at the back. We had breakfast, a little rest and then went down town. I gasped at the show of chickens and ducks – many roasted brown ready for serving; crayfish, lobsters and crabs and every known kind of good fish; cream cakes and shortbread; fruit cakes and pastries in all the confectioners; lovely toys and a wide choice of couponless net curtains; sweets and chocolates in pre-war profusion – fancy boxes of the latter. I felt I'd stepped back into the days of plenty. Edith said meat was scarce – since she had only had her joint and 1½lb chops and a kidney this week! Even the ironmongers, Woolworths, and fancy shops where things like gloves, beautifully crocheted collars, yokes and cuffs, and children's things were sold, showed not only more variety on their well-stocked shelves than Barrow or any Lancashire and Westmorland towns, but I didn't see the like even in London.

Tuesday, 18 June. We caught the bus to go to Portadown as we thought it would be nicer than the tram. There are a lot more new houses since we travelled that road on our way to Armagh, but the thatched cabins still gleam as white with the spring coatings and look as happy go lucky, however well kept. In the country poverty doesn't look as brutish as in the poorer streets of Belfast. I never recall seeing such half-civilised types anywhere, unless in Glasgow slums – heavy faces and vacant eyes, and ugly protruding lips hanging apart. The potato fields stretched in every direction, but Arthur said the grain was oats – wheat is little grown in Ulster …

I never saw so little make-up, even in Belfast, and none on Portadown girls. We came home on the 9.30 bus and the sun shone all the way. They seem very fond of inviting folk to 'Prepare to Meet Thy God', on barn ends and house sides and even on placards carried and sandwich boards. There was a good sprinkling of American soldiers about. They seem to be on leave. Some had Irish wives and babies. Edith knew many Irish girls who married Yanks in Portadown alone.

'We have met with such kindness and friendliness that I feel it's been the best holiday I've ever had,' she wrote at night on Wednesday 19th, as their visit was winding down. 'I've not had to worry if my husband was enjoying himself, for Arthur has been there and I've been "paired" with Edith.' She felt it had been 'a long care-free week'.

Two days later they were back in Barrow.

Friday, 21 June. To our surprise, Cliff met us. He had travelled all night. I think his main object in coming was to bring me a Siamese kitten. He always promised me one after the war but I always put him off, for I didn't want to hurt old Murphy's feelings – he is a very odd cat. Between his running wild for a week, Cliff and Mrs Pattison being about, and the kitten, he has held aloof and sulked in the garden all day. I've left the garage window open for him and his supper on a plate. I had to set to and do a biggish wash for Cliff – he goes back tomorrow night again …

This wee kitten is like a baby. He cries bitterly if cold or lonely, but in spite of only being eight weeks uses an old tin lid with ashes sprinkled as if very accustomed to a lav of his own. I felt so sorry for the little lonely orphan, I put an old tea cosy in my basket and tucked him up nice and warm. I brought him upstairs and put him on a chair by the bed. He was quite happy till I got into bed. Then with a joyful whoof he sprung on to the bed and settled himself close to my side as I write, beaming up happily through his slitted blue eyes and purring loudly. I hope the two cats settle down peacefully. I don't want old Murphy to feel pushed out for the little newcomer.

Cliff wants to 'buy everything you have ever wanted, Dearie. I'm going to see you never stand aside again for any of us.' I looked at my little cat with mixed feelings – he is a darling wee beastie, perfect in every way – but I had old Murphy. I wonder what Cliff has in mind – about things I've wanted in the past – and have I rather outgrown them if I get them now, I wonder? I cannot recall a real crave, except to travel and see the world, and who would want to do that just now? I've my little modern house, shabby, it's true, but things like carpets, etc. will come round in the ordinary way – be bought. I've simple tastes and little clothes sense. If my clothes are reasonably good I wear them long and carefully. I loathe 'amusing' styles. I've the garden – and the car, which, if it is 1934, to me is as good as a new model, and gets me to my loved hills and lakes. A Rolls Royce could do no more. I'm puzzled to put a name to one thing to add to my content, unless it's a fridge, and that's for family comfort on the whole. As to denying myself, it was never a hardship if it was for my two lads. It was a pleasure and privilege to help them in any way – and still is. Old Cliff over-rates me, I fear, but I looked at him in slight surprise when he spoke of 'making up' to me some day. I felt very touched.

Sunday, 23 June. Margaret came in with a friend who married and whose RAF husband has just been demobbed. He was going to be an architect but thinks 'there would be more in photography' and plans to set up in business, and he has only a small folding

camera, and never handled a studio one, done much developing
and no touching up. I felt amused as I thought of another young
fellow – also married who has bought a horse with his gratuity and plans to begin a riding school and teach people to ride,
running by the horse and rider presumably till he gets another
horse to ride himself. I often feel a sadness when I hear of the
many cases of unreality this war has bred in young fellows – girls
too – who have lived a sheltered life and had no chance of trying
out their mistakes as they went along. I felt glad Cliff has a vein
of practical common sense. He told of many ex-servicemen who
had lost their gratuity and very hard-earned savings in get-rich-
quick methods, toned down till they sounded genuine in the ears
of men who had not been in the rough and tumble of life for a
few years.

Another thing which Cliff was very bitter about – he says ex-
servicemen are being exploited. 'You cannot expect a real wage
till you get into civvy life and you have your allowance for a few
weeks', and then are only kept for a few weeks and another mug
comes along. He said, 'I never realised myself how dear things
were, or the many food problems. I honestly don't know how I'd
have managed if it had not been for the way you shop and plan for
me. Money goes nowhere in London. I've a good stock of clothes
too, thanks to you keeping them free from moths and dodging
new collars on to shirts and letting out the jackets. Some fellows
I know have no civvies but what they get when they come out of
the Services, and have to build up a wardrobe, both for work and
"best", and I don't know how they manage for that either.' Cliff
is like Arthur in that he thinks that the danger spot in human
relations has yet to be reached; that high hopes and joy at being
free again is carrying men along, but when they realise the scraping and pinching to start a home as well as keep on, men will

grow bitter, and if things don't quickly stabilise will tend to turn to anything that holds out more hope, from crime to Fascism or Communism. Arthur is convinced that we are on the road to inflation; that already there show plain indications of it; and the news in today's *Sunday Express* that inflation, in America will cut down the loan granted so niggardly is not good hearing. It seems a sorry business altogether. The seeds of ill feeling are not only being sown but show signs of sprouting.

Sunday, 30 June. I never saw so many people at Bowness and Ambleside even before the war. Hundreds had come by charas, more by trains and then steamer and even motor launch. Boat and rowing boat were reaping a good harvest of half crossings as at one time it would have been 6d or 1s an hour and 1s a shot per trip with the boatman. South Lancashire crowds don't behave 'tripperish' in the Lakes as they do at Blackpool. The quiet dignity of the hills and lakes seem to welcome and impress them. There never seem loud raucous voices raised in song. Perhaps, though, that type don't come. It may be that they who come have a love of calm serenity. Some who sit on seats in the sun look as one with we who feel the hills and fells holy ground, where all the peace and wisdom of life lie, ready for us if we can only reach out for it and claim it.

The heavy rains of yesterday had been a blessing to the little streams and falls. Everywhere the sound of running water, and cattle and sheep never lifted their heads as they busily cropped the sweet damp grass. Keswick was full of visitors. Moneyed foreigners always make for there. When we stayed at the Royal Oak last year, there were many who had been all winter. We picnicked in a quiet spot. Shan We had water and some minced cat meat and romped happily in the grass. This golden day will pass into rain. The purples and grey, green and brown of hills and bracken moors were too sharply etched against the blue of the sky for it to be fine for long. It was even lovelier motoring back than going. All was quiet on the roads. The charas had left. Only holidaymakers sat about and boatmen dressed up rowing boats and covered motor engines, and the two last steamers down the lake were crowded to capacity. As they passed I felt a God Bless in my heart, a wish that the memory of peace and beauty would linger through the busy week of bustle, queues and general worry.

My deep love of the Lakes never makes me want to shut out trippers. I feel 'Come and share it. Hold up your arms to the everlasting hills and draw their peace and beauty and healing calm into your tired minds.' To many heedless people I feel 'Go to Blackpool – you will be happier there', but I could never shut people away. My uncle is a rabid 'Friend of the Lakes' man. He would put a wall round if he could, so high that no one could see over. I would be very stern with people who wanted to build jerry† houses, make wide motor roads, build factories or works, or run a railway through, but I don't understand or agree with him in other ways. People who are shut in ugly soulless towns need our lakes and fells. I know I'm not consistent for I wouldn't 'tear down the ugly pylons' as he and his friends would. They are not too obtrusive, and I can only see the beauty and comfort they take to people whose lives have lacked much in amenities.

People have to live and work in far-off places. The farmers who are so important should not have to live like medieval peasants, their women folk slaves to hard work and having less comfort than the people whom they feed. I can see beauty in a tractor's moving its way over a hilly field as much as a horse straining out its heart. School buses to me are only a blessing. I never would long for the 'good old days of the village school'. My gran as a

Quaker was well educated by Friends and believed in her children being taught at home and then sent to school, but mothers of that day could not always teach their children. My husband's grandfather, who was reared on a lonely sheep farm, could not read or write till he was eighteen, and only his insistence and the fact he had a little money to pay for an adult school run by a retired school master in Bowness educated him in about eighteen months. Everything must be shared in tomorrow's world, beauty and peace, education and all that goes to make a happy child and good citizen.

Friday, 5 July. Jim Picken is eagerly looking forward to being demobbed next week or the week after, and I felt he didn't realise the difficulties he would be up against, poor lad. He talks as big as so many did. A fellow went into my husband's workshop and said he dreaded demob and scrambling for a job, as so many of his pals had been glad to take anything, whether suitable or not. Jim went off cigarette hunting when he had had his meal. He says the cigarette and beer problem is acute at Blackpool – long queues form for both. I thought of the oceans of drink of all kind I'd seen in bars and pubs at Blackpool, where it seemed as if one type spent their whole holiday! It beats me altogether. There seemed no shortage of many things in the war, and any temporary shortage was blamed on things going for the troops. There's bound to be a queer undercurrent of frustration in people's minds. We used at least to be able to say 'after the war', and use it as a cheer-up for everything. If all get demobbed by Xmas, as I saw in the papers, and have to come on the labour market and share in the scanty supplies and rations of so many simple everyday things, there will be more discontent than ever.

Tuesday, 9 July. By Gad, whatever else my men folk may be, they are not boring. I never know what they will do next. My husband bought another car today! I went down town early to take my grocery order so that it would come today, and going down Dalton Road I saw my husband talking earnestly to a tradesman we know, and as I would have passed on with a wave of my hand, he said, 'Just a moment – I want to ask you if you would like me to buy Mr Kirby's car.' Mr K.'s retiring and had mentioned he was selling his car and wanted £300. It's a 1935 Morris – only a year later than ours – but has only done 35,000 miles and been very carefully driven, laid up five years, thoroughly overhauled and got five new tyres. My husband fears the crown wheel and pinion they suggest fixing will not be satisfactory and that if 'we have to wait ten–twelve weeks we will miss the summer, and we have missed a lot out of life through the war and are not getting any younger'. I thought the idea well worth considering and Mr Kirby said, 'I will get it from the garage this afternoon. I've been having it greased and the oil changed in the sump. I'll call round and let Mrs Last see it'...

When I got in I slipped off my blouse and costume and changed my shoes and sat down to drink some cold tea I have in a glass, poured over mint leaves after breakfast when I put a little hot water on the tea leaves after breakfast. A car stopped and my husband came in and said, 'Come and see the car. Mr Kirby went for it straight away.' I had to go out and look it over and get dressed again for I couldn't go riding round in my overall! It seemed all right to me, but I don't pretend to be a mechanic and had not thought it over seriously, but my husband just bought it straight off and it was left in the garage! I said, 'What about the other?' and he said, 'If I don't sell it before, I'll push it in the empty garage across at Mr Howson's.' 'If you could only make up your mind often as easily as over this, life could be lots easier for you – and more profitable sometimes!' ...

My husband was as excited as a schoolboy to take the new car out. The gears are a bit different, but being synchromeshed, easier. He soon got into it and is so happy about it. I like him to be happy – he doesn't seem to get much fun out of life somehow.

Wednesday, 10 July. I didn't feel too good when I rose and eight o'clock brought a lad to the door with a request would I let five men have some boiling water. I looked out. It was a gang mending holes in the road with tarmac! I put on my kettle, reflecting there must be secret signs on our gate. It cannot altogether be Mrs Atkinson's idea that they know I'm soft! I had a cup of tea and some toast. I cleaned away and decided I'd make an early start on my bedrooms. The phone rang repeatedly. I had two garrulous callers to pay small bills. Shan We was a great attraction and I thought they would never go. Another start. The dustmen came. Please could they have a drink of water. They are such decent kindly men, and always shut the gate. The kettle had not been emptied. I switched it on and made them a jug of tea. It was such a hot morning and they looked tired out. The coalman came and said joyfully, 'TEA', so I made him a cup and started again. More phone calls. No butcher. Luckily the fish came, and I fried two nice hake steaks, and did cauliflowers and potatoes, and fried up a real good gingerbread from the beef dripping Mrs Picken sent, and made malt bread, to bake at the same time. Then the boy came for hot water again. I felt worthy and said, 'Everyone else is in the street', but he grinned cheerfully. I had enough soup for my husband and milk sweet from yesterday. I had a little fish and vegetables, and a cup of tea.

I'd said I'd go down to the bank for my husband and I'd to pick

up my bacon, or else I'd have relaxed quietly for the whole afternoon. It was hot, but a lovely breeze from the sea which made it
pleasant. Two encounters gave me lots of reflections. Both women
I've known from girls. One was a bar maid, and a very gay bohe-
mian who met an Admiralty man a lot older than herself. When
he announced his marriage, several took him aside and pointed
out she was not a girl anyone married. He gave the answer, 'She
will suit me – a virtuous girl would bore me to death.' He was
Harbour Master at Hong Kong and they had four of the nicest,
well-bred sons anyone could ever have. When she returned, no
one would have any more to do with her than formerly, and she
was a bit lonely, and always glad when I met her in the Park and
talked, when we had the children out. Her husband died. They
must have had lots of money, for all the lads had good schools
and the eldest is a naval architect and going back to Hong Kong
where she plans to go back to make a home when the two youngest boys make a start. They all adore her, and it's the happiest
family possible.

The other woman has never trod the primrose path, prides
herself on her respectability, and whined about her son getting
married after being a POW and worrying her to death – she
considers he owes his mother something for all the worry he has
been. She came up in the bus with me. I felt she was the last
butterfly on my wretched tummy. I came in and was very sick
and had to lie down for an hour, wondering what was virtue and
what was not! The first woman's gay, vivid personality, too young
dress, rather brassy dyed hair – and adoring family; the second's
sour Puritan face, whining voice, holier-than-thou attitude. Life
is odd, and seems to grow more so!

Friday, 12 July. I've had a job looking at me since I got back from

Ireland – an old fashioned 'play suit' of Edith's to cut and alter to an up-to-date sun suit – brassiere top and scanty pant skirt. At last there was a sketch in the *Express* I could copy, when I knew she liked it. I do dislike making new out of old unless I can have the wearer to fit, and the funny side struck me when after undressing and trying it on myself again and again, I wondered what it would feel like to be so scantily dressed and so much of me showing! It turned out really well. I felt really proud of it, and now I've only to hear if it suits Edith …

We have sold our former car! Someone had been advised at the garage where we serviced it. It's on the road and the noisy crown and pinion could last years, the proprietor of the garage said, and he told the would-be buyer it was a gift at £200. We said we would rather be paid £190 and get the new crown wheel and pinion when it came. I felt we owed it to the little car if not to a fair deal. I wished my husband had been a bit more patient, but he acted for the best – and it's not my money anyway. I dearly loved that car. Somehow it stood for more than a thing. It carried me to the lakes and hills when I felt I could not go on. I slept and dreamed beside quiet Coniston Lake, feeling my wild fears calmed. We came home in the quiet dusk and left a lot of 'bogeys' to drown in the peace of the quiet lake. We kept it so well cleaned and polished. It never had rough usage, and money was spent in garages whenever it needed it. It was never tinkered. I wanted to say, 'Be kind to it' as it was looked over by a mechanic and thoroughly approved.

The purchase of a new car, for £300, caused the Lasts no little bother, for in the following week they had to sell their old car to a dealer for only £150. A new crown wheel and pinion proved to be unobtainable and thus the prospective private purchaser backed out and the deal fell through. As

Nella saw it, she and Will were sorely out of pocket. 'It's his money,' she wrote on 20 July, 'but I thought of how I could have done with only a little of that wasted £150. My carpets are so shabby and my blankets patched – I've only three unmended.'

Tuesday, 23 July. We went to Spark Bridge. I got Joe an ounce of tobacco – such a scrap for 2s 5d. The poor dear only has what we take and it's his only little comfort or extravagance. I had the kippers and haddock, scraps of fat off my meat I'd not rendered down, a little cup of dripping and some loganberries and some Bile Beans as a different aperient for Aunt Sarah. I think their weekly ration of flour had been a bit of a shock when she saw it, bless her. She likes to give and I know a neighbour has always got a cob or tea cakes. I said, 'You will have to do as I am doing with Will's mother – ask her to send an odd pound of flour up.' She smiled but looked wistful as she shook her head. It worries her when so much that was the core of her very life is going – no sweeties for children, no rosy apples in the attic, no little pots of jam and jelly for wee presents, always dodging and contriving.

Suddenly I could have wept as she showed me a really beautiful rug, fit for anyone's polished floor in its faded russets and browns in a quite good pattern, all made from washed scraps of cloth, nothing of value, just bits. I looked at her little wrinkled walnut of a face as she said, 'We have yet so many blessings. It's not right of Mrs Marshall (a neighbour) to be so angry about bread rationing if it will help the thoughtless to share with the hungry.' If I'd put my thoughts into words, the rag rug would have seemed a symbol of my little auntie's life. She has had so little, yet from its bits and pieces made harmony, and a home for an old cousin where they are ending their lives in peace and, in the eyes of the understanding, real beauty. She is so frail, so poor, so old, yet is so strong, so rich, so ever young, so happy with each day's little efforts, so interested in all and everything, more alive at eighty-two than many young ones of today.

Thursday, 1 August. Mrs Whittam brought a jug of tea and we sat on the little wall of the garden. Some German prisoners passed, glum and miserable but thoughtful, ordinary men. They glanced at us. Mrs Whittam and I smiled and I said, 'It's a lovely day.' One replied in well-modulated English, 'It is indeed.' I wondered where he had learned to speak so well. We talked about the difficulties of life today when they had passed out of sight on their way to the fields, of all the unhappiness and frustration, heartbreak and misery, though we didn't use exact words. There's such a streak of wholesome sense in Mrs Whittam. I wonder if cows help country people to have it – or sheep? I've noticed people who have much to do with tending them have a clearness of vision and ability to think, however slowly. Both of her daughters rant and rave about German 'beasts'; she quietly talked of their homes and little children growing up without them. We talked of the misery underneath, the heartbreak and despair that passed unnoticed, little things in human relationships that meant so much, security in the love of home, planting things with the serenity of seeing them grow, of seeing days come and go without anything happening, of laughing without cause, just because you felt happy. Mrs Whittam's red jolly face, with its flying wisps of hair like a halo, saddened. She said, 'Never long for grandchildren, Mrs Last. What's in front of mine?' I thought of my baby of twenty-seven years ago and my heartfelt relief that war was over, never to return. People don't feel that sense of hope and thankfulness now. It's more a 'How long before it starts again?'

Saturday, 3 August. This heavy weather seems to press like a weight on people, making tempers short and heads ache. My husband feels it pretty badly and today I felt my patience snap. I listened to him with rising wrath and then said, 'What *is* this – a grievance airing? If so, trot 'em all out and by Gad I'll match them.' And proceeded to do so in real grand style, and he got a few things that had been coming to him. He whined because he had told me about some buttons and a tear on his working pants and which I'd quite forgotten, yet, as I pointed out, after thirty-five years of married life I'd never got a small clothes horse, an ironing stand to do my ironing on, or a decent tray or wardrobe. Anything in that line I had, I had bought – or gone without, as he never saw a lack of any amenities, and if he did it seemed too much trouble to see to in his own home! I felt wild. I thought, 'You are the most pampered, cared-for man possible, and the more I do, the more you expect – and the less you think I need.' I got right on my top note and said if he said one more word I'd not go out this afternoon with him …

The black mood seemed to lift off my husband a little, so when he suggested going to Kendal I agreed, feeling, as always, glad to see the hills. Bowness was very busy, and the station at Windermere looked like a seaside station with its crowds and queues of people. We picked up a young fellow who thumbed a lift. His home was at Windermere and he was going to Kendal. First glance he looked smart, prosperous and happy, but a keen eye could see his clothes were a little too tight and of too good material for being bought today, and I saw bewilderment and hurt in his nice blue eyes. He had been in the Navy and talked of the difficulty of getting a job. He seemed a bit vague – only had the idea of wireless operator – and, as he himself said, 'They are ten a penny now.' He loved his home in the country, but chafed to be off to a town or city, where, he seemed to think, were the only places for opportunities and a chance to make good. He was bitter about the way moneyed people exploited the country, living in big houses with dozens of shut-up rooms, while two or three families crowded into cottages, married sons and daughters having to live with their parents through housing shortage. He spoke too of people – he gave names though they conveyed nothing to us, of course – going about paying 1s each for eggs, £1 for chickens and ducks, and any price for sides of bacon and ham. I watched him as he talked, thinking again of the queer yeasty urges of today. People talk of 'this Labour Government', of Fascism, Bolshevism, etc. – one name for the surging sap that seems to be rapidly changing the world as we know it, more thoroughly than atom bombs, so relentlessly it bears all and everything with it, except those too broken, who are swept on to the banks and into backwaters.

Kendal always fascinates me, especially market days when scores of huge buses bring people in from miles around. Few stupid faces; many really handsome with boldly carved 'horse' features. Smart Land Girls, clergy, Boy Scouts, busy housewives and farmers and their families, all reduced to a common factor – ration books! No cakes at all – in Kendal! – home of such goodies as shortbread, pasties and plum cake. Not much bread either. I suppose people would have bought earlier. Apples were being carried. Not as many tomatoes as in Barrow, but the local potatoes were so nice and even sized. Lots of good dried fruit, but stoned raisins and prunes were for regular customers only – one shop had a ticket added: 'Sorry, short supply'. Beautiful Utility fur coats, up to sixty-eight guineas. Lovely tweeds, lots of biscuits, gorgeous flowers of every kind, very poor watery ice cream, 'amusing' hats I couldn't quite see on any of the country heads around, and lovely shop windows, none boarded halfway or empty as in Barrow. Our walk round was a real treat.

Sunday, 11 August. It's been a real summer day today. I rested till 11.30, had my bath slowly and lazily, and made lunch for 12.45 so that we could get out early. I packed pears and custard in separate jars, cheese sandwiches and cake and two flasks of tea, and we decided to go off to Keswick with it being so lovely. The sun shone so warm and seemed to tempt everyone out, either walking or cycling if they were only young. Farmers were taking advantage of the sun to toss hay to dry and, wherever possible, to load, but I noticed no one thought so much of future prospects to cut grass on any large scale. The hills stood out in their clear-cut beauty, with shadows sweeping over them from little swift moving clouds. Windermere was gay with craft of every kind, and in the huge bus park at Bowness there were charas from London, Liverpool, Glasgow and Newcastle, 'on tour' as well as the day excursions. Even Keswick, where either Dunmail or Kirkstone Passes have to be climbed over the hills between, had its share of charas. I wondered again, if Rogue Herries really existed, what he would have thought of Keswick and Patterdale nowadays.

Wednesday, 14 August. There was great excitement at North Scale – squatters were moving in to the RAF huts in Mill Lane. I feel shocked at the good Army and RAF huts that are going to waste while people are wanting homes so badly. Nissen huts could be made as comfortable as the hideous prefabs, I'm perfectly sure. One quite good camp seems to have got into bad repair alto-gether, yet it was ideally situated for, if nothing else, a holiday camp, for it was right on the Bank, only across the road from the sea. I felt, 'Jolly good luck to all squatters. In these days when we are anchored down with ration books and restrictions and growing into a nation of yes men, it's good to find someone yet with pluck and spirit.' I really enjoyed my afternoon. It nearly blew us away as Mrs Whittam and I strolled up the Lane to the fields for the cows ...

When war first broke out I used to feel wildly, 'Dear God, where has all the fun and laughter gone?' It crept back a little, if dressed in battle and service dress. I wish it could get demob-bed too. The lack of bright sunshine is, I think, the cause for fretfulness and gloom; a sunny day seems to wave a magic wand. Mrs Whittam said wistfully to me, 'We did have good times at Canteen, even if we had to work hard sometimes, didn't we?' They were such nice people to work with always. Yet now we are all like an untied bundle of sticks, all tired and busy with house-hold tasks and worries we took in our stride, or made them fall into the pattern that was our life for so long.

Sunday, 18 August. My husband was so moody. He hardly spoke and beyond a curt 'Yes' or 'Ah' didn't answer any remarks I made, but gets moodier if I'm quiet. We sat by Coniston Lake. I felt the healing, soothing peace of the quiet hills and lake, my little Shan We on my lap, his little sable paws curled round my hand. It looked very dull after we had tea and heavy clouds began to pile up behind the hills and we thought it best to start for home. I felt worried somehow. I felt my husband's mood had lasted too long. I felt it was the reaction of the car mishap, and having to spend money on a 'new' one. I felt for the first time I'd like to be lucky in the Irish Sweep and win enough money for a little income!

We were home by 6.45 and it had started to rain very heavily, and as my husband turned into the garage, a man spoke to him – someone he knew slightly – and asked if he had a drop of petrol in a can as his car had conked out – we actually saw it on the side of the road and his wife sitting in it looking very chilled as it was an open sports car. We had no petrol in tins, but as the man had some of his own at home, my husband said he would run him over Walney to get it. He didn't come back. I packed the laundry, weighed up ingredients for pastry and parkin biscuits and jellied my apples for an apple pie. He came in looking ghastly and said, 'I've had an accident to the car. A woman in a car turned out of a side street and ran full into me.' He had to go back and phone the police and get the car pushed into a side cutting. He says one wheel and the front axle and the side are badly damaged – the front axle broken. When I think of Mrs Picken and Jim coming, as well as Arthur and Edith, I feel it's a real calamity. I've felt a bit sick about the car since Friday when my husband had it in the garage for greasing and was told it must have been in a smash as it had had a new chassis! I would not have had a car that had been in any kind of an accident if I'd known, and the garage man said it must have been a smash. The worst worry is the effect it may have on my husband. He just cannot stand worry and upset.

Monday, 19 August. Such a load off our minds. The car is not as badly damaged as we feared. The axle can be straightened at the blacksmith's, the spare wheel put on while we get the other repaired, or a new one and bumper and mud guards straightened out, and they promised to do it for the weekend, to make it usable if not looking so good with damaged paint work, etc. It was such a relief to know my husband would not have as much worry as I feared …

My husband pruned the raspberry canes, and they look tidier, and took the worst of the weeds out of the crazy path – they grow so quickly. I wish to goodness I could get him to cement between the little flags. I came to bed early. No writing or reading till nearly twelve o'clock now for a fortnight. My husband is sharing my room again and he will expect the light out when he settles. I never thought I'd find it a bother to sleep with my own husband! He has preferred his own room these last few years and now I feel I like it best, although at one time I felt queerly lonely.

Wednesday, 28 August. There are a lot of strangers still in town on holiday. The bus I came home in had several families – mothers with small children. One quite well-dressed woman rose with her little boy of about four to get out at the station. She pushed him hurriedly in front of her, and he said shrilly, 'We didn't give the man the pennies, Mamma.' She took no notice – the conductor was upstairs – and as he spoke again as they got off gave him a push and said, 'Shut up.' I saw the look on that child's face. I'd not have liked to bring it to a child's face for more money than I could stuff in my purse. I wondered how long the episode would linger in his mind, and how it might influence his baby actions.

Most of later August and September were to be dominated by visitors, first Mrs Picken and her son Jim (from 20 August), and shortly after they left, Arthur and Edith (from 7 September).

Saturday, 7 September. The morning flew past. It poured with rain but my husband had to go down to a bungalow on the Coast Road to see about some windows repairing and we all went. It cleared up as the tide went out, and we got as far as Grange. We had a late tea and lingered talking. Arthur seems to be confident he will get his Higher Grade next year, with a rise in salary of £250 a year. I listened to their plans. When they have a little surplus money, they are going Youth Hostelling every fit weekend, buying a little car as soon as they can afford it, and having a fortnight in Switzerland in the near future. No talk or plans of beginning a family. I sat quiet and listened and watched their faces. Arthur seems to have a poor view of prospects of peace for long. He seems to think Britain has dropped to a third-rate power, and Russia and America the ones who will decide the future for some time. Without him actually saying so, he gives me the impression he thinks it folly to have children nowadays. Yet if they don't, their happiness will have no roots. Edith is very primitive and wholly natural. Her home is her delight and, to her way of thinking, children *are* home. It will be a sad mistake if they don't choose to have children, and, I feel, a tragedy if they cannot. We live in our children, try and help them avoid our own mistakes and failures, pass on the torch of faith and trust in God's goodness and plan. They are our standard to carry on and on, when we would sink and fall if we only had ourselves to think about. My Cliff was not a very lovable baby. He was nervy and difficult, with a tendency to fight and scream beyond belief – or patience! I was so ill after a major operation when he was eighteen months old, my one prayer was that I would be spared as long as my nervy, cantankerous scrap needed me. I had so little money. Life was a struggle, for my husband was never very strong. It was the need for my baby and my faith that kept me going. I'd have been unable to do it for myself. My longings for a grandchild recede. It looks as if my little cats will have to be my only pets!

This was a month devoted to family. Journeys to the Lake District occupied several days – Arthur and Edith did a lot of walking; some evenings were marked by entertainment (several films, a travelling dance company at Ulverston, another a dance for the younger generation); and many hours were consumed in dress-making. The weather was often disagreeable

– Nella mused on 19 September that if she were to win the Irish Sweepstake, 'I'd go and live in Cornwall or Devon, where the winds are not so searching and cold.' On Friday the 13th Cliff arrived for a four-day visit, thus bringing her sons together. That evening she wrote, 'I felt happy as a queen as I looked at them.'

Monday, 16 September. Cliff is an odd one. A wife doesn't seem to enter into his scheme of things at all. We were talking of Mrs Picken's fresh start the other day. Edith said, 'Mother says she wishes you could go in with her.' I said, 'In similar circumstances I'd not start a shop. If I had my health I'd go down to London, contact flats with bachelors or women on their own, and run a "Mother's Help" or rather "Motherly Help" service – do their repairs, see to rations, little parties – not big parties. I'd charge a small all-in fee, employ part-time help, in time have "sitters in" while parents went out, take children to the Zoo and all the places beloved by kiddies, change library books for invalids, etc.' Cliff said calmly, 'You would NOT. You would come and live with me and we would adopt one or two small children for our own!!!' I thought, 'Mercy me, that lad loves planning and organising as much as I do!'

Saturday, 28 September. It's a marvellous run up the Cumberland coast to Whitehaven, and today we felt in a dream. Deep blue skies, sunlight to etch the hills in terraces as far as eye could see, soft shadows of purple and lavender, blaze of gold from fading bracken, the whirr of hay cutting and creak of carts as dried hay was being carted, happy laughter of children and shouts that sounded like laughter, soft Cumberland dialect, bleat of driven sheep – a tapestry of sound and colour only called into brightness by the blessed sun. The grain is all in. It's the grass, poor as it looks, and the bracken for bedding that is the harvest home. Never in my life have I seen a haysel at the end of September ...

We had a good look round the narrow ancient streets. A lot of the very old premises are empty and almost derelict – not been used since the slump, Arthur says. He says when he was at Workington office, Whitehaven was a real heartbreak town. I'd have loved to go in what Arthur called a 'real low dive' a few yards from the up-to-date Globe Hotel. I wondered if Judith Paris's husband had sat drinking and plotting his smuggling activities there. We bought lovely ripe figs and sweet green grapes to eat as we went along. I felt as gay as a bird. I could have sung aloud. The sun shone so hot we had the windows as well as the top open.

Lakeland is never very busy on Saturdays, but Keswick, Cockermouth, Ambleside and Bowness were thronged with local shoppers. I must have a small-town mind, as Cliff says. I could settle down happily at Keswick if I'd a home there. I could never live in a hotel. We had our picnic tea by the lake at Waterhead. Two swans were so friendly I shared my tea, and we got ice cream, to eat with our raspberries. It seemed too bad to leave in such brilliant sunshine, but the shadows slipped down over the hills and shrouded the steel-grey lake, as smooth as metal. Boats left a pencilled wake that close and left it calm and unruffled. All was so still and mysterious looking. I'd not have been surprised if a white arm had risen out of the shadows – or a monster appeared!

It was nearly dark when we got home. I felt disinclined to get out my machine but gave myself a good poke and a reminder that I'd nearly finished my task of sewing, and I got on well. Arthur and Edith both had headaches. I made some strong tea and we drank it and all felt better. Edith is so quiet. I felt she was angry with me for something at first when she came, and she certainly looked happier when she saw I was going to be able to finish her dress and her mother's dress and little jacket, but 'dull' is the only word I can find to describe her manner. She doesn't seem interested in anything. Yet she eats like a healthy schoolboy, could go off tramping and climbing and seems well in body. I wonder if she is unhappy in some way.

The wind has risen but it's a south-west one and I don't smell rain. I hope it's fine tomorrow so that we can go off somewhere and make a nice wind-up for their visit. Already they are planning their next year's visit and the routes they will take when they go climbing and walking. Me – I've a queer feeling on me that there will be changes before then. I've a feeling a chapter has been finished. Arthur begged me to read their cups. I think they have a suspicion that Cliff got round me to read his – he did! – but I don't want to do theirs. I don't want to either see something they won't like or tell them a lie about it, and if I do see anything, I don't want the worry of it. I feel so highly strung lately, and could tell fortunes. I'll be glad when I can relax quietly and try and get into a less worrying frame of mind.

CHAPTER FIVE

STRESSES AND STORMS

October 1946–April 1947

Nella had not been well, on and off, for much of 1946. She frequently complained of exhaustion, and of various gnawing ailments. 'I realised lately a spring has broken in me,' she wrote on 5 August. 'Beyond a point, I just cannot stand things as I used to do.' As autumn began, she wrote on 3 October that 'I felt dead tired. My face has ached today. Perhaps I've got a little draught. I do so dread winter this year.'

Wednesday, 9 October. I'm cranky tonight. Mrs Salisbury came and I prepared to work with her but it was one of those days when the phone rang and people called on business. Beyond cleaning my bits of silver and brass, changing the beds and packing Cliff's parcel, I did little more. The butcher came early. I cooked the two wee bony scraps of chops out of some beef and mutton for stewing, with sausage and an onion for flavour, and set it to cool by the open window, and it got cool to put in the parcel. I must try to get it off on Wednesday. Even paying the express 6d doesn't ensure Saturday delivery in London if I post it on Thursday …

People are run down, but older people look ahead with a fear in their hearts to the new world. Restrictions and 'permits' harry and worry business people till it takes the sweet out of their brew. Young married people either cannot get a house or put money on a house that cost £650 and which they have to pay anything up to £2,000 for, and it's a drag on them, and in addition find the cheap jerry[†] house that has been up about ten years wanting quite a number of renewals, not just paint and paper. Younger still, adolescents don't work as they did for careers or trades. They have the unrest on them of going in the Forces and maybe going abroad. If they are timorous it frightens and unsettles them. If they are the adventurous kind, they cannot see today, only tomorrow. We are all in the melting pot of history, and that's always hurting. The best part of history is to read it out of books when things get more in focus …

I'd like to explain to Tom Harrisson just how laughter has fled – not through bombed buildings' 'clean cuts' of trouble but with the slow steady drip drip of little worries and anxieties that eat into one's mind and brain like water eats into a stone, warping and changing the shape, making clear a channel for itself and for all water – or worry – that comes after. When I meet old friends of Hospital Supply days and they say, 'Do you remember when —— and we all yelled with laughter till tears ran down our face?' I wonder if the crazy one they talk about was me. Did I really 'keep them alive'? And I long for a little of the vitality I must have had somewhere during those trying years – trying but strangely happy, when we all felt worthwhile.

Thursday, 10 October. Primroses and polyanthus are blooming with a summer show of roses, as well as all the autumn flowers and shrubs. The sun shone bright, but the cold south-east wind was cutting. I was glad to get in to a warm fire, which I'd banked before I went out. There was corned beef, tomatoes and chutney for tea, wholemeal bread and strawberry jam, buttered malt bread and fruit cake. Mrs Howson came in for the evening. She felt miserable. She said she has those 'after holiday blues'. We listened to the little thriller from 6.45 to 7 o'clock. The BBC would be surprised if they knew the great popularity of that little shocker. It's like a cocktail for the evening. Those who pretend to be too high brow listen in spite of themselves …

I'd like a real holiday in the sunshine, not bothering about a single thing, never thinking of meals or cooking and shopping. But I'd like best to feel I could do something for Cliff, in some way. One thing has ceased to worry me – old age – for we have this house, and if we had £2 12s between us, and what bit we have, we would not be badly off. I know well my husband is no money maker. He never has been. It's a mystery how he can work so hard and have three men and two apprentices yet make so little out of his business. The moon shone bright as day when Mrs Howson went home, but it's so very cold – everyone says so, it's not just my aching bones saying it. I must try and start my dollies next week, and then I'll not have to rush to get them done for Xmas. I've got my pieces all ready for making and dressing them. In all the long years I've made dollies, I've never felt less interest in starting. I really am in a lazy, indifferent mood. I feel as if I've no energy at all.

Friday, 11 October. The shop boy came up and helped me snip the remainder of the roses and take out all the annuals, etc. I dared not begin to bake this morning for fear they cut the electricity, so after a quick dust and vac I went down town and paid for my groceries and got a few vegetables, came back and kneaded wholemeal and also fruit tea bread and made a little cottage pie of corned beef, shredded onions and sliced tomatoes with a crust of potatoes, and heated the rest of the milk pudding from yesterday, added a little gravy and sliced tomatoes to a tin of vegetable soup, and lunch was ready. I relaxed for half an hour whilst waiting for the boy to come – such a nice willing boy, and used to helping in their own garden. The sun shone brightly and the birds chirped and sang. It was difficult to think it was October. I'd time for a bath before tea and cooked lemon soles, and there was wholemeal bread and butter, strawberry jam, new tea bread and fruit cake, and the blessed feeling of a job well done, a glowing fire, roses in my silver bowl and chrysanths in my pottery jug. I felt very tired and glad to relax after tea, my little cat on my lap.

Nella often wrote of her husband, sometimes sympathetically, sometimes not, and occasionally comically. 'It vexes and annoys my husband when I joke about growing old,' she wrote on 18 October. 'He hates to think of age, and seems to think if he doesn't notice or talk about it, it's not there – like the Victorian attitude to legs!'

That same day Arthur phoned to announce that Edith was pregnant; but shortly afterwards she miscarried. Nella was regularly worried about Cliff, his career prospects, his talk of moving to Australia, and his way of living, including his lack of a wife – on 29 October he told her he ' never was the marrying type'.

Saturday, 2 November. My head felt so heavy and I could hardly sit up straight, but it was worth the effort to go to Kendal to see that it was doing my husband good and helping him forget his business worries. It's so difficult to find comfort for him, but I did point out there was only the two of us, and dear knows I've always had to manage on little, and as I pointed out a bit heartlessly when he talked of a slump being inevitable sooner or later, that by then he might not have to give his parents £2 10s out of his business profits. When I think of his well-to-do chemist brother and one who left the business in resentment of what he called 'carrying a couple of passengers', and realise how my husband has it all to do just because of an argument when the business was turned over to the two of them – and the chemist brother can make his son a doctor, he has so much money – I feel I detest that family more than ever. I think as always how my husband has been the complete mug for them all his life. Some part of him never matured. He went into the workshop at the back of the house, never went away from home, never mixed in company if he could help it, never reads, never listens to anything he calls serious on the wireless, and has carried the domination of his parents all his life. Instead of making him more understanding towards Cliff, he goes on and on about 'If Cliff were only like other businessmen's sons', etc. Quite useless for me to point out so many sons who have not followed in the family business. Nothing wipes the look of injury off his face once he starts off.

All my life people had wanted to change me. My mother wanted a boy – or a blue-eyed, golden-curled child like the one of her first marriage, who died a gentle being of two. She could have forgiven my dark eyes and hair if I'd been a boy, but as it was I always felt her disapproval in everything I did, or how I looked. My husband was attracted to me because I was 'always so gay and lively' but has always disliked any gaiety himself, always pointing out that he was satisfied to be with me alone, he didn't want outsiders, etc., always wanting me to be different. It bred and fostered in me a real horror of trying to make people alter to please me – I'd not try and alter my little cats beyond training them to be clean and agreeable.

Cliff must live his own life. I stood it till my tired aching head could stand no more and then I said as I held out my left hand, 'Before I would dominate Cliff's life in any way, I'd thrust this hand into the fire, as God hears me', and then smiled wryly to myself at the futility of my remark. Cliff would never be dominated, by people or circumstances. Anyone who tried to do so would find they only held shadows. If circumstances held his body, the real Cliff would go. Oh dear, I could have shrieked 'Shut up' like a fishwife!

Will's anxiety at this time was partly because one of his reliable workmen, Norman, had just announced that he planned to leave and set up a joinery business of his own. Her husband's worrying got Nella thinking.

Sunday, 3 November. To hear him talk you would think he had a fire or something. Sorry as I am, I feel my patience already wearing thin, as he talks of having to cut down expenses. I thought moodily, 'Just keep your hands off my housekeeping money or else you will start something.' I said, 'Well, considering you and Frank carried on with two boys and paid your parents £4 out of the profits all through the war till Frank left, and you then managed to pay £2 10s yourself, I don't think you are near bankruptcy as you imagine. You have one good man, a last-year apprentice, another promising one, and a shop boy who is the handiest lad you have ever had.'

Always tomorrow, with my husband. When war restricted things he talked of how we would go off after the petrol restrictions were lifted – stay the weekend, have meals out, go on good holidays. To get him to Ireland was almost too much for me. He won't budge out to the pictures or anywhere else. I *will* go to London when Cliff is packing up, whether I feel ill or well. I can see a spell of grizzling economy ahead, though I am puzzled to know how he can cut down more. He never smokes, only has Guinness for supper, and never takes a drink at any other time. If we go to the pictures, we pay alternately. He never buys a sweet or a flower for me, or thinks I need any extra housekeeping or anything for my clothes, and just won't give me my income tax back – says he is getting too much money for any rebate. Nothing Arthur can say can convince him he should give me back the £12 to £15 every year that is stopped off my wee income. He says I've to ask him if I want anything. My cold made me feel cranky tonight. I felt I could have started a real row if the slightest occasion had risen.

Monday, 4 November. Cliff's letter came telling me he was spending Xmas at home and would be off to Australia by the end of December – dear knows how he has got his passage. I wonder if he will be better away from the London he so loves, and a lot of the silly useless people he calls his friends, and who don't seem of any value to him. Perhaps in Australia, where he will have to stand alone, my poor laddie will get his values finally sorted out. Weak tears streamed down my cheeks, I felt so very unhappy. My husband thinks I'm a fool not to put my foot down, for Cliff says he would never go if I was very set against it. I cried till I felt all life and vitality was drained out of me, and as I bathed my face I felt I prayed in my heart that I could keep in my mind how unimportant my little troubles were, that we were all part of the Plan, that all would work out some place, some day. 'I am the captain of my soul' is feasible, but 'I am the master of my fate' is not true.

Tuesday, 5 November. I dreamt Arthur and Edith came – wishful thinking; they will not have money to spare with Edith being ill. This time of the year so often brings change into my life – or worry. I'd two babies born in December – one died. My gran died in late November. Cliff was wounded and I got word on the 19th of November. I always felt glad when Xmas preparations could go on and I'd a little brightness to look forward to.

The North Lonsdale Hospital is on the verge of bankruptcy

1. Nella and Will.

2. 24 Ilkley Road (on the left), the home of Dick and Norah Redhead.

3. Nella and Peter in
Belfast, summer 1948.

4. Will, Nella and Peter,
summer 1949.

5. Peter Last, outside 9 Ilkley
Road, summer 1949.

6. Arthur, Cliff and Peter Last,
early 1950s.

7. Mr and Mrs Atkinson, Margaret Atkinson and an American soldier at the end of the war.

8. Abbey Road, at the corner of Ilkley Road, where Nella took the bus to the centre of town.

9. The Coast Road, a favourite drive for Nella and Will.

10. Shoppers in the centre of Barrow.

11. Laying a keel in the Barrow shipyard.

12. Home time.

13. Margaret Atkinson with Nella and Will.

and stern economy is the order of the day in every possible way. No one leaves money in their will to endow a cot, etc. There seems a general idea that the Government will 'see to all now' [*the NHS was set up in 1948*]. While I deplore mass nationalisation, I do agree about the state being responsible for hospitals. I've had so much illness and so often couldn't afford treatment I should have had, pulling through more by will power than care, always my little children to make me struggle to be well enough to rear them. I rejoice to think a time will come when women like me, too well off for charity and not well off enough for nursing home treatment, will be looked after in illness and operations.

I got notice today I was liable to be called up as a juror. Seems odd. I've never had word of such before.

Everywhere bangs and happy shouts of children. It's the first big Bonfire Night since war started, bringing back faint echoes of our jolly parties, and the last one, so wild and gay, when Arthur had got word he had won his Inspectorate exam – the second place in Great Britain. When he went for his Viva, he got more marks than the top one. It was a cheap party, sausage and mash, but so many rolled up with the 6d of fireworks they had agreed, and of course Jack Gorst's contribution was nearer to £6 than 6d! Of all that happy 'ignorant' crowd, eight didn't come back, one has queer nerve lapses and two of the girls were left widows. It seems so very long ago, so much has happened.

I'll have to bottle most of the apples Edith's friend sent from Ireland. They have got rather knocked and will not keep. They might do till Xmas, and by then I'll have a few jars empty again.

On 13 November Nella took the train to London, where she spent almost a week with Cliff. She looked around the shops in Kensington the following day. 'I coveted a fur coat I tried on – I couldn't resist seeing how I looked in it, £148!' She saw a play and two variety shows, went to the 'Britain Can Make It' Exhibition, visited Mass Observation's offices at Bloomsbury House, wandered about Portobello Market and travelled by bus to Camden Town and Putney – 'I felt shocked,' she wrote on the 17th, 'to see so many flats still unfit to be lived in and wondered wherever all the people were living.' Her stay in London got her thinking on the 20th about 'my father's people', who 'lived and were buried for generations round Woolwich. They were all seafarers, far back, working always for the Indian tea trade, any money in the family being an echo of "good investments" which enabled them to "die in their beds" and leave a little behind.'

With peace came little in the way of plenty in 1946–7. The lights had indeed come back on – to reveal a worn and shabby people inhabiting a nearly bankrupt nation. There was an impressive litany of woes, many of which got Nella's attention: a colossal national debt; housing shortages; thin or even virtually non-existent supplies of consumer goods; and austerity policies from Westminster that continued or even increased wartime rationing and added new regulations that constricted daily life. The burdens of existence fell heavily on housewives, for it was they who did most of the mending and making do and queuing, and it was they who dealt directly with new restrictions and unpredictable shortages. Bread had never been rationed during the war; now it was. In 1947 about half of consumer expenditure on food was rationed, and non-rationed perishables such as fish, fruit and vegetables were often in short supply or to be had only at alarming prices. Rations of some coveted items, including bacon, ham and fat, fell below wartime levels. The widespread shortages of consumer durables were exacerbated by the government's drive to revive Britain's exports of manufactured goods, at the expense of the domestic market.

Tuesday, 26 November. When I went down town I thought I'd never seen so many angry, baffled women – all except Co-op members! – who lately have been so well served. Tinned fruit was the bone of contention. 'Strachey [*Minister of Food*] said there was 2 lb per head for everyone and it was in the *Daily Mail* and the *Sunday Dispatch*' – yet my grocer, with hundreds of customers, had four small cases and we were told we would have to queue in the morning if we wanted one. If Cliff had been home for Xmas, I might have considered going down town at 6.30, though at that time I'd have had to walk, but I'll not bother. Someone with kiddies might get the tins I'd have got.

I stood amongst the women waiting to be served. Well dressed or otherwise, they all had one thing in common – a kind of look in their eyes and compressed-looking mouths, as if they had closed them tightly at times to keep back sharp words of irritation. I was covertly watching their faces through a little strip of mirror, rather badly lit, and one mouth looked particularly set. I looked again at the bit of chin that showed above a row of tinned pears, feeling pity as I thought, 'You *do* look repressed and irritable', till a corner of the hand-woven scarf under the chin caught my eye, and I recognised it for my own mouth, and wondered, 'Do I often look like that? Where, oh where is "Lasty's gamin grin" that seemed to amuse in those far-off Hospital Supply days, the "sugary smile" which at Canteen was said to spread over my face when Naval or Merchant Navy boys came in tired and hungry?' My face so fascinated me, I went into a chemist's shop next. I felt I must really see myself as others see me. I walked to the cosmetic counter and under pretence of selecting rouge under the daylight lamp, I looked closer at myself than I remember doing and was rather shocked to find how unlit my face was, so tired and shabby, so resigned, as if gaiety and laughter had fled – a November face. I bought a little box of rouge, feeling I needed it inside rather than outside, realising with a little shock how dead and heart-

a-cold I really felt, knowing suddenly what makes a man get
quietly and steadily dead drunk!

Both Cliff and Arthur visited their parents in early December – Cliff was
about to leave for Australia. 'I feel we four will never stand together again,'
Nella wrote on 6 December. 'I've such a sadness on me,' she noted three
days later, ' such a hopeless feeling, at the thought of Cliff going so very far
away – worse than when he went East in the war.' The rest of the month
was much less sociable and festive than the previous December had been,
and Nella's main companion was her reclusive husband. On 2 December
she had had 'thoughts of living on and on with someone who has lost interest in everyone and everything, except his food and warm fire, with not
the slightest interest in other people or their opinions or ways', and his sad
appearance on the 12th got her thinking about their lives together.

My husband looked so cold and tired. I often feel a sharp pang
as I realise how he has missed his way. Other businessmen have
arranged things that they don't work so hard as they grow older.
He has that queer mistrust of people, and plods on like a labourer,
though in many instances a younger and stronger man could do
things in less time. I thought of the muddle and disorder of his
parents' house and lives. He was never taught discipline of either
thought or action, and never left home or his parents' business,
to learn life's lessons for himself, except for those two blessed
life-line years of the 1914–1918 war when Arthur and I lived in
Southampton and the New Forest, to be nearer to him when he
was in 'Harry Tate's Navy' in the submarine chasm. I would have
been better if I'd been stronger minded and not, as he once said,
'so comfortable to live with'.

'I try in every possible way to keep him going,' she remarked on 18

December, 'feeling at times I'm fighting a losing battle.' However, Christmas was 'a very pleasant day, if rather quiet, after last year', and since Nella had persuaded her husband to close his workshop for the better part of a week, they (or at least he) had time to relax, and to take day trips.

Friday, 27 December. It was actually a fine day, and after a slap-happy tidy round with vac and duster, we set off at 10.30 to go to Ambleside to pay the bill for towing the car when the crown wheel went. They were very off-hand – said they would have sent it sometime but were very behind with all book-keeping and bills! It was a lovely day. We lunched at Ambleside at the White Lion, quite the best place we have been for years, and on to Kendal. The hills towards Scotland were covered with snow, but the sun shone like a blessing. Everywhere men worked at tidying hedges and ditches and road borders and carted huge drifts of leaves away.

To me it's really terrible to see German and Italian POWs, as well as Poles. Why oh why are they not sent home to work at repairing their own land, building up family relationships and doing a man's job? Whose idea is it, I wonder, to keep men in semi-idleness, destroying initiative, making them soft with regimentation and pampering? They cannot all be Nazis, and two wrongs never yet made one right. I look at their brooding sad faces with a great sadness. Human beings have no right to treat their fellows so. Hope deferred doesn't only make the heart sick, it withers and kills. My husband says I've always some bee in my bonnet, but nothing would make me feel it a right thing to do. I'm not sloppy about POWs, but you cannot punish a nation. What's the use of scraps of rations and old clothes in helping folks? Give them their men folk. Help in things like material to repair, seeds, livestock. Make all Germany on the same footing, not zoned so that one fares better than another. Help decent Germans and back them to accept authority – and start afresh ourselves. My husband says they must be kept for harvesting our food. Then how can we pray for good crops and fair weather if we use slave labour, and anyway how expect them to work 'worth their keep'? There may be Italians and Germans who, like many Poles, want nothing more than to settle in England. That's different, and surely work could be found on the land or in the mines, though from what I hear they are not wanted in the mines by the men who don't want their own sons to be trained for mines.

Whenever I've my WVS uniform on, it's almost certain at least one Polish soldier will speak to me. Last week I solved a mystery of quite a few weeks' standing as to whatever the Poles could buy to pack into parcels they are always sending home – it's second-hand clothes. They haunt the cheaper wardrobe shops in a rather poorer shopping street, and I feel sure the Pole was telling me of his family and their footwear trouble. His companion seemed to be telling me of his desire for work in a woodwork factory and insisted on showing papers – I could have read them if I'd had my glasses, the ones in English – and he drew a tangle of carved wood from his pocket and it was a chain cut out of a solid piece of wood, like Norwegians and Danes make. It's a very great problem no doubt, but it must be tackled. It's not good for anyone to have numbers of men herded together, growing bitter.

Kendal shops were an amazement as usual. Even shops like Woolworths and Marks & Spencer had things we never see in Barrow branches, and in one electrical shop there were electric blankets and bed pads with 'thermostat' control and three heats, yet both in Barrow and Manchester they told Mrs Howson none were made with them now. I always look covetously at the good antique shops: they always have such beautiful bits of furniture.

Today it was four Chippendale dining chairs and a little low long
stool I'd have liked. Modern furniture, unless copies, has to me no
grace or beauty, and steel tube furniture has real repulsion, and as
for twisted imitation wrought iron and plastic, a real horror.

Saturday, 28 December. It was so fair a morning – we set off for
Morecambe for a little day out. We meant to go about ten o'clock,
but Aunt Eliza came round and was a bit down in the dumps.
I'd had more fish than we needed, left on the window sill yesterday, so I gave her a nice fillet of plaice and a bit of dripping, a
mince pie and a sweet apple. Poor old pet; she likes eating, as she
admits, and it cheered her up and off she went. I took my little
Shan We – he refused to be left behind. Such an odd cat. He
either loves motoring, or my company, enough to conquer any
fear of the traffic noises, and when we had lunch at the Royal at
Bolton-le-Sands, he was tied to the table leg, but showed no signs
of wanting to stray. He had his lunch and bottle of water in the
car, but so strong is habit, I have to take a scrap of ashes in a newspaper – he must have at least one forepaw on familiar ground.

The shops at Morecambe were very attractive and, like
Kendal, still had tinned fruit like apricots and golden plums.
Either people had no points or there had been plenty. We walked
round the shops and along the Prom. There was a surprising
amount of visitors sitting in the windows having late lunch and
a lot of huge new cars about. South Lancashire people like Xmas
Holiday always. As I looked at them I thought, as often, how
silly and futile to lump people together and say, 'I don't like Lancashire people' or Germans or Poles or any country. There were
two South Lancashire men staying in the hotel where we had
lunch, and no one could have been favourably impressed, and I
thought, 'I'd hate to be classed among those men and typed as

from Lancashire.' They looked as if material things were their god; too well fed and too fat, too loud mouthed, far too expensive clothes and car, for the feeling of black market not to come into my mind, and I'd have liked to slap one of their faces as he leered at me and kept touching my hand as he petted and played with Shan We. A really horrible man. We were back home for four o'clock, both feeling better for our little trip.

Wednesday, 1 January, New Year's Day. It was such a lovely bright morning. We decided to set off at eleven o'clock and have lunch at Ambleside at the White Lion again. I took Shan We and nearly lost him – if coaxing could have made me part with him, he would be lording it in the White Lion, with several cat lovers at his command! He loved it, particularly when he got scraps of turkey brought to him. It was an 'extra' lunch – turkey and a choice of trifle or plum pudding, but I preferred cheese and biscuits. We would have gone off to Keswick, but snow powdered fields and roads and lay on the hills, and heavy clouds threatened more, so we turned back and came home by Kendal. Ploughing, hedging and ditching and dung spreading were all going on busily. Even the heavy water-logged land was being turned by tractor ploughs. Farmers are more behind than last year, for the wet autumn was bad for planting winter seed. We were in by four o'clock, and I made up a good fire and we sat down to get warmed ...

We sat talking of the coming year. He said, 'I wonder what it will bring?' I said, 'I feel changes all round somehow', and to amuse him I began to talk of 'If I won the Irish Sweep', or rather the share of a ticket I have. I feel so sorry he has lost Norman, for it means he has to work harder, and he did plan to take things easier after the war. His condition rather than his health gives me concern. I notice a big change in him – an ageing far more than his actual years, and he says he feels he is growing old quickly. If only he could take things easier, and think out his work better so as to minimise effort. He should have had a son to help him, though few sons would have been content with the muddling ways of that workshop, and he would never change in any way of anything; and it's difficult sometimes in the house, where I do insist it's *my* place, and as I don't interfere with the shop, tell him he should not interfere in the running of the house. I've fought my way to that stand, and anyway he cannot really prevent me giving things when I have to help his old ones. Never a day passes but a wee taste of some kind goes down to them. I never open a jar of jam, etc., bake or make anything, but they get a tiny share. I hoard my sweets or chocolate and they have little cheer-ups when they feel dim and have often eaten their share.

My husband needn't have been so short today when I gave some POWs all the sweets I had with me – they *were* mine. We had stopped to have a drink of tea out of a flask and two fair-haired lads – stupid peasant-faced children – came along. I let the window down and beckoned them and said, 'You boys like toffee?' I felt a little twinge of real fear at the wolfish look in their eyes when they saw the handful of sweets I held out and, knowing boys, divided them equally. There were two coloured tinsel-wrapped chocolates – they were 'Quality Street' mixture – and the anxious look on one boy's face till he got his would have drawn a rebuke of 'Now, greedy' from me when Cliff was small. I could only feel pity for the two grown children. They spoke quite fair English, but very slowly. I said 'A Happy New Year, boys, and good luck.' They gave a funny little bob and one said, 'And to you, good madam' – I thought, till a little while after I realised it was 'müdder'.

Gradually a feeling of pity rather than let-them-suffer towards

POWs seems to be creeping into people's attitude. Mrs Whittam is very kind to those at a nearby camp. They made rope slippers very skilfully and asked three packets of cigarettes for them, and Mrs Whittam gave everyone a pair for Xmas so that those poor lads could feel they were capable of earning something if it was only cigs! Yet at Canteen she was really bitter against all Germans, and very angry with me for the notion that there could be any good ones. What interests me is – nobody has a good word for the Poles and I never see anyone talking to them. Yet any I've had speak to me are quite nice friendly boys or men, and if our eyes have met and I've smiled they have seemed eager to return it. They walk about like shadows, rarely conversing, and the look in their eyes, sometimes of far horizons, grieves me sorely. Someone once said to me, 'Those Poles might have fought against us', yet I know that same woman feels sorry for German and Italian POWs.

I always remember Margaret Atkinson's cousin telling of a little incident. He had been a POW for years and was taken at one of the Greek Islands and held in many places before ending up in a forestry camp in Germany. He was good at catering and dodged up Red Cross parcel oddments into square meals, and swapped things with the eager and not unkindly guards for vegetables and fruit from the surrounding district, but his greatest need was salt – the Germans seemed to lack any for themselves. He was a 'trusty' and the guards took him to carry the loaves of bread from the village bake house and he decided he would 'try and find some salt for Xmas anyway'. He took a small Colman's mustard tin and as he waited in the doorway of the bake house, managed to reach the box of salt and get it back into his pocket. A wrinkled old gran brushed against him and muttered 'God bless – I've boys of my own' and pushed a packet in his hand.

When he got to the camp, he found it was about one ounce of salt, carefully wrapped. He said, 'I never felt so mean in my life, Mrs Last – and pray I don't ever again. It wiped all bitter feeling from my heart. I seemed to have a window in my mind opened.'

Friday, 3 January. I had no shopping to carry so went for a ream of paper to the printing works, wondering just what weight of paper I'd covered with scribbles since the beginning of the war, and how much postage for letters, air mail and parcels! The girls in the post office used to laughingly tell me I was one of their best customers. I was in again before four o'clock, so got my ironing done before tea. I fried bacon and sausage and thick sweet apple slices, feeling my husband would need a good hot meal when he came in, and he ate a good one and the warmth brought back colour to his face. He seems to have too rapid a metabolism, for his good meals don't do him the good they should – they never did …

Today I was approached again by the Secretary of the Women's Unionist Party and asked to take the Chairmanship of a Ward. I held it for two years before the war and did quite a bit of speaking, but always shied from a real political speech, feeling I was a sad 'wobbler' and had no hard and fast conviction or the real bigotry necessary. It was no use arguing with Mrs Finlay. She used steamroller tactics of 'splendid organising ability rusting', 'having the tact and gaiety so necessary', etc. I weakly pleaded health reasons, wishing heartily I could have gone in for politics again, but knowing it would only be a source of real worry and annoyance to me now.

On 19 January Nella would say of her resistance to this political overture, 'I don't feel a good enough Tory to do it.' Later still, on 18 February, she allowed that the Labour government 'are trying to work to a goal, where no one will be hungry, and all will have work to do. I've a deep admiration for their ideals and aims. If I began to speak or work for the Conservatives, I feel I'd have just that sympathy to opponents that would make anything I said or did of little value.' This sort of open-mindedness tended to moderate her anti-Labour inclinations. 'I've a fatal gift of seeing both sides of a question,' she confessed in a late 1948 Directive Response. Still, she was decidedly not on the left. 'I'm a Conservative,' Nella wrote on 18 October 1945, 'or maybe a Liberal at heart, like Arthur says. Anyway, I'm *not* a Socialist.'

Nella's sympathies were clearly towards individualist rather than collectivist values; she wrote in her Directive Response for October 1942 that 'I'd rather live in a hut of my own than share a palace with others'. Her empathetic qualities may, though, have steered some of her thinking to the left. On 21 December 1948 her friend, Mrs Newall, said to her, 'You crack on about being a Tory, but you are an out and out Socialist sometimes'; however, while this remark touched on Nella's eclectic and flexible thinking about politics, there was no doubt about her approval of prudence, restraint and personal responsibility, and her hostility to bureaucratic controls. (Revealingly, Nella disliked the novels of Anthony Trollope, and wrote on 28 December 1947 that 'I always feel Trollope portrays a period from which sprang "socialism" in its more rampant form.')

Monday, 6 January. It's been a dreadful day – snow and driving wind. I woke cold in the night and lay awake for a while, trying to think what I could turn out for my parcel for Save Europe, and when I'd had breakfast I turned out everything I possibly could spare, feeling it wasn't right to have two woollen jumpers, a woollen dress and stockings lying about – I've not worn them lately – and if I do want them, I've other things to wear. I packed good khaki shirts Cliff left, both drill and woollen, and my WVS raincoat, and made a really decent parcel – 1s 2d postage …

Mrs Atkinson really annoyed me. She came hurrying in to
borrow some starch – but was unlucky. She walked into the dining
room to warm her hands and saw the half-packed parcel and she
said, 'You're surely not giving those two woollen jumpers. Why
our Margaret would be glad of them.' I said, 'But she has piles
and piles. Come to think of it, she could turn some out.' Mrs
Atkinson tossed her head and said, '*I'd* watch she didn't give anything that might be given to a German – I'd burn it first – and
it's a bit heartless of you when they did what they did to your
Cliff.' I opened my mouth to speak and closed it. All the talking
in the world wouldn't convince people like her. Then I said, 'Cliff
doesn't bear ill will – he thinks like I do – that good is stronger
than evil and only by turning to good, in however simple a form,
will we find strength and a way out of all the mess we are in',
and let it go at that; but I felt glad in my heart that my careless
Arab,[†] wounded and injured for life as he has been and is, could
feel strongly the unhappiness of the POWs, and could condemn
the luxury of the Army of Occupation, lavish food in NAAFI[†] –
so much better even than we get at home – and would talk of the
Germans, Jews and Italians as people and not as something alien
and set apart – and I'd rather be a fool, judged by Mrs Atkinson's
standards. I thought when she had gone out, 'You would be worse
off, you know, if I wasn't a fool. What about buying a big pan and
a jam pan for your own use?'

Three days before, Nella had written of Mrs Atkinson, 'I like her as a neighbour and she is very kind, but she is certainly very trying.' Nella, perhaps
unfairly, thought Mrs Atkinson insufficiently careful in her household man-
agement, and she objected to her neighbour's penchant for borrowing. 'If
she was poor or old I'd give things gladly, if it meant self-sacrifice, but it does
irk me when I know she has more housekeeping money to work on than I

have … She says, "You know you are welcome to anything I have", but when you don't happen to be a borrower the offer has no value.' Nella revisited this issue in her Directive Response for September 1947 when she wrote about neighbours, and her remarks then were fairly objective. 'We are on very good terms but at times I have to withdraw a little. She is such a chronic borrower. I'm not. I dislike having to use anything of anyone else's and have a finicky distaste of lending personal things like blouses, scarves, etc. Luckily we are not the same size in much – I'm much smaller. Pans, dripping, garden roller, cooking tins and dishes, mincer, tapes, cutting-out shears – she regards as communal', an attitude that was bound to conflict with Nella's view that 'my things are mine'. Still, Nella said of the Atkinsons, 'I would like to be friendlier. I'd like us to exchange bi-weekly evenings and perhaps play cards. They are good company but my husband prefers his fireside unshared.'

'What a day,' Nella wrote on 7 January. 'We woke to find all covered with snow and a cold wind that seemed to drive into the house and take all warmth away.' The rigours of this exceptional, almost unrelenting winter persisted for weeks, with various consequences. On 18 January, en route to Spark Bridge, she noticed that 'The flooded fields and meadows were pitiful. No dung spreading has been possible – the heaps either lay in islands or washed away. So little ploughing was possible last autumn and now, when the ground should be getting into shape, it's under water.' 'Bitterly cold' were the words she often used to describe a day's weather. She kept only one fire going in her house, in the dining room; and she saw how her Aunt Sarah struggled to keep the cold at bay in her small cottage. 'I shuddered to think of the squatters in the RAF huts over Walney,' she wrote on 29 January. 'They could not keep fires day and night as the servicemen did – and still complain of cold and discomfort.'

These were grim weeks. Coal was in short supply – some women were routinely going to movie matinees in order to save on fuel – and from the second half of the month there were intermittent power cuts, which meant, among other things, that these cinemas closed. On 24 January, 'When the laundry man brought my fortnightly parcel, he said, "Go as slow as you can with laundry – if we don't get more coal this week we will have to close down.'" Nella found on 29 January that 'water spilled outside glazes into ice almost at once, and when Mrs Salisbury was doing the step, her cloth kept freezing to it!' It was all rather dispiriting. 'It seems as if Nature herself is part of the out-of-joint tenure of our lives,' she wrote on 6 February. 'When blinding snow was swirling down yesterday afternoon,' observed the *North-Western Evening Mail* on 10 February, 'Barrow Park resembled a scene in Switzerland' and 'tobogganing was in full swing'.

Friday, 31 January. We had our first 100% cut in electricity, but it didn't affect me as I have gone back to my wartime ways of cooking on the hob of the dining-room fire wherever possible, and I never use the bedroom or bathroom radiators unless for a very short time, and my husband always writes in the dining room, to save electricity for people who haven't a fire. I wonder what folk will do in those lovely all-electric blocks of flats, and on some housing estates. I've my one coal fire for warmth and water heating, and, with the little stool in front, do the bulk of my cooking, when it's mostly stews and soups.

Wednesday, 5 February. Mrs Salisbury came and we worked busily together. Snow fell all day, but the wet kind and kept melting. I stared in amazement at Mrs Salisbury. She has always seemed sensible in the way she tried to make the money go round her family of four children, for her husband is only a labourer in the Yard. I've often told her she would be better to stay at home now she has the children's state allowance, cook meals and bake, etc. I can tell beyond potatoes, bread and jam and corned beef they don't get much of a midday meal. Today she said, 'I'm trying to get a vac – pay 5s a week for it', and she only has the very old carpet I gave her off our dining-room floor and with no pile at all except round the edges where there was no tread. I said tactfully, 'Don't you worry about the house. You get a really nice rig-out for yourself this year and pay in to the "club", and get Phyllis something nice. Don't forget what I say, that in a few years the two oldest boys will be bringing home wages to help you.' But I saw her mouth set. If she can get a vac, she will.

Friday, 7 February. The cold has been arctic – glassy roads and a bitter south-east wind that swept through unexpected crevices and doors. The screaming gulls fought over my boiled vegetable scraps and wheeled and swept overhead all day, and the starlings, tits, thrushes, blackbirds and robins fought over the sheep's head bones I threw on to the lawn. I felt I'd no clothes on under my cotton overall. My wretched bones felt they creaked, and my hands swelled with the pain when they got chilled. I was thankful I could stay indoors …

The news of the cuts in electricity was a shock. I thought of the poor people who were in all-electric houses or flats. As it is it will mean cinemas, hairdressers and many confectioners at a standstill in the day, and be a problem to housewives with only an electric stove for cooking. I began to plan. I'll bake a batch of bread tomorrow and a good gingerbread, for I've plenty of dripping and some brown sugar. My butcher brought a piece of brisket beef and I'll cut off any bits of lean I can and stew it with vegetables and pot roast the fat end with potatoes. I can always do a casserole on my dining-room fire stool.

The next day her husband joked about her fondness for plans, saying, 'You should have been married to Shinwell [*Minister of Fuel and Power*]. You would have seen he never landed us in this mess. Your love of planning would have been of some use there.'

Saturday, 8 February. My husband has a queer dislike of seeing me asleep. He woke me anxious as I slept on the settee and said, 'Are you sure you feel all right?' I blinked and said, '*No*. I'm cross you woke me. I like to wake up myself.' He said, 'You looked so far away from me I was frightened', and he really looked upset. I said, 'Well, someone once said sleep was a "little death"', and was sorry I'd been so flippant when he whitened and said, 'Don't say such dreadful things!'

Almost every day this month was a struggle – a struggle to keep warm (often not possible), to prepare food, to keep the pipes from freezing, to get out and about (Nella was housebound most of the time). People's spirits were low, their energy was sapped and physical complaints were commonplace.

Wednesday, 26 February. It was a very wild night and I heard the heavy swish of snow, but I wasn't prepared to see it as high as the front palings. I always bring in the garden spade and the stiff brush I use for the paths if it looks like snow, so my husband dug himself out to the middle of the road where it wasn't so bad and then got a bus to work. The snow plough had been out all night so men could get to work all right. I was surprised when Mrs Salisbury arrived, all bundled up in scarves and a big coat. I said 'I hardly expected you this morning.' She scowled from under her ragged scarf and said, 'I nearly didn't set off and then I thought, "She'll only try and shift this bloody snow and make herself bad" and I thought how good you always were to me', and she grabbed the spade and brush and went snow clearing. I went on working inside and she stayed for lunch before going on to another place.

Saturday, 1 March. My husband had to go to Ulverston and we decided to go on to have a look at frozen Windermere, if the roads were not too bad. We felt a queer awe at the steel grey sheet that was the friendly rippling lake of summer – it looked austere and remote. The sun was smiling behind a shoulder of a hill, and its slanting rays seemed to lick out every shorn hillside, every ugly gaping gully where trees had been dragged to the road. There was not a sound anywhere. An awful stillness seemed on everything and that queer atavistic desolation gripped me. I felt I wanted to lift my voice in a wild 'keen', if only to break the silence. We seemed the only living and moving things left on the earth. I felt thankful to leave the unfamiliar scene. The hills around were patched rather than crowned with snow. The fields were white instead of freshly ploughed as they should have been by March, and heaps of dung stood frozen and useless. I wonder if it will mean a bad crop and harvest, with so late a season. Heavy sullen clouds rolled in from the sea, looking as if we would have more snow, and we were glad to get home to a fire and our tea, with the table drawn close to it.

Friday, 7 March. The blizzard reached us last night and we woke to find all snowed up. While my husband dug a way out, I rose in my dressing gown and hurriedly packed soup in a jar for him to heat at the shop, and made beef roll sandwiches for him. I opened the door and passed out the milk bottle to put on the window sill 'in hopes'. Shan We seemed to lose his head – he took a header into the deep snow and disappeared, except for the tip of his brown tail. I leaned forward and heaved, and we both fell backward into the hall, bringing a pile of snow. The cross-eyed look of reproach he gave me and the anxious look he gave his tail, as if surprised to find it still on, nearly sent me into hysterics of laughter – helped by the same 'Why should this happen to me?'

look on my husband's face as he shovelled snow. He said, 'I don't see there's anything to laugh at', but as I said, he wasn't standing where I was!

Snow ploughs kept the bus routes open, but two cars were stranded in our short road. I was surprised when the Co-op lorry came, but the driver asked to phone for a motorised lorry to come as it was too much for the horse. Poor beast, he was getting snowed up, and I persuaded the driver to unyoke him and bring him into the comparative shelter of our path. He had a tarpaulin over his back, but I offered the kitchenette matting to cover his neck and head a little, and Mrs Atkinson and I fed him bread and apples. He was a nice old spoiled horse – he raised his shaggy hoof to shake hands. I made tea for the driver and boy, and Mrs Atkinson and I had ours, and later the lorry driver.

Friday, 14 March. More snow, to add to the piles of frozen snow on the roads. I rose feeling tired to begin the day. I'd not slept very well. I gave all a general tidy and dust, cleaned silver and brass oddments, and took the worst of the snow off the front paths and had an early lunch. The sun shone brightly and I was down town for one o'clock, to keep an appointment at the hairdresser's. The roads were a horror of slush and melting snow. It poured off roofs where gutters and spouts were still cracked and broken after 1940's bad winter, and queues of women stood nearby on the kerb to escape the dripping eaves. That meant passers-by had either to walk under the drips or step down into the flooded gutters. I didn't bother. I had Wellingtons on so just splashed along, but women with only low shoes on complained to a passing police-man. The women in the queue lost their tempers and everyone shouted angrily. I thought the policeman acted really well. He said, 'Now, now, ladies, it's not my fault the gutter leaks or the sausage and black pudding is late, but you cannot expect to have these others ladies get wet – now, can you?' If he had taken a high hand, I felt the angry women would have been capable of rolling him in the slush and snow.

It was only after the middle of March that the harsh wintry weather retreated. However, flooding presented new perils: some land was under water, and many farmers were struggling to contain the damage. 'Towns-people cannot realise the devastation of floods that take off good top soil and utterly ruin rich pasture and crop land,' Nella wrote on 22 March. 'My husband's insistence it's the atom bomb that has caused the dreadful winter makes us at times wonder.' In the evening on 28 March she and her husband drove to Spark Bridge. 'It's pitiful to hear of small farmers I know well, who have lost over 100 sheep and lambs, and one young fellow who built a little house on a hillside had to take his children to a barn higher up, as the snow, melting, washed through their home like a river.'

Sunday, 30 March. Mrs Higham called in to tell me her mother-in-law was dead. I felt very glad – she has known no one for nearly a fortnight, and she was eighty-two or eighty-three, and Mrs Higham could not have kept on for much longer. She looks worn out. She will go to Liverpool tomorrow to make all arrangements for the funeral there on Monday. Gert, the sister-in-law, will be a problem. She is a very plain but conceited and touchy woman of over forty, always telling someone off. If she is wise, both for herself and her brother, she will keep on the house and get someone to live with her for company, but there again, no one could or would stand Gert for long!

When Mrs Higham went I sat by the fire – my husband was reckoning up bills in the next room so I didn't put on the wireless. I reflected how, looking back, I could see people have changed as much as fashion. Everyone asks more of life and that they should be let to work out things for themselves. When I was a girl, for a woman to live alone, even if she had money to do it, which was rare, it would have been quite unthinkable. When Aunt Sarah's husband died and left her alone, both Aunt Eliza and my mother offered her a home, confidently thinking it was their duty to 'poor Sarah'. When she calmly refused, there was shocked amazement, and questions how she possibly could. The situation was saved, after wrangling, by a bachelor cousin, whose sister died, going to live with her. People offered homes to old people and children left without parents, as a matter of course, never stopping to ask if it would upset their arrangements – and 'fit in' – and old people seemed to settle and make no fuss.

Tuesday, 1 April. I feel sorry for Margaret, and these two last times she has been in have given me an insight into her wanting to get away from home. I thought it was merely restlessness, but she is unhappy at home. Her father hasn't spoken to her for weeks – just ignores her. I said, 'What did you do or say in the first place?', but Margaret said she was really unable to say … She said, 'It's daft to say it, but I believe Dad was vexed with me when I peeled an orange and ate it in bits. He and Norah were sucking theirs and he said I was "la di ah", and' – she paused and blushed deeply – 'he said I was trying to be a lady but I'd not catch Cliff that way.' My nebulous dislike of Mr Atkinson crystallised. I felt at a loss for words, poor dear, for her own father to be so mean. I began to talk of Cliff, of his roving ways. Half seriously, half jokingly, I began to tell of the escapades – some of them – of Cliff's great-uncle, who, I often reflect, he looks like resembling more and more, and sighed as I thought how match making had its good points. Margaret's 'hero worship' would have been a greater happiness maker between them than any forthright qualities. I looked at Margaret, wishing more than ever she was my girl to love and make happy. I won't lose patience with her again, now I know the root of her unhappiness. It's so easy to misjudge people, however we try to understand them.

Wednesday, 2 April. Sometimes I feel there is a real jinx on us lately. Nothing goes right with my husband's business, poor dear. He now is losing another apprentice, a lad of eighteen–nineteen, whose friend is going into the Army. He seems to think they can always be together if they both go into the Army together. My husband was going to get him exempted till he was twenty-one, but if he wants to go he cannot stop him. That makes three in a very short time – first Norman, then the Manx boy who went back to Douglas and now this one. It's impossible to get a man, and big work beginning again, like shop alterations. I sighed as I looked at his poor worried face and wished I'd won the Irish Sweep!

Thursday, 3 April. I had a very restless night. I turned things over and over in my mind, unable to forget how worried my husband was about Alec leaving. I decided I'd go and have a talk with his mother, so rose early, put potatoes in the pan with the stewed mutton and vegetables and left it on a low heat on the stove, feeling I just didn't care about fuel restrictions. I'd bigger worries. Alec's mother turned out to be a very nice woman and we knew each other by sight. I tactfully pointed out what a disadvantage it was to boys returning from the Services who had not finished serving their apprenticeship and how lucky Alec was to have the chance to finish his, and I told her my mistake with Cliff, when I let him over-rule me – leave school before he took his matric. I don't think she had thought much about it. I could see my ideas were new. I told her what a promising boy he was and how my husband regretted his decision, and let it go at that, and went shopping …

When my husband came in his face was radiant. He said, 'Alec has been thinking it over, and has realised it would be better to finish his time when I *can* get exemption for him till then', and he went on to say he had sent in the form for applicants for exemption for him straight away. I recognised in Alec's mother an artfulness I always possessed dealing with my lads. I bet that Alec thinks it's entirely his own idea, and unless it comes out any time that she and I had a little talk, it's best forgotten. Men don't like 'managing'.

CHAPTER SIX

'SUNSHINE IS LIFE TO ME'

April–October 1947

On 5 March, after weeks of the plodding grind of daily life, Nella had written glumly about her feelings, and perhaps her changing outlook:

'Perhaps if this bitter cold would go, we would all recapture a little sense of humour. Tom Harrisson is right – no one laughs much now.* I feel as if I've had little unnoticed grains of sand drop on my head – unnoticed till it's a burden that is not easily shaken off. All my life, illness or trouble, shortage of money, moods and queerness, have never got me down. Doctors have remarked on my "amazing vitality". I've always been welcome in company because I always had something to say. My company has been sought because I was always cheery. My "gift of laughter" was an asset, and my sense of humour at times deplorable. I calmly look back on what I feel was quite a gallant person, and realise what a contrast to the tired, resigned old aching bag of bones I am today. I always liked my quiet moments and circumstances tended to drive me in on myself, for my husband never takes much interest in things, and when the boys went, there was no one to argue with or talk things over. How at times I feel I've the makings of a real recluse growing in me. I never strive to get into company, and have settled down to the fact a social life for me is impossible, but the

---

* Tom Harrisson, one of MO's founders and leading lights, who returned from service in Borneo after the war, had recently observed of postwar Britain, 'I noticed how much less people laughed than when I had gone away, and how very much less than we laughed in Central Borneo' (from a broadcast on the BBC Home Service, reprinted in the *Listener*, 23 January 1947, p. 136).

screamingly comic side of it all is that now I walk alone and never strive to alter things, my husband is less suited than when I was always fighting. Sometimes I feel I'd like a tiny cottage in the country amongst the hills I love, and quietly dream my life away. So little seems to matter really. Things break and grow old. However people plan, there's something to turn plans away. I feel a deep abiding when I look at the quiet of hills and lakes, a quiet peace. Perhaps I'm low in health – I know I am. The lowered vitality makes me like this. I think of others who feel like me, and long again for something nice to happen.'

Her spirits did in fact improve – and the summer of 1947 would prove to be as sunny and warm as the winter had been bitterly cold.

Saturday, 12 April. I told Aunt Eliza I was thinking of going to Ireland for a week in June, and she was delighted to be asked to look after my husband's lunch each day – and the cats. She told me neither of her daughters would let her have the run of everything – they have a curious way of locking everything away. Knowing they had little of value, I laughed, but Aunt Eliza reminded me of her husband's odd secretive ways and said both girls took after him, making secrets when they had none ready made!

No letter from Cliff. I wondered if the strikes at Melbourne could have anything to do with any delay. I'll be glad when I get a letter. I sensed a feeling of Cliff being out of tune in his last letter.

I packed a little tin of salmon, bread and butter, fruit bread and cake, and two flasks of tea, and we went to Kendal. We had the top off the car, and even then too warm, in our winter coats. The sunshine and the smell of newly turned earth with the sun on it and the happy faces of people who sauntered along or sat about was different from last weekend, and it seemed as if a golden breath had been on every hedgerow, field and wood. I never remember such a show of daffodils, celandines and coltsfoot, sprung as if by magic, for on Monday when we passed there was no sign of them. The ploughs were everywhere, and grain has been sown and harrowed, and lime and fertiliser being spread from little tippy carts. Kendal was full of country folk, come to market. I'm always fascinated by the types of faces, from patrician to serf, only the dress making them different from bygone ancestors. There is an old-world air of kindliness and leisure everywhere. Come to think of it, I've never heard a raucous voice, or one raised in anger, in either Kendal or Ulverston. I'd like a holiday in Kendal, and time to explore all its old courts and alleyways …

Just as I picked up the local paper, Mrs Atkinson came in, asking me if I'd read the deaths. I was shocked to see that of a neighbour in a nearby road who had put her head in the gas oven. She is only forty-eight, and since the war, when her husband got a very good job – permanent – at a wine and spirits merchant's, her daughter, a friend of Margaret's, a good job too, and she went back to an office where she previously worked, the poor woman seemed really well off. She scorned women who like myself 'worked for nothing', and when her job finished when an ex-soldier came back she was unhappy, for she missed the company. Just before Easter I met her and she said how bored she was, and asked me how I filled in my time now WVS had packed up. I told her how I'd not felt too well and things took me longer to do, and confessed how I too missed the fun of working together, but she didn't seem unduly despondent. Margaret went to a big twenty-first party of her daughter's last week, and said Mrs Senior was jolly and gay. Perhaps a sudden brain storm came over the poor woman.

Friday, 16 May. I got my permit to fly from Liverpool to Belfast today, so now I can really make plans. I feel so excited about going, especially when I'm going by air. It will cost about £7, I think, and then there will be little expenses. I took £10 out of the bank, after all. I'm not going to buy a new costume so my extra holiday is my own affair. When I felt the surge of joy run through my veins, I thought surprisedly that I'm not as old as I thought, that it's rather the monotony of my life that tires and ages me.

By Gad, if I won the Sweep my poor husband would get a shake up. I'd try anything once! I always drilled it into the boys it was all the things I hadn't done and nothing I'd done that grieved me as I got older. Ill health, little nervy and giving way too easily about any little change all combined to make me walk sedately, but if I had the chance I know I still love travel and change as much as ever, and that dullness breeds dullness in me.

Wednesday, 28 May. I've everything packed and ready except a few sandwiches and a flask of tea, for I will not be able to eat much breakfast and will be ready for a snack about ten o'clock. I'd had my bath before tea while Aunt Eliza boiled the kettle and set the table, and I rinsed my Celanese undies through and they dried in the warm air and will go in my case. Mrs Howson called in to tell me I had an invite to Manchester to some WVS meeting next Tuesday. I was sorry I'll be away. I love a day out with them but it would be hot and tiring if it's as warm as this. Shan We knows well there is something in the wind – he has never left me all day and been tiresome when he would take a running jump on my shoulder when he was not getting enough attention. I'm very glad Aunt Eliza will look in – he loves her. This time tomorrow I'll be with Arthur and Edith, after all the looking forward for so long. My husband was quite nice tonight, but it doesn't look as if he is going to give me anything towards my holiday. Never mind. What you don't have you can do without, and if he is awkward, I can be too when we go to Scarborough. I'll insist on having my housekeeping and buy something I need, to wear, and not let it go in the kitty. I felt annoyed when Mrs Atkinson said she wanted my pan to bottle rhubarb for herself and Norah. It looks as if she doesn't intend to ever get one – and she could do it in her gas boiler quite well and do more at a time.

Thursday, 29 May. I'm a lucky traveller and always meet nice people, and my whole journey to Liverpool Exchange was pleasant. A very nice RAF fellow, like myself a stranger to Liverpool, shared a taxi, I to Lime Street station and he to a medical school where he hoped to continue his studies, if passed by a Board. A bus picked up passengers to Speke airfield and I felt caught up in really pre-war courtesy and efficiency as everyone spoke so kindly and wanted to be of every assistance. I was one of four passengers going to Belfast, the other three being men. One young man about Arthur's age was really a dear. He seemed to think I'd be nervous and showed me how to buckle my belt and sat beside me. I'd imagined a 'whoop' into the air, but we took off so quietly we were in the air before I realised, seemingly flying slowly, over cotton-wool clouds, with only a brief glimpse of the sea. Refreshments were served – coffee and sandwiches and cakes, which looked very nice – but I'd had tea and sandwiches while waiting at Lime Street. The air hostess came round to make sure we had our belts fastened as we were soon to land. I'd begun to read the paper and had a feeling '*Now* the unpleasant feeling would start', but I saw the edge of the wings open as if in some kind of brake and we went down easier than going downhill in the car. Mr Graham, the nice young man, said, 'Well, how did you feel?' and I said, 'Cheated – never got the least thrill.'

Nella liked visiting and meeting new people, and being with Arthur and

Edith, and not having to worry about whether her husband was enjoying himself. 'This week has passed very quickly,' she wrote on 4 June, 'yet England seems strangely far away. I couldn't have had a better break and I've begun to sleep better.' The next day she was bound for home.

Thursday, 5 June. I'm getting the thrill I hoped for as we sight Liverpool and look down on the lovely little estates of houses. The sun is shining on them as they are laid in segments, half moons, or scattered in gardens – so beautifully planned. I'd not realised we had such well-planned building estates. They look more like America.

I had a very good journey home. There was a taxi waiting at Lime Street station and when I got out at Exchange station and asked the next train to Preston, I found I had about a minute to catch it – the guard's whistle was beginning to toot. He flung open the door and the porter passed my case in and as it was the Liverpool to Glasgow train I went straight through to Carnforth. There were Scots folk in the carriage and one young fellow had evidently been discussing his life as a soldier and I gathered he had been taken POW at Dunkirk. The man to whom he was speaking asked details about treatment, boredom, etc., and got non-committal answers, but I felt an echo from the past when the speaker said, 'Only Red Cross parcels kept life in us at times.'

Sunday, 22 June. We set off to Silecroft, at the foot of Black Combe. The hot sun after the shower of rain brought out the scent of new-cut hay, honeysuckle and clover till the air was drugged with sweetness and the larks seemed singing in competition, so sweet and shrill they sounded. The sea rolled up with little waves, flopping on the shore. Bathers and happy paddling children were everywhere. A lot of German POWs strolled about, a surprising number on their own and quite plainly letting any of their countrymen know they preferred it that way. I never saw such a mixed lot, a number had such brutish faces. I felt they were the type that would look on at the Belsen camp, so utterly insensate their expressions, their huge outstanding ears and flat-backed heads making them look subhuman. Yet amongst the group were men who looked like musicians, thinkers, scholars – and aimless boyhood. One, perhaps on a farm, had a working dog with him and I bet it had never known such fondling and affection. They sat in deep content, looking out to sea. They were better dressed – in dyed service clothes, but quite good fitting – and only a few had small POW patches stitched on. A number had jungle jerseys on. I thought of the WVS who had patiently put on the shoulder patches, never thinking Germans would wear them. It brought back Hospital Supply days, now so long ago. Our work and effort seem only a dream that has faded. So too has my family dream – that I had little happy boys around me. I've often longed for Arthur and Edith near, but a growing suspicion makes me feel it would never bring happiness to either Edith or I, unless Edith has children of her own. She will grow very jealous. I've always tried so hard to make her feel a daughter, but I fear she would get the music-hall idea of a mother-in-law and resent Arthur's deep love for me.

Monday, 23 June. My husband put his head round the door this morning and asked plaintively if I'd seen his grey trousers. I said, 'No. But why worry? Put on another pair.' But he said his bunch of keys were in the pocket. I helped him search, but without any luck, and he went off worried, and after breakfast I hunted in every likely and unlikely place and still couldn't find them, and felt the mystery deepen, for in a small modern house where everything is always kept in its place there are no hiding places! I looked in drawers and cupboards, behind doors – everywhere – but had to give up and go down town shopping. I took my grocery order, got fish scraps, went to the library and came home, and began to hunt again, feeling completely baffled. I told my husband I hadn't found them and, short of throwing all out on the lawn, couldn't think where to look. As a last recourse I went to the drawer where he keeps his books. They were all stacked neatly away, the big ledgers on top. I lifted all out and there were the missing pants, for once neatly folded at the bottom. I said, 'I've got so used to tidying up after you, I'd much rather go on than you putting things away and forgetting where you put them!' The time I wasted was unbelievable. I didn't find the darn things till mid afternoon.

Thursday, 26 June. Mrs Higham and I sat on her lawn in deck chairs. She had been down to the Social and Moral Welfare[†] this morning and was a bit downcast. She spoke of two 'wasted' young lives and blamed mothers going out to work and their not having a home life. She is like me and bigoted about the importance of home and mother for young things.

The curate came. He is so deaf he wears an ear appliance and has odd mincing ways and affectations. I looked at him as he girled and gushed, with the feeling I could 'throw up', and when he said, 'What is the matter with dear Mrs Last?' I could have leapt in the air. I felt he was the answer to 'Why Christianity has failed'. Thank goodness he didn't stay long. I shuddered to think he was going to a living of his own shortly. He is called 'little Tom' in the parish. I prefer dignity and someone to respect. I looked at him and thought of the dignity and reserve of my two cats!

When he had gone, we talked of the lost dignity of the clergy, wondering if the 'jolly good fellow' attitude had been the cause of a lot of the casualness of today. Mrs Higham always causes a little resentment in me when she insists I *am* a Christian. I say, 'I'm not, you know, and haven't been since I was a girl of twelve–fourteen', but again today she said, 'Nonsense – you are one of the best Christians I know', and went on to talk of our war years together and said, 'Only a Christian could have said that – or done so and so', as if conduct depended on any creed.

Wednesday, 2 July. It's been wet and foggy, and poor Mrs Salisbury was in a worried mood when she came. I've always advised her very strongly against making a change just now, telling her to be patient till the boys of thirteen and twelve get to work before she commits herself to any further expense. I felt she has been rushed into buying this house and selling her own, for the man gave her £5 off hers and bound the new one with the same £5 she put on it. Now her lawyer, the building society and the insurance man all tell her she has taken too much on and the house dealer is keeping out of her way and she cannot contact him. You cannot point out to anyone how ragged and unkempt her little family are, how uncouth her husband, how shabby her curtains and furniture are – and how all will combine to make her unhappy in a smart neighbourhood – but I stressed the many coppers needed for bus fare for the children going to school and shopping, adding my advice to all she had already got. I do hope it will straighten out for her. She so wants to get on for the sake of the children …

I went down town for some cat bits, the last I'll be buying for some time, and then went on to Walney. Talk about salons and witty and interesting talk in them – I'd back Ena Whittam's tatty untidy kitchen against *any*. If it's not politics – Ena is

Secretary of the Women's Unionist branch for Walney – it's a discussion on clothes or domestic economy, and there is always her sister and several friends drifting in, and Wednesday afternoon, when they expect me, seems their At Home day. I was later today and found them deeply discussing of all things – Lesbianism! I sat and laughed and my amusement and my 'Well, well, and all respectable married women' didn't offend them. Maisie, one of Olga's friends, had had a book on sex sent from America, and a chapter was given up to the subject. I could add little knowledge, beyond knowing several 'kinkies' and having a strong suspicion of a few more. Maisie spoke of a 'somewhat unhealthy curiosity about private parts' – she is a solemn-eyed little mother of two children and her husband is even more solemn and is a Youth Club Head – a paid post. She said, 'I don't quite see why you laugh, Mrs Last. It's a very serious subject.' And when I said, 'So are the Pyramids', she stared. I could tell she thought it a phase of modern times. I thought of the utter ignorance of my young days, and the horror there would have been if such subjects had been discussed openly. I thought how much better it was nowadays when curiosity was not a crime.

Nella and her husband had for months been planning a holiday in Scarborough. Despite car troubles, they arrived there on the evening of Saturday, 5 July, and settled in for a fortnight of relaxation. It was a pretty typical seaside holiday – lots of eating, evenings out, taking it easy most of the time. Sunday, 13 July was 'Such a nice warm morning', she wrote. 'We sat on the front and read the papers, feeling it was just what we had hoped we could do – laze round in the sun.' The next day, 'another lovely heatwave day, we had deck chairs on the sand to meet the incoming tide this morning, moving them back as it rolled up' – she felt 'utterly detached and carefree'. Her husband, freed from his workplace, was much less gripped by anxiety and moodiness, and during these two weeks she reported no marital tensions.

Friday, 18 July. The memory of the lavishness of Scarborough will take some forgetting – the stacks of milk bottles in milk and snack bars, the milk shakes, the cheap and good ice cream, the blackboards outside the cheaper snack bars offering bacon, mushrooms, ham and at least half a dozen varieties of fish – all served with chips – even fresh eggs and chips at several shops. The gorgeous dry cherries and plums, strawberries and raspberries, huge stacks of tomatoes, well-filled pea pods. The really remarkable show of shoes – many folk seem to recall last year the same and are buying shoes. Hot-water bottles, Wellingtons, plenty of stockings, marvellous Shetland knitted garments and lengths of wonderful tweed, rug wool in great bales, Angora wool in every possible colour, 'quick knit' too, and today there must be hundredweights of wool in the wool shops, just stacked in original great bundles, no display attempted. Fish of course should be plentiful, but even so the shell fish of every kind, prawn and lobsters, crab and dressed crabs, also dainty sandwiches, all fresh every day, sold by wives and daughters of fishermen who wrap all daintily and hygienically in cellophane wrappings. I'm sure a lot of jewellers, etc. must have pre-war stocks – nothing yet has been made like their necklaces, brooches, etc. – and they are fairly reasonable.

I've packed everything I could and when we go in for tea – we are on the sands – we will pack as much as we can in the car and pay the bill and get as early a start as we can. I'll be glad to see 9 Ilkley Road.

Friday, 25 July. Mrs Howson came in. She hindered my work, but the rest was welcome. She asked me if I'd seen last night's *North Western* news and if I'd seen Eric's death in it. Poor creature – he had gassed himself. He was one of life's misfits and I bitterly opposed him coming to the Canteen as cook. He had the reputation of being a 'kinkie', and certainly kept strange company. Yet at Canteen he worked well, and would do anything for anyone who gave him a kind word. He was always a grand help to me when we gave the Canteen parties in the Warden's post, and would see to the fires and get the cups out and help wash up.

Saturday, 26 July. Mrs Salisbury came, full of news. She went in for the £1,400 house after all, putting the money she got for her other – £600 clear – and the £300 repaid to the building society, on to the new one. There's a lot of sharp dealing with houses, clever ones skilfully working up prices and snapping down on deals, before folk have weighed things up. How Mrs Salisbury will pay interest and something off capital, rates, extra bus fares, the very necessary extras in such a better neighbourhood, and the repairs that are needed now, and which will increase in a twelve-year-old, very jerry-built house – they were built with a garage for under £600 – and then on top of it all work on such a close margin, I don't know. She has two half days a week and that twelve shillings is vital, and as her husband is only a labourer and liable to 'pay off', it's a great risk. I hope all goes well with her …

We listened to *Journey's End*. Perhaps the dour grey day helped to bring on the fit of miseries, but I couldn't bear to hear the finish. With startling clarity I seemed to recall my girlhood friends who died in the 1914–18 war and the memory of this last war seemed to rush back in a flood of sadness to choke me. The utter futility and senselessness of mankind, the cruelty to each other, the utter waste of it all, and not one lesson learned – unless it's to do more destruction in less time with atomic warfare. I felt I caught a glimpse of the despair that had made poor Eric put his head in the gas oven. I felt we were all like struggling flies in a web; if we escaped for a while, it was as much as we could hope – or expect.

Sunday, 27 July. After the nine o'clock news we went and picked the raspberries that had ripened and I got a 1 lb jar and ½ lb jar filled and covered with sugar syrup to sterilise tomorrow. I felt I didn't want to leave my quiet fragrant garden to come to bed, and my little Shan We felt the same. He had been out with me, but plainly showed he loved the cool grass to roll on and the mystery of shrub and bush to play his own little games of hide and seek. The evening seemed to carry on the sweet nostalgic memories called up by the lovely music and opening tune of *To Let*. Were Edwardian summers warmer, times more gracious, or only so in memory? To each his own.

My earliest Victorian memories are of being a somewhat spoilt crippled child, of plump women who seemed to jingle with what they termed 'bugle trimming', a vague smell of caraway seed, quite a few parrots at different houses where we went – how I hated and feared them, dear knows why – of lots of men with beards, of flannel petticoats and the weirdest washday articles on the line, too much to eat, and horrendous stiffly starched pina-fores, which were a stern test of a little girl's niceness in keeping them clean. I was nice once for quite a while, till my horrified mother found out I was leaving it folded on a shelf in the pantry as I went to school, and donning it as I came in. Perhaps the fact I could walk without a crutch when I was eleven, began to go off on business trips with my father when I was twelve – five years or so after Queen Victoria's death* – made for a 'lightsome' outlook, a quickened interest in life. The hoof beats in *The Forsyte Saga*, the perfect, perfect productions of a land where it was always summer, thrill and hold me as nothing ever before on the BBC. Did fires burn more brightly, people always sing sweetly old ballads when asked out for the evening? Were the new-fangled Viennese bands that were brought from London to big garden parties in the country so very good? Were there so many raspberries, damp fragrant mushrooms, juicy blackberries – and so many wild sweet chestnut and walnut trees? And do children now ever discover the rows of Dickens, Thackeray, Dumas, Harrison Ainsworth, Scott or Brontë on the higher shelves of the bookcases?

When the boys were small and begged for stories, they loved best to be told 'when you were a little girl', of life on Gran's farm, of trips to London and Ireland. Arthur said as he grew older, 'You had something Cliff and I never had', not realising they too had different memories than their children will have, that time speeds by, and only by comparing can we see how swiftly, so swiftly that as we grow older there is a little confusion. Sometimes when I've had a sadness, I look at my treasured snap album, often feeling my little boys nearer than my grown sons, often, alas, feeling I've dreamt it all, now I see them so rarely. All the striving and worry, the anxious love – all passed. Only two wise, kind little cats about now.

Monday, 28 July. We went round to see if we could find where Mrs Salisbury had moved. I cannot do with her on Saturday as my husband will be off, and will want to go out early. She lives in a big estate, built before the war, on the outskirts of town.

---

* Nella was actually eleven when Victoria died in January 1901.

I really gasped to think of anyone asking, never mind getting, £1,450 for the tiny, poky little jerry-built house, built originally for £450 or less. It's nearly half a mile off the main road, and up and down hills to her house. Then there's about 100 yards to a bus stop – or across the main road to a Co-op, built at the same time as the estate. It was planned to have a shopping centre, but only a shop where groceries and vegetables are sold, and a little sub post office in one corner of it, an outdoor beer licence where odd packet goods are sold, and an Army hut recently converted to a Methodist chapel, offer any amenities. Small children have all to go by bus to school, and I don't remember seeing for years so many small children playing round. It looked to me as if an infants' if not nursery school was a real need.

While many different types of houses are on the estate and there are different sizes, the one Mrs Salisbury has bought is amongst the poorest and pokiest, the kind where any ordinary furniture is almost useless. She hasn't much, dear knows. But everything looks overcrowded. I felt a real dizziness for her when I looked round. She doesn't yet realise what she has taken on.

Thursday, 31 July. I worked busily in the garden from six o'clock to nearly nine o'clock. I knew my husband's love of fault-finding too well to expect praise for all my work, but Hell's blue light, even I was not prepared for the list of my left-undones. I left him and went to water the rockery in the front, but he followed out nattering. I raised the watering can and said, 'If you don't go in this instant I'll pour this water on you, you nasty, disagreeable little pest. You came home with a black dog on your back. Next Thursday I'll consider going to the whist drive with Mrs Atkinson and leave you to it all and then it will be right.' When I thought of Mr Atkinson getting up lettuce and salad and

finishing the garden to wash it in time for when Mrs A. strolled
in complaining how stuffy it had been in the whist room, I saw
red. I must have looked as if I meant it. He held his tongue and
did the lawn …

I feel better in every way for my holiday, but strangely edgy
– don't know why. When the sun shines so bright, it's not often
I lose my patience so thoroughly with my husband. I generally think something has worried him at work, or he perhaps
doesn't feel well, but tonight I felt completely out of patience,
realising well Cliff's words once, 'You don't know what it's like
working with Daddy. No one ever pleases him and you wouldn't
care so much if he was very capable himself.' I stalked upstairs
to have a quick bath and came down to make supper, feeling
my thin woollen dressing gown irksome. I could have wandered
out into the garden in my nightdress, so loath to leave its sweet
earthiness.

Saturday, 2 August. I feel a sadness when I look at my husband. He
was so different on holiday. I began to feel it had done him lasting
good, but now he is back his little worries have piled up into an
overwhelming flood. I often wish I was clever and could help do
books and bills, but know in my heart, however clever I'd been,
it wouldn't have been really practical. No one could work with
him. It's best I'm good at cooking and housekeeping perhaps.
Today as we sped along in silence to Morecambe I built a little
dream – that we went to Australia and made a home for Cliff. I
feel often so useless, so selfish; there's so little to do in Barrow
in the way of any voluntary work and it's pounced on by women
like myself who have learned the real joy of service and working
together. If we could go to Australia, I could make a home where
Cliff could bring his friends and work happily, and I know well,

if my husband could potter in the sun, his health, mentally and physically, would be better. Some people need a certain amount of stimulus of routine, but others, as they get older, love best to just sit. It's always a deep-seated worry in my mind, and rarely lifts for long.

There was a constant stream of holiday traffic, and, to me, more huge transport lorries on the road than ever, and our narrow winding roads are not really suitable. Before long this question of roads will have to be really tackled – bypass roads through narrow country towns like Kendal and Ulverston. It's a marvel how the huge industrial loads get through. I've seen loads from our Yard that must have only got over some bridges, under others, and round narrow awkward bends with inches to spare.

Monday, 4 August. As long as I've memory, the 4th of August 1914 will stay in my mind. The shock when war came seems to always remain. In fact, I think the years make it stand out more clearly. And mankind never learns, and women bear and rear children unthinking of what lies ahead. Life has to be lived with courage, and then we have to pass on, but it grows more complicated and puzzling. It's been a really wretched Bank Holiday, dull and overcast, with heavy showers.

Tuesday, 5 August. I met Mrs Thompson, who was the Canteen manager. She is one of the unlovable type of Scot, and we often had little wrangles, but I felt sorry for the way she had been ignored in the winding up of Canteen. What bitches women can be, especially if they have snobbish daughter-of-a-bank-manger, wife-of-a-Rotary-member views like Mrs Diss, the head of the WVS, and Miss Willan, a retired school teacher who comes from Ulverston, that little town of snobs and worshippers of 'the county'. I've come to a very catty conclusion about Rotary, if our town is any guide – *super* snobs, the lot of them, with a more feudal manner, a holier than thou, that is very at variance with its brotherhood policy. Mrs Thompson says they have wound up Canteen affairs in their own way, which puzzles me, for after all there would have to be auditors and she holds all the bills and several of the books. Her husband, an Admiralty man, is in poor health – he has 'cardiac debility', the result of war strains. She is still teaching and they plan to go to her people in New Zealand, who went out in a family of eight, and the parents, and who have all done well. She said, 'Wouldn't it be nice if we could go out on the same boat?' I thought, 'Yes, if it was a very big one.'

Sunday, 10 August. We were out before two o'clock and went to Arnside. It was scorching hot and a lot of people were there, mainly visitors. Scores of German POWs sauntered about, looking so happy and well kept now they can buy hair oil and blacking, light shirts – and ice cream. I looked at them, many such pleasant healthy lads, and thought if I'd to choose between them and 99 out of 100 Poles, I'd choose the German every time. I'm really getting a prejudice against the loutish, unmannered Poles who lounge in the buses, while women and old people stand, and walk three and four abreast on the pavement. Why don't they either send them home or let them work? They slouch so aimlessly about as if with no hope – they are dying slowly. If there is a risk of what the Russians will do to them! – well, all life is a risk. They are men, and we have no right to spoon-feed anyone. What was once 'Britain's sheltering arm' and so forth tends to be interference to a degree nowadays. I often wonder in a 'maze' why on earth we don't get out of Palestine and leave Jew and Arab to batter each other instead of using our poor soldiers as 'in between'.

The tide slipped silently in, as it generally does in Morecambe Bay. Soon happy bathers were playing and swimming round. We had our tea, and left for home just before seven o'clock to travel slowly to be sure to be home for 8.30 to hear *To Let*. Somehow I felt as if I was part of Galsworthy's 'golden age' tonight. I felt sun soaked, and the westering sun still warmed the dining room and made for that feeling of well being when all is glowing and warm. The very music is a triumph, a mental magic carpet to carry me back, and the tempo of their lovely voices is perfection. I got my husband to carry a bucket of water for each of the little fruit trees and I watered my leeks and broccoli and the little rockery walls and rose trees at the top of the garden. All seems very dry and it looks set fair for a day or two.

Wednesday, 13 August. Mrs Salisbury didn't come. She said she might be having a day at Lancaster with her sister-in-law, so I began to do the bedroom. There was a ring and Mrs Whittam's agitated voice begged me to come over early and give her a hand. She didn't know where to turn. The harvesters had come two days before expected and Ena had been up all night with a cow that had developed mastitis and there were sandwiches to cut for eight of them working in the fields …

What a mix-up and mess they were in, and Olga does get cranky. I persuaded her to take her little girl and Ena's three children off to bathe. I simply couldn't have done anything today with them all squabbling round me. Mrs Whittam and I make a grand pair – I love to plan and 'boss' someone round, she loves to be told exactly what to do – and then she works like two. She said I could do what I liked and there seemed lots to go at, so I said, 'We will bake for two days and then it will help Ena tomorrow.' Mrs Whittam looked after the coal oven. I got all ready. Two big tins full of date cookies, three of cheese scones, three of plain to have cheese between – Ena cut into a 12 lb cheese she had saved for harvest. I beat up a batch of dough for little crisp rolls, using new milk, made a four-pound gingerbread, two big tins of jam pasty and two of apple, and then the rolls were ready for the oven. A pleasant Jewish-looking POW came from the field to carry the big enamelled bucket of tea, and he took one side of the big basket of food with Mrs Whittam. We had washed crisp lettuce hearts and there was a bag of dead-ripe tomatoes and we didn't forget to put in a little box of salt.

I took Ena some tea into the cowshed. She was so upset over the cow and the vet didn't come. He had left pills yesterday and it seemed a bit better, but as I told Ena, she shouldn't have let her drink. The POW came and I asked him to go gather an armful of marshmallow and we boiled it and laid big poultices on the cow's swollen udder and we all helped to bathe her all over and put cold compresses on her poor hot head. They call the POW 'Youbie' or something like it. He had real kindness and patience with that cow. I said, 'You should have been a vet' and he said quietly, 'I would have been by now if the war hadn't come.' He spoke very good English. I looked at his intent face as he bent over the cow and at his long sensitive hands, and felt I'd have liked to know all about him. Oddly enough he knew Gran's way with mastitis in a cow. He prepared the marshmallow as I'd have done myself, and I could see he thought the cow had been neglected. Ena is slapdash. Kindheartedness is not enough with animals. As much common sense is required as with children. My husband called for me, and we sat on the seashore for a while, but I was tired out and I'd my potted meat to make.

Saturday, 16 August. We didn't have the news on last night, so it was seven o'clock when we heard the pitiful account of the trapped miners at Whitehaven. I felt sick at heart as I thought of those waiting wives and mothers. I was once in Whitehaven when there was a pit disaster. I'd gone with my father on business, and was only a little girl, but I can remember the hush over the little town and the waiting crowd of women. They rarely spoke. Many had shawls over their heads and their faces looked as if carved in ivory, and they strained towards the pit head ...

We had all windows, the windscreen and the top open, yet it was only when we were moving we felt it bearable. Harvesters, road menders, bikers and hikers and drivers of heavy lorries looked very un-English with only singlets and shorts – many only the latter. Their golden brown bodies gleamed with perspiration, but they looked as happy as I felt in the lovely sunshine. I never saw so many tramps. They shuffled along, the only overdressed people about, for most wore tattered overcoats and had heavy packs that could have been a makeshift tent on their backs.

We went to Arnside, thinking to find it cool by the estuary, but it was very airless. We had tea. The ice cream made our simple meal very festive. Scores of POWs from the big camp nearby sauntered about or sat on the wall. I felt really happy for them, to see how getting a little money nowadays had turned them from sad sullen prisoners into ordinary citizens. Granted, this life-giving sun would lift up anyone's spirits, but the gleaming oiled hair and polished shoes, light, open-necked shirts, and some odd looking white linen caps they had bought from some queer source, made them look usual in spite of coarse POW pants. Some had sunglasses, many ate ice cream – but it came to me suddenly that I rarely saw them smoking. A wide-mouthed lad with gleaming teeth and long sensitive hands sat near, so like my Cliff when he went overseas – even his burnt orange shirt made the likeness more plain. Cliff loved to feel different …

My husband said suddenly, 'This weather agrees with you – you look ten years younger.' I laughed and said, 'Only ten years – I feel as gay and light headed as a girl, and feel like buying a bathing suit and going swimming again!' I feel my body is soaking up sunshine like blotting paper. Work is a pleasure, simple, well-cooked food a banquet. I feel it will build us up for winter and help us face any crisis.

We wouldn't have come home as early, but wanted to hear Churchill's voice again. I'd a queer little sadness when I heard him. I felt he was worried and heart sick, and baffled when he had no authority to sound the clarion call as formerly. Bless him for his faith and courage that we *will* pull through. I share his concern about so many who want to go abroad, but what can we do? Youth is so fleeting. This generation has lost so much, and dear God they ask so little – just that chance to work and see something for their labours, a share in those simple good things in life in the way of food that the colonies offer. I've never yet heard anyone speak of making a fortune or of big wages, only the chance to get on.

Nella was one of those who, in post-war grimness, often remembered Churchill fondly. 'If only we had a leader like Churchill now, whoever he was,' she wrote on 14 January 1947. 'When I think of a tired, ageing woman, driving herself with a whip, always, as I had to, I remember that husky, rather stuttering voice acclaiming we would "fight on the beaches, on the streets". I felt strong, my little hands with fingers that ached so badly, curved as if round a weapon. I felt my head rise as if galvanised and a feeling that "I'll be there – count on me; I'll not fail you." That, looking back, was a bit comic, for I couldn't have done much fighting.' On 6 November 1946 she had recalled his 'stirring, rousing speeches in the war' and 'feeling a surge of strength coming over the air, flooding not only the quiet room, but my tired body'. Later, on 5 August 1947, she thought of 'the electrical feeling of expectancy when Churchill was announced as being on the air in wartime'. Her declaration on 23 October 1946 would have been widely shared: 'What a grand leader he was in our darkest days – long may he be spared.'

Sunday, 17 August. We met Jack Hunter's sister and a friend by Derwent Water and, somewhat to my embarrassment, she insisted on telling me all about her divorce. At the time she was married I told her straight she was a fool. It was doomed from the start. She was a very nice but not very attractive girl, and it's no use denying, but there's a lack in the Hunter family and a downright taint in the kindly gentle German family of his mother which seem to make for idiot children and peculiar old maids. Jack is undeveloped somehow. He would never have married Isa if he had been 'all there', and the sisters seemed to have the same curious lack of judgement, and this one at thirty married a peevish-looking, sickly mother's darling of nineteen! They met on a cruise. The Hunters have more money than they can spend, and I could just imagine how lavish they were. The lad was studying for an architect and was not fond of work – mentally he would no doubt be the elder. Her money and connections, plus her mothering for fifteen years, have made him a prosperous man, and they had a lovely home in Weston-super-Mare.

She said today, 'You said he would realise some day I was so much older and he did and then began mental cruelty that nearly drove me insane. He was always trying to get even with me for marrying him, shutting his eyes to the fact that it was my help and money that had made him.' She let him keep it all and didn't sue for alimony. Her kind stupid eyes, so like Jack's in their puzzled bewilderment, blinked back the tears. She said, 'I've only kept the name "Mrs Round", and the few oddments of jewellery he bought me.' I recalled that old Mrs Hunter had paid for the engagement ring. Luckily she has a good home, the grocery business of Jack's to potter round in and draw a salary – it's the dirtiest, most badly managed and run and most prosperous one in town or the outlying districts – and there will be more money when her mother dies. Now at forty-five, she can relax – not *too* much, I hope – she has put on two stones since she came last October. They all tend to put on fat, because of self-indulgence, but Jack has made a determined effort to reduce since they went to live in Ulverston.

Isa has got her way at last – she has persuaded Jack to let her go back into business and has opened a little gown shop in Ulverston. I'm glad. It will keep her out of mischief anyway, and she always had a flair for clothes and made a success of the shop she had before she married. A thought struck me though. She will perhaps fall between two stools. The 'county' folk are inclined to stick to their own modishes and the country folk buy at old established shops, so that only leaves visitors and people who come to work – not a large source of custom. But I bet because she has no need to make a success of it that she does. It's often like that.

I've always said there is very small litter left about the Lakes. Today I saw that if you are litter minded you can ride in a Rolls or motor coach or tramp the roads. Few little streams are running into Thirlmere, and only one where there was any coolness from its wetness or enough to bathe sticky hands. A very big car with four well-fed adults and a chauffeur were just pulling out, and I suggested we park a while. Thrown carelessly out, presumably from the car just left, were paper drinking cups, a small cardboard box which had had sandwiches in, two empty chocolate carton-boxes and crumpled paper napkins. A passing tramp paused shyly as if hoping there would be something he could pick up. I smiled and picked up the sandwich box, which had two in it, and said, 'This box might be useful for you.' He came across and we looked down at the litter and he shook his head and then picked all up, and said something about 'being kept busy', as if he held himself to be the salvage collector of that piece of road, but when I looked at his grubby, shabby appearance, I thought he had a finer 'inside' than the untidy ones.

Monday, 18 August. Another lovely day. I seem to have packed in two days' work! I decided to go down town shopping before it got too hot and put some clothes to soak, dusted round, and was down town by ten o'clock. I bought 4 lb tomatoes and 2 lb pears to bottle, left my grocery order and got fish bits, etc. The town seems full of strangers, and scantily dressed women and children in bright colours made such a happy note.

I stood waiting for the bus and met an old Barrovian whose family and my father were connected with the railway when it was local and called the Furness Railway. He is staying at a nearby hotel and I've often chatted to him going down town or waiting for the bus. He seemed lonely, for he has spent his life abroad on tea plantations. He is older than I am. He married a friend of my father's youngest sister, who was not ten years older than I am, and she died years ago and they never had a family. He has always asked after various relatives and friends – if my husband had been more sociable I'd have made him welcome and invited him round, but it's no use denying the fact I'm giving up the struggle as regards visitors. The bridge was evidently up and buses delayed. Mr Jefferson suggested strolling on to the next stop. I remarked how I loved the sun, and how happy and well I felt in sunshine, spoke of when I lived down south and of envying Cliff in Australia – just talked idly as we strolled. He said something about me going back south to live, perhaps Devon, but I said if I made a change, I thought it might be Australia. I recall something about going for a long visit to Australia and coming back – 'After all, you have your own life, and interests in England' –and then I couldn't believe my ears – he asked if I thought I could consider marrying him!!!

Such a mix-up. I've had a suspicion sometimes he was getting me mixed up with Aunt Mary, whose husband was killed in an accident in Abbey Road in the blackout in the war. I can remember telling him I was going to Ireland on my own, and how he teased me about always being independent. It was such an embarrassment to us both, and he apologised so sincerely for his mistake. I could see how lonely he has been these few months, for I've often seen him round town and always alone. I was so upset I got a bad attack of hiccoughs when I got in. I wish I knew some lonely friendly soul who could marry him. He's a dear.

Wednesday, 20 August. I've been nattering about the lavatory seat and lid ever since war ended. I hate shabby things and try and dodge some way to make them better, if I can. My husband never had that pride in his home to make the best of things and says, 'Ah, don't bother – it's right enough' as long as it holds together. I wanted him to have the seat and lid French polished, but today I got on my top note and decided I'd do the darn thing myself. I unscrewed it off and partly stripped off the polish with a piece of woollen material, wrung out of warm water and ammonia sprinkled on, and I'll sandpaper every scrap off. It's mahogany. I think I'll just oil dress it, giving it repeated stains of linseed oil, and

then Mansion polish will finish it off. I love a Chippendale polish
on wood, or beeswaxed oak, far before a hand gloss …

I was washed and changed before lunch, and off to Walney
before 1.30 to Ena Whittam's. The cow is better and out in the
field again and today they were not so busy, for it was a little
spell off in their harvest, for the two north fields are not ready
till Friday or Saturday for cutting. There's a lot of chinks in any
scheme, rationing especially. Olga and Billy, two of Mrs Whittam's family, have bought a pig between them to fatten and kill
about Xmas, to ensure they have plenty to eat all winter. Olga has
one little girl, Billy as yet no family. The pig weighs twenty-two
score pounds, and they paid £25 and will feed it till killing, and
there is all the waste weight. Ena says she estimates their bacon
will work out at at least 3s a pound before they get it, and they
will only have to give up their bacon ration!! I helped pick pears
and beans for two orders besides my own, and then we stacked
up a pile of untidy raspberry prunings and potato tops, which,
to Ena's mirth, annoyed me as they lay around. She said, 'You'd
never make a farmer. You are too nasty particular about dirt and
untidiness.' I smiled, but thought of Gran's farm, tidy to a degree
and as sweet and fair, in its own way, as a well-kept house.

Monday, 25 August. Another lovely day. A pleasure to get up and
face the day's work. I decided to take all my curtains down, wash
them, and left them in water to soak while I went down town
shopping. I met Mr Jefferson and quite simply got to know how
he had got me mixed up with Aunt Mary. On the boat coming
over, Amy was talking about people and families she knew in
Barrow and the district, and Mr J. and she found they had many
mutual acquaintances. He asked if she knew anyone called Lord
– Mary Lord, who had been a young friend of his wife and her

sister. Amy said, 'Ah yes, very well – wasn't it dreadful about her husband, but it's a happy release' and told of Uncle Jim's death, and how very lonely Aunt Mary would be now her family were either married or, in the case of Molly, working away from Barrow. Then he said, 'I was walking down Abbey Road and saw you laughing and talking to someone and your whole appearance in your summer frock brought back a memory of before the war, when we were over. You looked so like Mary, and when I met you the first time and said "I'm sure you were a Miss Lord." I never thought of any other Miss Lord, or of the years between my visits.' I told him about gentle, sweet Aunt Mary, who, through all her bitter troubles, married to a brilliant clever man who was a dipsomaniac, loved and shielded him and only fifteen months after just stopped living and laid back in her chair without a word and died.

Sunday, 1 September. Mother's birthday today. She would have been eighty-five. Odd she should die so young, only fifty-two, and her three sisters and brother live above the allotted span. Even the senile invalid sister who lives out of the district, and whom we have not seen since before the war, is over seventy. Mother wearied her life away. She was never a happy woman. Her life really ended when her first husband died when she was only twenty-one.

In September came a two-week visit by Arthur and Edith, who arrived separately, he on the 2nd, she on the 5th (after a holiday in Scotland). In the midst of recording details of daily life, Nella was, from time to time, introspective. 'I hope I don't live to be over eighty,' she wrote on 10 September, 'but then I like reading and cats, and being alone has no terrors for me – there's so much to think about.' On the 16th she was contemplating her 'uncongenial in-laws'. 'I remembered my own "let me alone" streak and my frenzy at people always poking sharp fingers into my soul case and leaving little scars, as they accused me, silently or vocally, of "being different".'

Wednesday, 17 September. Such a nice letter from MO. Arthur can see a value in my endless scribbles. He told me long ago they were of more use than 'clever' writings, as they wanted an ordinary woman's viewpoint and routine. There's so little help I can give now. It gave me a grand feeling I *could* help someone. An idle thought struck me – the weight and volume of over eight years' scribbling must be surprising. Supposing I'd been clever, there could have been a few books! Always I longed to write, but there was something missing. Only in my letter writing and MO have I found fulfilment of my girlhood yearning to write. Anyway, they might have been good books. At least my letters have cheered and comforted – the boys always like them.

Sunday, 21 September. We came back to Thirlmere to eat our picnic tea, and sat in the sun, then came slowly back, pausing a while by Ambleside lake. A car pulled in beside us and I heard a parrot screech, which I knew could only belong to one person, and sure enough it was Isa Hunter and her husband, and Amy and her husband in the back. We passed a few remarks. She had the audacity to ask why I'd 'not brought Arthur and Edith up to see me'. I bet the little toad thinks I've forgotten her monkey-shines enough to be friendly again. By Gad, I'd like to meet her on her own and then if she 'Dearied' me I'd let her hear something she'd not forget.

Nella's hostility to this woman was exceptional, and re-emerged a few weeks later. 'Whenever I think of Isa Hunter,' she wrote on 11 November, 'I feel again that cold rage she always arouses in me. I feel she has less right to her twisted, thwarted life than one of my little cats. I shall always blame her for making mischief at a time when a happy friendship was developing between Cliff and Margaret.'

Wednesday, 1 October. My husband came rushing in excitedly and said, 'How would you like a fridge for your birthday?' and said a shop had four in and the proprietor, an electrician who often works on big jobs my husband has, had promised him one for a long time. In fact, he first did nearly five years ago, but any that have come in have been either 'shop' ones or priority. I feel a bit dazed and a bit indifferent, as I think if I'd been let have one and paid for it myself by instalments when the boys were home, it would not have cost so much – £29 10s – and I would have had it when most needed. I've done so long without it, I could have gone on doing so. I didn't voice my thoughts. If we have another hot summer it will be grand for we both like ice cream, as well as the advantage of well-kept food, hard butter and marg, and crisp salads. It's my birthday and Xmas present, so I'll buy my shoes, and if I decide on a costume, out of my year's income – this year only £19 odd.

Poor Dad. I'm always glad he died before he saw his investments dwindle and crash after the 1914 war. They had begun to weaken in 1919, when he died suddenly. In a queer expansive mood on the cold wild March day before he died, when I sat on a low stool with my sleeping baby on my lap – Cliff was fifteen months old – he said he knew he would never realise his dream, to retire to Cornwall, and live retired, but he said he realised it was 'much better to journey than arrive'. He had had a queer unhappy marriage. Mother should never have remarried. Her thoughts and heart were for ever in the never-never land of her idyllic short marriage. She thought married life would always be like those few months. Dad puffed at his pipe as he rather shyly said, 'You were always a blessing and interest to me. You know I've only really had two women to mean anything in my life, you and my mother, and it makes me very happy to know I'm leaving you comfortable. I can see Will will never get far, and I know you want to help the two little boys.' If he had lived to see how money and investments went down so rapidly, it would have grieved him.

CHAPTER SEVEN

'I CAN BE REAL BITCHY'

October–December 1947

Thursday, 2 October. Mrs Higham came in to see my fridge. Like Mrs Atkinson, she has that feeling I have – that we could have bought it years ago ourselves out of housekeeping money by instalments. 'When things pass, both good and bad go' – by the wee man.[†] I'd not go back, wars, atom-bomb threats or anything else. I'd like the more leisurely days, the plenty of simple amenities, of quantities of plain food like butter, milk, coal, etc., cheap. I'd like the ignorance that really was bliss, when war was something in the history books for ordinary people. The South African Boer War only touched a few deeply. To the rest and especially to we children it was a confusion of flags waving and 'Soldier of the Queen' and happy cheering, cakes in bags and mugs of tea sent to outlying fields in beer barrels, which made the tea taste very odd.

But under all the freedom, women could only speak and write, and *all* men were tyrants, however loving. I see red when a silly song out of, I think, *Annie Get Your Gun* is sung, 'The girl I will marry', is drooled over the wireless. It sums up the Victorian-Edwardian attitude so thoroughly, and I was one of the unfortunates who 'looked like a doll'. I've always looked incapable, or something, for added to my weak streak, I've been over-ruled by first my father and then husband, 'taken care of', 'far too attractive to give much education – she will only marry and it will be wasted'. Men folk of my day had a very 'Man of Property' outlook, 'I earn the money, I must know where it all goes' attitude. No housekeeping savings could possibly be spent on anything not liked or approved by the lord and master of the house, father or husband. A woman's place, unless sickness or loss drove her out to work, was, except in districts where women worked in mills, decidedly in the home. When my husband had such a lot of rheumatism and was off work six months at a stretch, he would never let me have boarders to help out – there were only men boarders in any quantity in Barrow at any time, with there being no work to bring women into the town. I was not let take advantage of my father's offer to put me into a little shop of whatever line I chose. Every idea that didn't coincide with his was condemned utterly. If the boys had not backed me up more or less by their outlook on life and their ambitions, I couldn't have gone on – and I saw to it they had no false ideas of lordly superiority towards women!

Mrs Higham and I talked idly of our girlhood, of men's really harem outlook. She said, 'I often wish I'd stayed in Liverpool, you know. I could have felt in things as I grow older.' We talked of Hospital Supply, Canteen and Red Cross shop days, when we felt worthwhile. Now there only seems the daily round, and to take each day as it comes and do the best with it. Neither of us are the 'Housewives' League' type who could fight for causes.

Wednesday, 15 October. Mrs Whittam and I sat and talked. She has had a wonderful lot of things sent from America lately – it cost her nearly £6 for duty! Her daughter has sent shoes and a dress, stockings and rubber overshoes, and stacks of food – dried fruits and chocolates, meat, milk and jam. She is wisely putting some on the shelf. We had a real good grizzle as we conjectured about the austerity ahead, wondering how long it would last. She had backed Firemaster and it came in second – she never seems to back a loser in a big race …

It's a fearful and wonderful thing the way the Russians have emerged from serfdom in so short a time, but virgin minds like virgin soil, and can nourish quicker than old. The Russians are unique in this swift moving modern world. With that clear-cut opportunity to go from night to day, they are not cluttered up with the perplexities and complications of mind the rest of the world have accumulated in the last 200 years. I always have a feeling that Russia is a potency of good or ill, and can swing civilisation as never before, I've a feeling for right or wrong. Communism is THE force in the world, and the worst of it is that it is one of the few creeds (?) or beliefs (?) – perhaps force is the right word – that in this world of inertia of mind and muddled thinking is a living urge. Just as Christianity took a deep hold on people by the sincerity and belief of people who would go to their deaths in Rome, making them feel 'it must be right', I've a feeling that the very fanaticism of Communism is like a torch on a dark journey for a lot of people. Sometimes I feel as if life baffles me. I sit and think and think, trying to fit things together, feeling I look through a kaleidoscope that changes before I've seen the last pattern and making little sense or cohesion at that. Ordinary people can do so little.

Wednesday, 22 October. Lately I've been amazed at finding so many people with old relatives of eighty and over. At one time it was seldom, especially when, as now, they are active. The other day Aunt Eliza was grumbling about her thatch of brown hair, with only a few grey ones sprinkled through, saying it grew too quickly and a perm lasted no time and that by Xmas she would be ready to have it done again. Aunt Sarah is failing, it's true. In her note the other day she complained of the mists off the river and how frost gripped her bones, yet she bakes and washes, reads a lot and loves visitors, and her cottage is kept trim and clean. There's something in life today that suits old people. I often think it's because they are compelled to lead a regular life. They cannot choose the somewhat indigestible dainties the very young and very old prefer. They cannot sit in the chimney corner, and if they did give up and stay in bed, as old ones did up to the last generation, the modern hardness and the undoubted lack of endurance their daughters were expected to have wouldn't encourage semi-invalidism. So unusual was it to have an active gran of over seventy, when most girls at school had grans sitting round in shawls or in bed till lunch, if not all day. I swung between pride and a queer kind of shame. My little gran was so active and busy. I felt it was not quite right she should be the first one thought of or sent for in illness.

Things were different then. About fifty-two years ago, she came to visit Mother at Rampside, just outside Barrow, and to go and see an old friend who had changed farms from Greenodd to near Rampside. I can remember plainly how upset and worried my mother was when Gran stayed overnight to look after a sick child and when next day two more were ill and it was scarlet fever. We used to go and talk with Gran over the garden wall and she was there nearly six months as one after another went down – milk and butter, by the way, were sold as usual and no one seemed to think it odd! No breakdown for Gran. Mother went and brought her cat that had been going to have kittens, and kindly neighbours who had been going to stay the fortnight Gran had planned to be away shut up their cottage and stayed the full time till Gran got back – and no one saw anything odd in any of the arrangements.

Nowadays, unless it was in the backwoods, no such state of affairs could exist. We cannot hold more than a given quantity in our hands. If we pick up one thing or choose another, we have to put something away to do so. We are getting pensions, medical care, school meals, do this and do that, and you cannot have this and only a wee bit of that – all very nice and easy in some people's minds, but it lessens personal responsibility and kills that kindliness to each other, even in the country villages. I heard Aunt Sarah say once, 'No one watches for smoke from a cottage chimney, knowing if a fire is lit all is well, and if no smoke from the chimney of a person living alone, it's your duty to go and see what is to do and if help is needed in any way.' People carried buckets of water from the well for each other, hung clothes out if anyone had bad colds, kneaded and baked bread for old people or expectant mothers, cut up an old warm coat and remade it for a shivering child. Time brings changes. No doubt all will work out.

Sunday, 26 October. We went round Coniston Lake, paused a while in the stillness that always seems a part of the charm of that quiet place, and then round by Ambleside. The sun shone, but from behind the hills, and made Windermere at Waterhead like a faintly coloured steel engraving. Little boats, landing stages and the hills across were a silhouette of dark colourless angles. The lake was pale grey, only a faint colour in the sky and where the sun tipped the hills with metallic gilt. It looked strange and remote, as if all the gaiety and welcome of the summer were gone and the hills and lake preparing to live some somber, withdrawn life of their own. I often wonder as I glance towards the field on the side of the lake where Roman remains have been found, how those exiles from sunny Italy, cultured Rome, fitted in, if they liked their life so different here, or if their hearts withered and died with longing. Times like today I feel it was the latter!

We didn't take tea – with no visitors in motor coaches, or at least very few, it's easy to get a meal anywhere. We went down through Hawkshead and Lakeside and had tea at The Landings, a wonderfully restored, old, early Victorian house, which has gone all out to attract the quiet visitor. Mrs Woods' brother, the Chief Constable of Fleetwood, spends weekends and all holidays there, and as we went round to the tea room, which when I was a girl was a huge useless conservatory, no use to anyone, but is now a wood-block floored, flat concrete-roofed place where small dances can be held, we saw the luxury and comfort of the two lounges for resident visitors, who sat in big easy chairs, with a leaping wood fire, though the sun was on that side. We thought how cosy it looked and realised why people went again and again.

The tea was really amazing – tomato sandwiches, with the crusts cut off, little hot French pancakes, bread and butter, slices of sweet tea buns buttered, apricot jam and little homemade pastries and cakes. The tables were mostly set for dinner. They must have a regular feature of dinners, judging by the number laid. The china and silver were like the tablecloths – pre-war in their condition. Everything was exquisitely kept and served, a treat if it had only been bread and butter and the really good hot tea, with unlimited milk and sugar – and the tea was 2s a head! I felt I wanted to linger and then walk round the well-kept grounds, down to the water's edge, where the lawn sloped to the quiet backwater end of the lake. I enjoyed the food I'd not seen before it was set before me, but even more the luxury and comfort. Not one little hint or sign of utility or make do and mend. I felt I'd have liked a holiday there but realise it would pall on my husband. He doesn't like to have to amuse himself and, unlike

Mrs Woods and her relations, wouldn't like sitting round talking or playing cards in the evenings, and of course when the car couldn't be used, there would be nothing at all for him …

I finished two more dollies as I sat listening to the wireless. What a grand talk about craftsmanship after the news. I'd like it printed and put in the 'lessons to schools'. Every word in the rough North Country burr was like a message, and so very true. I'm not clever beyond homely things, but if I'd not the delight in a well-cooked and -served meal, and well kept house and my odds and ends of sewing, I would have nothing to make me happy at all now. My dollies are very homely craft but are a joy to make and seem always a pleasure to kiddies. I looked at the two smiling faces as they sat perched on the sideboard and felt they were a little craft. They were my creation. I often feel glad I never snubbed the boys in the mess and welter of stage making, clay and plasticine modelling, and every doll-eyed homemade thing they insisted on making. They loved to make their own Xmas cards, calendars and presents. I feel Arthur with his love of drama and glove making has good escapes from dull income tax, and Cliff's childish crafts have turned out well for him. If I'd been unusually tidy and resented the mess, I could have robbed them of something very precious.

Monday, 27 October. What a day, though dear knows it started off calm to dullness! Last Thursday Mrs Higham and I were talking of the coming opening of the Children's Ward, for which the WVS had handed over monies left when Hospital Supply, etc. was wound up and 'efforts' and the sale of the WVS van brought the sum up to about £800, which furnished and redecorated the Children's Ward. Invites have naturally had to be kept severely to a limit, but we quite expected one, she as Secretary and I as the money raiser for Hospital Supply. I said, 'Oh, we will get them on Monday, perhaps. They will get them ready at the office and post them at the weekend, but if by then we haven't had one, I'll ring up Mrs Diss.' When the postman passed the gate, I rang up Mrs Diss and asked if Hospital Supply were not being represented. Mrs Waite couldn't go and I knew Mrs Lord, the Chairman, was going away to a wedding next weekend. Mrs Diss said, 'Mrs Lord has invites for both of you. Get in touch with her.' I did and felt very taken aback when her 'Mrs Feather' voice fluttered over the phone telling me she and Mrs Waite, who is a cranky, rude semi-invalid, snubbing anyone who calls, if she will see them at all, had talked it over and decided Hospital Supply would not be represented, and burnt the three tickets.

Suddenly I realise why men strike, against all reason. I felt there would be bother if two more tickets were not found for us. I was determined that neither Mrs Higham nor I, who had had to do so much alone, should not be snubbed by either of those jealous, bigoted old women. I went down to the WVS office and spoke my mind, asking why tickets should have been given out like that and not sent by post, etc. etc. etc. A little later I couldn't think I'd been so snooty. I think it was the memory of all Mrs Waite's underhand tricks, her hatred of a committee, not having all her own way, come what may. I felt, 'You shan't have the last laugh, you hateful old woman'. Anyway, phones buzzed and first one and then another was rung up and two tickets found that could not be used.

Mrs Higham was waiting when I got back. I had remembered to put in my grocery order and get my hungry cats some fish bits and two packets of grease band for the fruit trees, but hadn't paid my electric light bill or ordered vegetables as I'd intended. We had a cup of tea and a real good laugh – a triumphant one, as we talked of the time Mrs Woods, Mrs Higham and I resigned and only went back because of Mrs Diss pleading we '*were* Hospital Supply and couldn't possibly "desert"'.

Tuesday, 28 October. I've often had a little example of hair trigger temper lately, both in myself and others, and this morning had another. I did not feel too well and planned to turn out my cupboards and pantry as I rose. I put on my dressing gown and heard a commotion and shouting from Mrs Atkinson and Mr Atkinson's quiet voice raised in anger. She has only had a few outbursts in my hearing since they came – real shouting temper – but this morning I felt there *was* something to do, when she went into the garage, shouting. I went down in my dressing gown and really felt afraid of her glassing eyes, till I saw she had Murphy hanging on her arm. She yelled, 'Murdering little beast – he caught a poor little sparrow and I've hit him on the head with the sweeping brush.' Mr Atkinson followed, looking upset, and said, 'Oh, I do hope the poor cat's all right. You will do someone an injury in one of your nasty hysterical tempers some day.' And turning to me he said, 'Should I phone for the vet, Mrs Last?' Cold rage flowed over me like a current of air. I said, 'If that is necessary, Mr Atkinson. The Cruelty Inspector will be called too.' And I turned to Mrs Atkinson and in a cutting tone said, 'If there was less bread wasted on your shed and lawn, the birds wouldn't come and feed till they are too stark fat to fly easily – and remember, it's a cat's nature to catch birds if it can.' Luckily for things the poor cat opened its eyes and huddled under my arm. I've never felt before I could have had a real row with a neighbour – a real fight!

Later she came in very apologetic, with some meat scraps on a plate. She said, 'Charley and I have been wrangling for days and it came to a head this morning. He knows I've set my mind on a fur coat and he won't give me anything towards it – says we might need money for something more than a fur coat.' I felt very stiff with her but could have laughed out loud when she said quite artlessly, 'Did you get any currants from your grocer? With you having made your Xmas cake and mincemeat, you won't need them, will you?' I said, 'With dried fruit being so short supply, unless I get some from Australia from the Sydney firm who promised to replace the damaged parcel, I don't think I'll have any to spare. Remember I make fruit bread and any cake I can.' She collected my shilling for the big race – we planned 1s each way between us on Wild Child – and went. I felt, 'There's nothing as queer as folk' …

Arthur's letter distressed me today, far beyond the surface of it. He is so bothered with persistent impetigo, and while I still think a neglected liver could cause it, plus too much grease from fried food plus too much cake, the doctor speaks of poverty of the adrenal gland. The word 'gland' strikes cold. The Lasts as a family seem to have some kind of glandular deficiency. It worries me to think he could take after them. They age so quickly, seem to have so short a sex life, go grey far too young. When Arthur was here I noticed with a little sick pang how thin his neck had grown. He still looks young and virile, but he is thirty-four. Sometimes I have a feeling I'm getting a pile of little stones on my head. My husband says sometimes how lucky he is because I'm always 'serene and calm' and 'there's always home, thank God'. Only the good God knows inside my head. I'm not really calm and strong, and I sometimes feel tired out with being so. I must be a very good actress, for inside me I feel worry and more worry about little things. Now it's Arthur's health as well as my husband's. I turn to thoughts of Cliff, that gay Arab, knowing well the shortness of his life line, which curiously shortened in the war. He used to say jokingly, 'Don't worry, Dearie. It looks as if I'll live to forty–forty-five, a short life and a merry one. I'll have to work overtime if I've to achieve anything.'

I sat quietly after I'd ironed and stitched my dollies. Their pleasant little smiling faces from the sideboard seemed so friendly and cheerful. I wonder just how many I've embroidered from this transfer. Cliff traced 200 before he went overseas in the war, and I've made some dozens of gollywogs, whose faces couldn't be traced on the black material and had to be done free hand. I do try to reach out into the Rhythm, where all courage and hope lie ready if we can only submerge ourselves. I do pray earnestly for courage and gaiety, kindness and strength, feeling my little lamp flicker so often, feeling I'd like to sleep for a week and get everything in focus before I woke.

Wednesday, 29 October. When I was at the WVS office the other day, they told me they were trying to get collectors at the various picture houses for the proposed memorial to fallen American soldiers, and I took it they meant young people. Today they rang me up, asking if I could possibly take a turn, and get anyone else, as no one wanted the job. I said I'd go tomorrow night, and Mrs Higham will come. I've broken it to my husband, and he is not very pleased. Although he works in the other room when book-keeping, he likes to feel I'm in the house! I was very airy about it – wouldn't notice his hurt look. I've felt lately as if I was being slowly strangled, and when the car is laid up for pleasure motoring, it will be worse. I must build up some kind of reaction.

Mrs Diss is beginning to regret a few things. She has a little love of authority and when just after the war her mother's health failed and she became an invalid and needed a nurse constantly, and Mrs Diss only had one maid for her big rambling house, she had to turn over a lot of WVS work to her deputy, Miss Willis. The latter is sweet, a retired school mistress, good to work with but fussy and afraid of any kind of effort started. I feel, between the two, a lot of chances of service went adrift. Then again, after the war ended a 'bank manager's daughter married to a wealthy jeweller' complex raised its head in Mrs Diss. She recovered her pre-war snobbery and lost touch with the rest of us, all of whom I used to feel she considered much beneath her. I laughed and went my way but often regretted the break-up of such a grand lot of women ...

Mrs Diss talks vaguely now of trying to revive the old wartime spirit, and hence this proposed trip to Preston to hear Lady Reading speak of the future of the WVS. She speaks of some kind of service to old people, doing their shopping, etc., and seems quite willing for anyone to start something now, and looked at me speculatively. I thought of the way we longed to keep together, and wondered if I could rally my good Canteen squad. Mrs Higham would work happily with me. The trouble is that many women have found matinees at the pictures, little bridges or whist fours, joined classes at the Women's Institutes to make up clothes in the make-or-mend class. Mrs Diss said, 'Couldn't *we* have a make-or-mend class, or toy or rug making, or something?' If she had listened to a suggestion I had, to let us have the top room of the WVS office, the Club would have been formed long ago, and all the women with ideas would have worked out something to keep the WVS alive. It's easier to keep a thing alive than to revive it.

Thursday, 30 October. Although it was Thursday, the night when most picture places are full in Barrow, there was a poor audience for first house and we soon collected and then sat down to wait for the second house collection. The programme was a double feature – Bob Hope in *While There's Life* and an adventure of someone called *The Falcon* – and we realised why there were so few people in. Of all the weak drivel I've seen, these two pictures took a bit of beating. Not a titter from anyone for Bob Hope's efforts. My idea of Hell would be to go to the pictures every night, as many people do. It often puzzles me when people say, 'It passes the time away.' I never feel I've enough time and what I have seems snatched away before I've done what I want to do. I rather expected people to refuse and pass the box along, but only one pimply-faced youth waved me rather grandly away. When we counted it, there were a lot of sixpences and shillings and I had two two-shilling pieces in the £2-9-0 I sorted. Mostly it was copper – three-penny bits – but there were eight foreign silver coins, six ditto copper and two farthings. I said, 'It looks as if some people keep dud coins in case there's a collection.' The manager, a somewhat disillusioned-looking man, said, 'I think, madam, you have the same dim view of human nature I have myself.' We got just under £9. The most they got was £10 Monday, since when the houses have been poorer each night. We did feel our luck out when we saw the trailer for next week, *Moss Rose* – it looked pretty good.

We were out by 9.30 and had a cup of tea at the ice-cream shop, feeling very gay and carefree. Somehow wearing our uniforms brought back a feeling of comradeship and we felt 'let off the chain' and not at all like going home. We sat and talked. I'm sorry Mrs Higham cannot come next Wednesday. Her husband will be away next week and get in tired out on Wednesday noon and she wants a hot meal ready for him. The cold was like winter and reminded us of coming home after Canteen parties, though of course it was not so late. Mrs Howson said suddenly, 'Do you ever look back on Canteen days with regret?' I said, 'Oddly enough

I was just thinking of the days when the Scotties were here and loved farewell parties. Yes. I had quite as much out of all I did as I put into it – but life's like that. It's what we do rather than what we get that is the real heart's-ease.' And rather to my surprise she agreed. She said, 'Yes, and looking forward to a thing. I always wanted the day when Steve was out of the Navy and now I don't know. It isn't going to be very easy to settle down in any way.'

Friday, 31 October. I'm tired out tonight. It was such a lovely morning. I hurried round with vac and duster, kneaded my bread and left it by a little fire to rise, and was out by ten o'clock. My husband was lucky enough to see some good carving tools, second hand, and I packed them, together with a mallet to replace one Cliff broke, and took them to the post. Never in the worst of the war did I see so many queues – or such long ones. In their order they were fish, sausage and meat pies, potatoes, fish and chips, cakes, wallpaper and children's shoes. I stood a few minutes in a fish queue for some fish bits and a bit of filleted plaice and was struck with a little incident. An elderly woman, obviously rather feeble minded, walked into the shop without queuing, saying vacantly, 'I can't stand out in the cold. I'd be badly.' There was not one look of pity or tolerance on one woman's face, but there was resentment, annoyance and real anger, and remarks of 'cheek', 'she always does that', as they moved up to keep her out of the queue inside the shop. The shop man said, 'Couple of herrings?' and she said, 'Yes – and I've got my paper ready', and she had exact coppers ready. I thought he showed wisdom in removing an irritation but the women weren't at all pleased. It was such a trivial thing to cause anger. We do seem nervy nowadays and little kindly acts and tolerance grow more scarce …

I remarked to Norah [*who was pregnant*] how well she looked these last months and she said, 'I feel it. I'm sure I've been calcium short for years and I've had calcium injections and vitamin tablets, cod liver oil and orange juice – everything there was available. I feel better than I've done in memory.' She didn't mention the chop or juicy steaks her husband [*a butcher*] brings every day! She brought a plate of scraps for the cats – more meat than I generally have for two meals for both of us. Mrs Atkinson has been very gushing since she hit Murphy, and brings him scraps. I wonder how much meat above ration they all have. Nowadays to have a husband – or any relative – in any branch of food distribution seems the best way of being well fed!

Saturday, 1 November. I'd got a good start when Mrs Salisbury came just after nine o'clock – beds stripped and all mats and rugs on the line – and she was in a lot better working way. She has got someone in for a fortnight and it will give her a chance to get a 'permanent'. With so many less working at the Yard though, and no Service people wanting to bring wives or families, there is not the demand for lodgings and apartments. She brought me a pound of bananas – she wanted a swap for a bottle of fruit. I let her choose, and she took sweetened damsons, so both of us felt satisfied with our respective treat. I'd planned my work so that I could have my bath before lunch and get shoes and stockings and underwear changed. I slipped on an overall again to work and serve lunch. I'd cooked a wee piece of shoulder of mutton with vegetables and a jar of tomato puree. Today's soup had a tin of vegetable soup added to a little Oxo and shredded onions, and I fried sausage 'pats' and some potatoes from yesterday's casserole, boiled cauliflower and made a cup of tea.

Mrs Higham called at 2.30, and I was waiting ready, and we parked her car easily, with going early. Everyone was amazed at the beauty of the décor of the Ward and upper passage. It was all a pale luminous turquoise with gay little stencils of fairies in every pose, while on the big blank wall of the Ward, Peter Pan played his pipes to the rabbits and birds around his pedestal. The new up-to-date cots were primrose yellow, and the newly equipped bathroom had primrose-yellow raised baths and wash bowls. The children were all so good and looked happy to see the crowds walk round. The various branches of the WVS were represented. Governors of the hospital, their wives, doctors and Committee and their wives as well as nurses and sisters.

Tea was served in various rooms on the lower corridor. We – Mrs Higham, Mrs Howson and I – were in one where photos of all the head surgeons since the hospital was built were hung. It's not a very old hospital – eighty years at most, I think – and I knew by sight all the doctors of the last fifty years or so, some of them grim and stern in their whiskered dignity, but there was a curious resemblance difficult to define. I looked across at old Dr Livingstone, the head now, and he had somewhat the same look – so absent from the younger doctors around. It was a look of purpose and dignity, a look of a calling. I looked cynically at a group of younger doctors boisterously laughing by the door. Two are well known to be 'too fond of the girls', two showed unmistakable signs of hard drinking, several had weak faces and rather a nervous manner. I thought suddenly, 'If I had to rely on a doctor to save my life, I'd choose one of you two' – a coal-black eye specialist, or a brown Jamaican with the kindest, firmest mouth of the lot. I was quite lost in my thoughts, but Mrs Higham's were straying the same way as she whispered, 'What a bunch. I'd sooner trust those two coloured doctors. They seem to radiate strength. They would give me confidence far before, for instance, Drs Moore or Ronald.' We were interested in the type of nurses too. I've spent so much time in hospital and nursing home; Mrs Higham has visited her sister in hospital. Now the bright little nurses look 'ladies' as against the rather rough Cumberland and Irish ones who at one time seemed general in our hospital, and who took a lot of training. Perhaps better wages have attracted a rather better type of girl.

In a speech made by a member of the Committee, she spoke of her admiration of the WVS for all their faithful unpaid work all through the war, and her feeling that 'service' couldn't have been better remembered than in seeing this lovely ward so bright and gay. Mrs Higham and I could have had a silly fit of the giggles. We could see Mrs Waite and Mrs Lord's face as the WVS were extolled. They had a curious reaction to the very title and refused firmly to wear WVS uniform and lost no chance of malicious and biting remarks. They had run a 'Queen Mary Sewing Guild' in the 1914–18 war and 'There was no daft talk of WVS then and we don't want it now and for two pins we would sever any connections with it.' She (Mrs Waite) was ranting once, saying she was 'not WVS and never would be', and I quickly said, 'We, as a committee, acknowledge and belong to the WVS and so it will go on', and I think her dislike of us as a committee grew from that day. Today they sat with sour, pursed lips, waiting for some separate mention of Hospital Supply – and none came. When Mrs Higham and I spoke politely to them, only Mrs Lord replied. I felt so sorry for their bitterness. They are very alone. Mrs Higham was the last to try to keep contact with Mrs Waite, but rudeness and real insult made her say 'never again'.

We felt so happy to renew old acquaintance. Odd how in such a small place as Barrow one can lose touch with one another. It was like a fashion parade with most of the women – such lovely new fur coats, tweeds and coats, shoes and hats – and my sharp eyes recognised new strings of pearls on two old friends and a new diamond ring on another, jewels I knew they didn't possess a short time ago. Matron asked anxiously about her Xmas dollies. I told her they were all ready and being kept aired well in the top of my airing cupboard. We were shocked to hear in a governor's speech that the hospital is losing £400 a week. There are several thousands less employed at the Yard, but I felt it was the raised cost of every item, including wages, that was the real cause. I thought of the army of cleaners necessary to keep that rambling old place reasonably clean, and the big increase alone paid to them. We were home by 5.30, feeling that blankness of being transported to another plane and then back to everyday life.

A day's outing was set for the following week, and this prospect alarmed Nella's husband, whose distress annoyed her. 'I'm only going away for the day on Wednesday,' she wrote on 3 November, 'and I'll leave everything planned for his lunch and tea and bank a fire that he can see to at lunchtime. Times like these I understand every revolt, strike, assault – yes, and even murder!'

Wednesday, 5 November. It was such a lovely morning – more like September than November. I rose blithe and gay. I do love a day out. I felt I could have sang over my breakfast! We were down in town by nine o'clock, and the journey to Preston was wonderful in the early morning, with the sun shining on the autumn colours of trees and fells. We were there by twelve o'clock and had lunch first. The luxury of Preston shops and our really good meals added to the enjoyment of the day …

The shops were a delight – such luxury things displayed – and hats we never see at comparatively reasonable prices to ours. I've such a love of luxury in me somewhere. I coveted a night blue silk velvet gown, with severe classic cut, only draperies round the hip caught by a sparkling diamond clasp, before falling in folds to the ground. We all picked luxury shoes, furs, hats, feeling there was wide choice for our assorted sizes and shapes, losing ourselves in 'buying' happily, like children in our make believe, not really covetous – they seemed so utterly outside our ken or possession.

The County Hall was a delight in its solid, worthwhile furnishing of real wood in profusion and its real leather seating. I smiled to myself at one thing we all had in common – a 'those were the days' as we admired work and craft made to endure, to wear better with polishing, etc. Preston has such splendid stained windows and the double windows of the Council Chamber with the sunlight through their glowing colours, touching the lovely gold and coloured tooled leather on the backs of the row of chairs where the Mayor sat, seemed to give another note of difference to us all.

Lady Reading [*founder of the WVS*] spoke well as usual, but even she could not hide the fact she thought the future prospects a bit dim. She spoke of the ideals of WVS, our oath to serve in however humble way, how by example we could teach the simple homely things, be kind and help wherever we could, not waiting for the 'big chance to serve' which only came to the few. Her talk had more uplift and influence than most sermons. I glanced round the curve of seats, feeling she had given a message. Saying WVS had earned respect and admiration, she begged us to keep our standard high, shun black-market and spiv[†] dealings, and help others to do the same. Barrow is not as affected by real black-market as much as fiddling. We talked to a woman WVS from Bolton and she said it was rife in that area, accepted often as the only way to obtain logs, paraffin, etc. – simple necessities of life. Lady Reading fears the whole world is slipping in its spiritual

and moral values, and believes in each and all doing all they can
in their own corner, and handing on true values to children as
they grow …

Dusk fell quickly. We set off at 5.30 and as if to make our
luxury day still more unreal, we drove through bonfires and firework displays all the way home. I'd never seen the like. Most of
the fires must have been branches and brushwood and their clear
red and gold fires burned a hole in the blackness of the night,
which made such a perfect firework night. Star shells and rockets
streaked in grand display. As soon as one fire and happy group
was passed, another came into view anywhere where there were
houses, and in the country districts several times we feared ricks
were on fire. We all said quite sincerely we never remembered
such a day out. There was only one rather unpleasant woman in
the coach, who, to hear her talk, had done more than three times
her share of war work, but when we snubbed her by silence, and
refused to take up her challenge when she averred she 'should
have had the OBE – everyone said so', she piped down. Anyway,
poor thing, she was a devastatingly plain-faced woman, with horrible jumbled teeth, unmarried and getting fat. She had not got
much out of life. Times like that I believe in any kind of a marriage where a home is made or there are children.

My little cats rushed to meet me as if I'd been away for a week.
Mrs Newall and I sat in a corner to have our tea and I hastily
slipped the bit of chicken skin and a wee bone into an envelope
when no one was looking, wishing I'd the courage to offer to
buy a few kitchen scraps for my little friends. Their delight was
comical to see, though Shan We plainly showed me how 'moreish'
he considered his tit bit! I was in by 8.15. There was a good fire
and my husband forgot my fault in going off and only showed his
satisfaction I was back. Times I get so impatient, realising I was

never beautiful, never flighty. Men have always liked but never pursued me, and the only time I was 'insulted' was when I was living in the New Forest and a very odd Channel Island captain of a ship – married with a lovely blonde Devonshire wife and adorable little girl – told me calmly I was the kind of woman he had always dreamed about and asked me to let him take Arthur and I away, and presumably we were to sail about together all over the world for the rest of our time! Beyond that – and my husband wasn't told for years after – there has never been the least cause for my husband's wildly possessive attitude. I sat down opposite to him tonight, my cats on my lap, and looked across at his tired face. Suddenly I felt a sincere prayer in my heart that I could outlive him, could always look after him – after all, it's my job, and I like a job well done and finished off. He would be a desolate lost man on his own.

Thursday, 6 November. It's my going out alone that makes my husband so moody. He clings like a frightened child. If I'm irritated I think it's because I spoil him, looking after every comfort, and make his meals and home as attractive as I can. Any 'sex' has long died and I aver to myself it's because he hates any discomforts, even like waiting for the tea being brewed, and he thinks lunch or a cooked tea can be served easily, half an hour late – or early – just the same. But when I'm not cranky at his attitude, I feel such a deep pity, wondering just what caused his fear of life or change.

Life was still difficult. Scarcity continued to be a nagging worry; manufactured goods were more and more costly; and there was at least one power cut. 'People do seem gloomy and depressed,' Nella wrote on 8 December, 'and I've noticed those who rely on pictures or whist drives for their

pleasure get far more so than anyone who sews or reads.' On Saturday, 29
November she made a rare reference to football – Nella was no sports fan.
'Barrow won, so all those thousands of Carlisle supporters – 2,000 alone
came in coaches from the surrounding district of Carlisle, and then there
were the long line of cars and the trains – had their long journey to see their
side win in vain, and they drop out of the Cup final.' Babies were much
mentioned: Norah had a baby girl in mid November (Nella saw a lot of both
of them); Aunt Eliza was to have another great-grandchild in the spring; two
new neighbours, both reckoned to be in their thirties, were expecting (late
by standards then); and Edith announced that she was again pregnant. Nella
was a great admirer of babies, and quickly became attached to Norah's
'adorable' infant. She sometimes thought back to her own babies, though
rarely spoke of the one who did not survive: 'I buried my first baby on a
Boxing Day,' she recalled on 7 December (and said no more).

Sunday, 30 November. At 7.30 we sat quiet to listen to *Cavalcade*,
which I feel, like *Journey's End*, will never date or die. I felt a
great sadness when I heard some of the high hopes, the certain-
ties war was finished. I contrasted that hope with the feelings we
all have today in some degree – France trembling on the brink of
civil war, wild unrest in Pakistan, a blaze of religious war ready
to sweep the East, when Palestine is divided. There's no place –
unless it's little pockets of peace like the quiet hills – where we
could point and say, '*There* is peace.' Unrest is in every mind and
heart, and until it passes there will be visible discord. The old
ones who wrote, 'And renew a right spirit within us' wrote for
all time. Only right thinking and a sense of responsibility and
personal endeavour can lift us all out of the mess.

Wednesday, 10 December. I didn't feel like going over Walney. It
was a cold, raw day, but Mrs Whittam has had an ingrowing toe

nail off this week and I couldn't disappoint her. I felt so very sorry
for her. She seems to have suddenly turned into an old worried
woman. Olga and Ena are still on bad terms and go their way,
not trying to make up, and it worries Mrs Whittam till she is
really ill. There's an odd bitter streak in the family. Mrs Whittam
and her only sister once disagreed over a trifle, and never spoke
again, though they lived in the same road. The old mother lived
at Mrs Whittam's home – a holy terror who lived to ninety-seven
– and when the sister visited her, even if Mrs Whittam sat for
hours in the same room, they never addressed a remark direct,
and any business that couldn't be directed by a third member of
the family was done through their lawyer!

I felt a sick sadness for that joyous, gypsy, carefree life that
has flown, never to return, but to me there was always a streak
or touch of unreality, even distortion, in their 'ecumenical' way
of life, when children, food, work and every interest seemed to
be shared and discussed, by the two sisters and their children. I
often wondered how the husbands reacted, or if in the evenings
and weekends, when they were home, things were different. I feel
that unconsciously there must have been little resentments which
have accumulated and boiled up like milk in a boiling saucepan,
and that the trivial quarrel was an effect and not a cause. If it had
been my boys, I'd have been able to talk or reason – I couldn't
imagine such a situation with them anyway – but Whittams are
so uncontrolled, living in their passing emotions. There doesn't
seem 'depths' to draw upon. I felt the tears roll down my cheeks
as Mrs Whittam talked – pity for her distress, a deeper grief for
the happiness and gaiety I felt had gone for ever, and nothing
to take its place. The mists and fogs of the Channel, the mud of
the receding tide, and my aching bones, all seemed part of the
so dismal day as I came home – and misery in the form of Aunt

Eliza waited on the step. She hates this weather and it makes her unhappy.

Tuesday, 16 December. Such a mild day – I'd really like winter if it was no colder. I dusted round and left a little beef casserole on lowest heat with a deep soup plate with soup in and the pan lid over it, on top of the pan, a well-banked little fire with the kettle by the side, and caught the eleven o'clock bus to Ulverston from the corner. Farmers were busy all along the roads to Spark Bridge. More pastures are being ploughed, dung carted and spread, hedges and ditches trimmed and drained, making the most of this grand spell before winter breaks. Snow ploughs and their blades are at their posts. Thin threads of smoke from pockets of common land show gypsies have settled in their winter quarters. I had three-quarters of an hour to wait at Ulverston, for the Coniston bus, and wandered round. I like Ulverston best on working or market days. I feel so at home with the country people, who shop. Many I recognise, and still more know by sight. I got half a dozen nice little boned Finny haddocks. With it being cold weather, Aunt Sarah and Joe could keep them a day or two till eaten.

I travelled in the bus with an old retired doctor. He must be even older than Aunt Sarah. He spoke to me as if I was too young to remember some of the things he talked about, as he chatted of Gran and a horse she used to lend him, when his own went lame, called 'Bouncer'. He seemed one with the blessed peace that seems to cling round Greenodd and the quiet villages round the sleepy slow river. I looked at his quiet face and recalled he had had two marriages, one happy, one a tragedy, where a dipsomaniac had trapped him into marrying her by spending the night, unknown to him, in the bedroom next to his, which had a door between. Her story was that she had been taken ill – too ill to call the young maid before she left, or make the old deaf housekeeper hear – but 'she was ruined for life when her people knew – she dare not go home', etc. etc. He only knew her slightly and doctors of those days were even more marked men. Only loyalty of patients and friends kept him sane for years. He met a sweet frail woman, daughter of a retired colonel, and for thirty years to my knowledge they were the closest friends. By the time they could have married, she was a hopeless invalid from a kind of arthritis. He lost his only son in the 1914 war, and a grandson in this last war, yet his old age was serene. I wondered if God gives forgetfulness of hurt and grief, and only leaves tiny grains of memory of happiness, like grains of gold. We spoke of wood smoke and the smell of baking bread which always greets you in the little valley village of Spark Bridge, and which seems to cling to cats' fur and dogs' coats. He likes the motors off the road – hopes we will all start horse riding if our feet won't carry us! When he shook hand and wished me 'All the compliments of the Season', it sounded – and felt – like the blessing of a priest.

Thursday, 25 December, Xmas Day. Not one carol have I heard today, except on the wireless. No bands or waits – the war seems to have killed all that. I thought it would have killed more Xmas customs, but this year fir trees decked with lights and crackers could be seen in most windows of the rather poor neighbourhood we walked through on our way home [*after visiting her parents-in-law*]. I was rather amused to see how many children had had clothes sent from Canada and America – long pants and blouse jackets and caps to match, in gay coloured cloth or corduroy. Margaret's auntie in Canada sent a splendid parcel – hardly worn clothes of her well-to-do sons' wives and out of her own wardrobe, a really lovely dress and good waterproof that fits Margaret, a costume Norah claimed, a dress for Mrs Atkinson and a coat that will make a good pinafore dress, and piles of good underwear. Apart from the coupon value, they were so well cut and made. Linda came in with Margaret and we talked interestedly of a small new block of flats – the first private buildings in Barrow to have concrete stairs and all floors. I should dislike that. I could not imagine any floor covering either lasting long on concrete or being at all comfortable. I had a letter from a Scots woman in Australia who has met Cliff – such a pleasant letter of her family – and who sounds an interesting person. My post came very 'Xmasy', for I had four letters.

It's often the way, if you look forward to anything you are disappointed. I felt indifferent about Xmas – 'detached' would be a better word – and yet I seem to have had a very pleasant one, and my husband is so uplifted about the car,* he is being quite pleasant about my little party on Saturday night – and when I got an invite to go to a party in Mrs Diss's big new house in the Park on the 7th of January. The other night when we were down at his brother's, Harry said, 'Ah, Nell, we did have some jolly times, didn't we? And you know you and Xmas are always associated together, for we never had any kind of Xmas fun till you married our Will. I remember the first time I saw you. You had a white fur muff and cap and your hair was so black and your eyes danced with fun. You seemed so strange in our dull gloomy house. Tell me, did you never regret marrying into such a dull family?' Harry has at times been my one ally, when whatever I did or I said was condemned. I said, 'No-o – not for the dull part, Harry, but it

---

* Two days before, Will had phoned Nella from work, for he 'had just had word the ten-horse Morris he had ordered two years ago had come in!! We thought all hopes of it fled when the export drive was intensified.'

was a bit hard going when I felt your dad and mother were trying always to kill all the gaiety in me, and what was worse in my eyes, make my little boys "like other boys".' Harry said, 'You should have been a businessman's or soldier-traveller's wife, you know. You have had a "wasted" life.' He is not often talkative and I said, 'We don't really matter much individually, Harry. It's the pattern on the carpet that matters, and I am beginning the home stretch, I think. I feel as if I see clearer the real values – of doing the things at hand, of liking the things we have rather than having the things we like.' He smiled and said, 'In other ways, polishing up the dark side.'

When we came home my husband looked thoughtful and he said suddenly, 'I've always tried to give you everything you wanted. You have a nice home, a car and all your own way in things.' I half opened my mouth, but shut it firmly again. It's Xmas, and we have been over the ground so often. I could have pointed out that it had been my own money that bought the car *and* the house! – that only sheer fright had made him buy the car in the first place, when I had heart trouble after an operation, and the house was bought after a serious talk by the doctor, who wanted to order me 'a trip on a slow boat to Australia', an odd but favourite prescription of his, which, he maintained, had 'saved life and reason' on several occasions! I felt Harry's remarks had helped me about my little party, and I need not worry in any way. Tonight, too, when Linda and Margaret were in, he joined in talking and sat all the time they were in, never once looking at the clock or fidgeting. I feel girls like Margaret have such an advantage of those of my generation. We were 'tweenies' – between Victorian submission and today's career girls, and if you were at all weak minded and passionately loved peace and a pleasant atmosphere, you tended to have individuality squashed somewhat.

Wednesday, 31 December. I'll remember this Hogmanay all right –
it's been a day. I felt conscious of my bones when I woke. I knew it
was a cold raw morning before I got out of bed. I planned to tidy
up thoroughly with vac and duster, and settle down to sew in the
afternoon. I'd just finished breakfast – before washing up – and
kneaded a batch of bread, when Mrs Atkinson came in, looking
so drawn and tired, and as if she's been crying. She said, 'Be a pal
and come and help me get Mamie ready for the ambulance. The
doctor insists she goes into the hospital without delay.' She had
her breast off in Christie's Hospital in Manchester, and when she
was in, someone told her that her husband had to have a bladder
operation, and she insisted on coming out, against every advice
from doctors and nurses. At first she seemed all right, though
she had ghastly wounds that would not heal. The last time I saw
her was three weeks ago, when she brought Norah's baby a little
knitted coatee and bonnet, and she looked ill, and her husband
looked as if he could hardly crawl round, for he had only come
out of hospital. She said that she couldn't sleep for the pain in her
arm, shoulder and neck. Last night they sent for Mrs Atkinson
and the doctor, who said firmly, *'Hospital* – I'll be round at ten
o'clock, when the ambulance will be there.' Mrs Atkinson was
tired and upset. I helped wash and change Mrs McLachan, get
her few toilet things ready, shuddering to my soul case at the
pitiful sight – her arm had swelled to a large alabaster-like limb
and her neck was level with her shoulder, and she couldn't speak
plainly. Mrs Atkinson said the conditions had worsened while
she watched in the night. The doctor gave her an injection before
she was lifted on to the stretcher, but it didn't seem to take well.
He said, 'One of you had better go in the ambulance', and Mrs
Atkinson looked pleadingly at me, so I went. I was asked to wait
a few minutes and then went in to see her, in a side ward, put

her toilet requirements handy and asked if there was anything needed, or any message to deliver. The sister shook her head and I saw her take screens and arrange them round the bed. I realised I'd no hat with me.

Mrs Atkinson was so upset as she talked of her cousin and her troubled life – infant paralysis of their only child in America, where they had gone after the 1920 slump, an accident which resulted in a tumour in her husband's head and all the illness and operations, the bitter struggle to get her son walking and to educate him and train him for a chiropodist. She cried so bitterly as she told me, and spoke of death as if it was a punishment and an end. I've noticed so often the same attitude to death and the hereafter in Christians, but do realise that any real orthodox Christian has little held out to make him otherwise – green pastures, 'no more sea' of St Paul, streets paved with gold, harps, angels forever singing, etc., so far removed from every human idea of bliss they could well be a punishment.

I'd not washed my dishes, and left them while I hurriedly dusted, heated soup and fried sausage pats with a sliced potato and two sliced sweet apples, and I'd pudding enough. I felt all jumped up and only had pudding and later a cup of tea. I'd washed the crocks and was beginning the pans when Mrs Atkinson dashed in, shaking and white, and squealed, 'What shall I do? The chimney is on fire.' I said, 'Well, what' – and glanced through the kitchenette window and felt she had cause for upset – her tall chimney was the 'stalk' for a huge bunch of flames like flower petals. I said, 'Did you shut the dining room door after you?' and we ran in, and not a minute too soon as huge lumps of red hot charcoal, which the sweep tells us is the result of burning so much wood, plus the bad soft coal, rolled down the chimney, burned on the tiled hearth and would have been scattered all over the rug. We turned the rug over and fielded the red hot lumps as they fell. Our hands were scorched. We grew blacker and blacker. But gradually the loud roar lessened. A passer-by rang to say she had heard the chimney pot crack, and when we went outside we could see it plainly, as the red-hot lining of charred soot glowed through. It's a very smoky chimney and this tall pot had little ventilating louvres, and it helped keep the soot alight. We felt terrified that as the pot cooled it would snap and crash through the roof, and it would have been through the next-door roof where Jessie lives and who expects her baby early in January. I phoned my husband, asking him to get in touch with a builder, which he thought unlikely at three o'clock on Hogmanay, many of whom had already packed up if they lived out of town and planned to spend New Year at home. He promised to send a man and boy by to take the pot off anyway, so we felt we could leave it at that.

We were black as two sweeps. I said, 'I'll put my immersion heater on and you can have a bath at our house', and I suddenly said, 'What caused such a blaze? You had hardly any fire in the grate.' She said off-handedly, 'Oh, I threw the fat out of my roasting tin on the fire.' Words failed me. I thought of her everlasting dripping scrounge – she has had two whole tins of Australian dripping lately. I felt it greedy to keep it when I'd two or three on the shelf. I said, 'You *burned* FAT', and she nodded and said, 'I had such a lot about with the goose and the beef.'

I felt words failed me, but from now on I'll hide my tins of dripping, or give them to someone with more sense. I let her have the first bath and I made up my fire and finished washing up. Mrs Howson came across and burst out laughing when I opened the door. She said, 'I never saw you look as dirty and cross. I saw you in and out of Mrs Atkinson's. Whatever caused the blaze? It's a wonder the fire brigade wasn't around, never mind the policeman.'

Mrs Atkinson was coming downstairs and heard my reply. 'Oh, Mrs Atkinson threw some fat on the fire.' 'FAT,' squealed Mrs Howson, 'on the FIRE.' And I felt it let Mrs Atkinson see how her crime was looked on by another woman. Mrs Howson said, 'If I'd known you had enough to spare to grease my baking tins I'd have been across.' She said, 'Go and have your bath and I'll make you a cup of tea', and Mrs Atkinson stayed.

Hot baths are not for me. They either make me feel dizzy and faint, or else sick, but I was so very dirty and had to rub and scrub myself and perhaps stayed too long in the water, or it was my upsetting day. I felt ill as I dried myself and put on my dressing gown. Half dressed, I'd my cup of tea and then began a bad gastric attack. Mrs Howson got the table ready and I laid down with my blessed electric pad on my clay-cold tummy. Mrs Atkinson brought me some hot brandy and water. They both were scared. They hadn't seen me ill before. By 5.30 I could crawl down, feeling like chewed string, shaking so I daren't lift the kettle to brew tea, so my husband did, and cut the bread and butter when he came in. He had to have cheese and salad again, but he enjoyed it, and all the bits and bobs of cake, shortbread, jam, lemon cheese and Xmas cake Mrs Howson had put on the table. She came across later and was surprised to see me sewing – a bit less quickly, I felt I couldn't care less. She said, 'Are you sure you are all right? What are your lips like under that lipstick? You frightened me when you went so blue.' By the nine o'clock news I felt I'd better get off to my bed, Hogmanay or no. I sent my little prayer winging into the Infinite Rhythm, with Big Ben strokes, no New Year resolutions in my heart. Each day begins a new year, each day we must begin again.

CHAPTER EIGHT

BABIES

January–June 1948

Friday, 2 January. I looked with amazement at the slashing reductions in coats, dresses and suits – up to a third of the price – but, contrasting them with the 'new look' ones, they did look dated. I knew if I'd been buying I'd have not been tempted to buy out-of-date clothes and give up coupons. I am so lucky. I've no middle-aged spread and a dart each side of my corsets gives me a waist. I've a good hem on my costume and with dropping the skirt from the top to the bottom of my waist belt and putting on a velvet ribbon belt from a belt I have, I can lengthen my skirt to London length, and with my new dusty pink and altered best dress I feel quite up to date.

Nella's Spirella corsets were, she claimed on 11 December, 1947, 'museum pieces'. She had only two and was frequently repairing them, so that by now they looked, she said on 11 January, 1948, 'like a patchwork quilt'. Late in the following year she revisited this matter of scarcity – rubber was in short supply and was needed during the 1940s for 'essential' manufacturers, or those related to exports. 'I met my Spirella corsetiere the other day,' she wrote on 23 November 1949, 'and she told me no doctors' permits were to be given before an order of Spirellas. I bought two pair in January 1940, and none since. I thought I was a good advert for Spirellas, for I've worn them constantly, except for the hottest part of last summer when I turned out an older, thinner pair.' Nella was advised that 'it takes two to three months for delivery and they have been told a drastic cut may come again in spring. I need the under belt carefully measured and adjusted. Dr Miller advised it rather than another operation for "dropped" stomach.' (She probably suffered a prolapsed uterus after Cliff's birth.)

People seem to take their jobs so casually nowadays. Employers complain on every side, saying better pay, shorter hours, paid holidays and less and less interest taken – and more impudence given. I often hear little remarks about rude assistants. I'm lucky, for at all the shops I deal, there are such nice assistants. It's a real pleasure to be served at my grocer's and to hear the kindly patience they have with old ones, and men folk, having to do unaccustomed shopping and at a loss about coupons and points. As I sit quiet, the day's events often flit through my mind. Little incidents and remarks come back. A woman I know was in the grocer's. I asked after her son, away at sea, and as I left I said, 'A Happy New Year, Mrs Jones.' She said, 'And to you, Mrs Last. It's the first time this year I've heard anyone say that.' And it suddenly came to me that I'd been the first to say Happy Xmas or New Year, and I thought of the greetings of other years, even war years, at Hospital Supply. We set our faces against drabness and clinging to old customs of happier days was one little gesture, even in the darkest days. I sighed as I thought the so-called peace was robbing us of things that war never did. I often look back on the war years personally and think of the exhilaration that filled my veins like potent wine, carrying me over rough places, helping me to laugh and joke however dim I felt inside, giving me courage to do whatever came along. Perhaps the curious loss of that exaltation of spirit makes me feel emptier and more dead than I otherwise would, feeling as if I'm beaten and tired out, that my bones master me when they ache so badly.

My husband said tonight, 'Get the garage floor cleared early in the morning for I'll bring the new car home', and I felt I couldn't care less. I was ashamed of my lack of interest and excitement. I felt complete indifference whether we had a car at all! Anyway, I've very common tastes – I love buses. There's such fun watching people and overhearing remarks and trying to picture what is behind them.

'My husband brought the car home, looking as excited as a schoolboy,' Nella wrote the next day. 'I do hope his car worries are at an end. I pointed out he cannot blame a previous owner for faults and failings now, and that with care, this car should last as long as we need one.' On Sunday the 4th they had tea at the Atkinsons. 'Jessie Holme, Mrs Atkinson's adjoining neighbour, and her husband were there, a very nice pleasant couple, who expect their first baby this month. I hope it's the boy they both want, though she said when she looked at wee Ann' – Norah's baby – '"No one could help loving a baby, boy or girl."'

Monday, 5 January. Mrs Whittam wasn't her bright self. She said Ena and Olga were getting her down. They spoke, but as acquaintances only, none of the old love and friendliness. I felt there was so little I could say, that saying about blood being thicker than water is a queer, misleading saying – who wants water to be thick anyway? And if people related turn, they can be bigger enemies and more bitter than any stranger. Again, Mrs Whittam, perhaps unconsciously, likes her sons better than her daughters, listening to their advice, etc., and that doesn't make for peace. I tried to talk of old times in Canteen and Hospital Supply, but found I'd started another annoyance going – one of our members died suddenly two years ago this Xmas, and her husband married in less than a year and brought his wife to live

near Mrs Whittam. I felt really amused at her intolerance. I said,
'It's better so. If I died I'd like to pick a woman to look after my
husband and care for him as I'd done. It would be dreadful for
me to think he could be lost and lonely. You cannot live by the
dead – they have gone beyond worry.'

Tuesday, 6 January. We were at Mrs Diss's party by soon after
seven o'clock. The lovely big house was ablaze with lights, big
fires in every grate, huge expensive gas fires in bedrooms and at
the ends of the long rooms. Since I'd been in the house – when
Cliff was small and for a while it was used as a massage electrical
sun-ray place, and where my husband used to attend frequently
– the Head of the Yard lived in it, and as always under those circumstances, money hadn't been any object in any décor, electric
or gas fitting, or improvement, and the carpets, at today's prices,
worth a king's ransom. Mrs Diss bought all fittings and quite
nine-tenths of the carpets, for the occupants were moving to a
much smaller house. All heavy brocade curtains, door curtains,
two huge folding Indian screens and several big fitments had
been left – and not been priced at an exorbitant sum, for the
Callenders and Disses were friends. Added to all the priceless cut
glass, antique furniture, china, etc. of Mrs Diss and her mother,
who has recently died, few houses today look so pre-war. I'd have
loved a few of the Indian and Chinese carpets, and several pieces
of cut glass, which I like better than silver or plate, but when I
heard some of the women's envy I realised there's lots of gaps in
make-up or perhaps my tastes are so simple – the only thing I
really coveted was a Spanish bitch about eight months old. I half
wished I'd accepted the proffered one at Xmas when Penny was
such a nice dignified little lady, puzzled at the crowd, accepting
it, and conquering her puppy shyness by an effort.

There were about fifty–sixty there, yet so large the room we were not crowded, even when twelve tables were set up for whist, while those who didn't play sat round talking. We had refreshments – piles of good but dainty sandwiches, with real meat in, no made-up filling, lots of too gaily-coloured iced cakes, Xmas cake in segments, trifles and jellies. My sharp eyes had already said 'British Restaurant' when I saw the too-bright-pink icing of the too-lavish 'hundreds and thousands' on the cakes, and I heard later it was correct. I don't believe in British Restaurants. They undercut traders, get preferential treatment and lose money. No other caterer could help Mrs Diss out for this big party and one for the Inner Wheel[†] tomorrow, and I know well if they had done, there would have been no roast beef sandwiches supplied ...

Mrs Howson sighed all the way home about the 'lovely big house', 'gorgeous silver and cut glass', 'marvellous carpets'. She said, 'That would be my idea of heaven.' I sniffed as I said, 'With coal and other fuel rationing, shortage of labour and the cost of keeping up rooms never used unless like tonight, it would be my idea of hell.' What queer snobbish streaks we all have. I looked at Mrs Diss's two quite charming young people: Julia, settled now to her 'domestic science'; Geoff, content in the family jewellery business. And when I recalled Mrs Diss's horror of and superiority to trade – one would think sometimes she was the daughter of a belted earl instead of a bank manager's daughter – I thought of all the money and influence in the family, and of my own two, getting there in 'professions' unaided. Times were when I'd have given years of my life for money to help educate them and give them a start in life. Things work out queerly sometimes.

Nella had mulled over these matters of ambition and social status a few weeks earlier (1 December 1947).

It's odd, but money doesn't always help like the will to get on. The Disses are very wealthy people. He is Barrow's leading jeweller and there's a lot of money in both families. Mrs Diss always spent hundreds of pounds on expensive boarding schools and brought Julia up with the fixed ambition to be a doctor. She was both a clever and charming girl. We all felt sorry when she failed her prelims – and women don't get a second chance. The son went to Cambridge and then into the Fleet Air Arm, and Mrs Diss spoke of him going back to train for 'optics', which we took to be a kind of eye specialist. He calmly told his people he only wanted to go into the shop, as he wanted to marry and settle down. He is only twenty-three but his wife-to-be is an orphan and doesn't like Domestic Science teaching. Mr Diss will not mind, but I know the slightly snobbish streak in Mrs Diss will have had a blow. She makes such a sharp distinction between trade and 'profession' – she was a bank manager's daughter. In the WVS office Mrs Diss had said a bit morosely, 'It's no use planning for your family.'

Thursday, 8 January. Margaret came in to have a new dress she is making fitted and a little cut out of the armholes, and we discussed a few dodges to let dresses and skirts down, but Margaret, in spite of her square sturdy shoulders, loves padded shoulders, and I insist they will have to be taken out, or only as they used to be, to hide shoulder defects. The 'new line' seems to have ousted points problems, the poor quality of coal and even the weather, when women are talking, and I feel wildly amused when the only ones *in* fashion, or not caring, are the dowdy old grannies and maiden aunts. It always amused me to see Aunt Sarah's upswept hair, the latest fashion, but which she uncompromisingly stuck to between the Edwardian and these days.

Friday, 9 January. I had to wait in the shoe repairer's, which was full. I felt a bit snooty. I could have given a woman a good dressing down instead of the sympathy her goggle blue eyes, swimming with tears, asked onlookers. She put a pair of dreadful low shoes on the counter and before the shoe repairer's wife handled them, I saw her shake her head. The soles were worn through the inner soles down one side of each shoe, and the heels were so bad it was a wonder anyone could have walked like that. Big 'easy' tears filled the woman's eyes and she wailed, 'Can't you do something? They are the only pair my poor husband has, and I've no coupons and he is home ill with a cold now, with getting wet feet.' All eyes travelled over her really smart get up and then to her little girl, equally well dressed. She sensed the looks and said, 'My husband said I could have his coupons. He never plans like I do, or buys things he should.' And she pushed the broken wet shoes in her bag and went out. I bet her ears burned with the remarks passed about 'silly selfish women'! I had good bone and vegetable soup, and enough potatoes to fry up, with bacon, and sweet apple slices, and enough semolina sweet from yesterday to heat for my husband, and hurriedly tidied round while lunch cooked and heated. My husband was very wet and had to change, but there was the good soup and a warm fire.

Jessie Holme came in for the afternoon, and Mrs Atkinson came in, so distressed. Her sister-in-law who went back to Canada sent parcels and a whole ham to be divided between Mrs Atkinson and another sister. It looks really perfect but is salty as brine and curiously tasteless. Even Norah and Dick hadn't eaten two thick slices Norah cooked, and when I tasted a wee piece I couldn't wonder. I could only suggest she boiled the whole piece after soaking well, with vegetables to add flavour. She had looked forward to it coming so much. It could have been such a grand standby. Jessie was so delighted with a dressing gown we partly dodged up some time ago and finally fixed this afternoon – a few hours' sewing will finish it. She had a very good but shabby raglan camel-hair coat. The cuffs and collar were worn, and she had only worn it about the garden when she lived in the country. Her sister had a nice wine-coloured one, with an overcheck in fawn, equally good but old-fashioned and worn. Between the two, after we had had them cleaned at cut price, we've made a dressing gown both smart and better than money could buy nowadays. It's got a deep border, wide deep cuffs, and roll collar of the check material as well as the big patch pockets Jessie wanted and made from the fawn front facing which we discarded, with a band of check material. She didn't want a belt, so I fitted it slightly with darts.

She is tall and stately. I said admiringly, 'Jessie, you look as if you had stepped straight out of *Vogue*', and she was delighted as she prinked and preened. Suddenly I realised why I had liked her as soon as I saw her. She is 'my kind of folks', perhaps because of her country origin, for she has always lived in Broughton, a very small market town just up the coast from Barrow. I gave her a piece of Xmas cake with her cup of tea. I wished suddenly Edith was as friendly and showed signs of liking me. I couldn't imagine Jessie showing resentment or jealousy in any way. Her husband's mother is coming to be in the house, and she has a good visiting nurse, and Mrs Atkinson and I will see to anything she needs till her mother-in-law gets here from Whitehaven. I opened a small tin of salmon for tea. Jessie had to go to make her husband's tea for five o'clock, and I gave her a tin of cheese and macaroni out of a parcel from Australia. She has an appetite like Norah and a good digestion. My goodness but I hope baby Holme is a boy. It's not that she hopes it will be a boy. To hear her talk, there's only one sex! I recalled my own calm assurance – I wanted boys myself – so hope she too has boys. She wants two or three children.

Tuesday, 13 January. Jessie Holme came in. She feels restless and unsettled, now her time is near. She looks very drawn and ill. I looked at her in pity today – thirty-four is not the time to be having a first baby. Apart from the physical side, babies and young children need the patience, or rather the joyousness, of youth, to rear them. Jessie would be sedate, though sweet, at any age. Young wives of today have a lot against them, if even they are born home makers. Jessie has some good bits of furniture from home, but her house has such a cheerless look, so few rugs or carpets, and poor skimpy curtains. The polished lino looks so cold and bare. I thought of the houses that are going up now with concrete floors. Some very nice maisonette type of flats are going up nearby, on the main road. I look at them every time I pass – concrete floors and stairs, and all woodwork eliminated that is possible. I thought of stepping out of the bath, or warm bed, for I cannot see any floor covering making concrete 'warm'. We sat and talked of babies, and little children and their odd sayings. It was a pleasant afternoon, and after a cup of tea, Jessie went at 4.30. Her husband has such odd hours for work.

Thursday, 15 January. I didn't feel too well, but got dusted and vacced and all tidy this morning, including two neglected cupboards and my pantry shelves. I went out into the garden to dig some leeks. The sun shone fitfully and patches of blue sky showed in rents and holes of the sullen clouds. I've known an April day feel colder. There was that drop in temperature that could mean snow or storms ahead. The rooks cawed lazily and happily. The thrushes and starlings chirped happily, as if telling each other winter was past, but great black-backed gulls ranged on the roof tiles and chuckled evilly. They knew it was only a breathing space. I have primulas and polyanthus budding and a soft greenness on pansy clumps, and round the dead stalks of chrysanths, new green shoots are thick.

Mrs Atkinson called over to say her cousin died in the hospital. She has never been really conscious since I went in the ambulance with her. They kept her drugged and free from terrible pain and she died peacefully. She was such a sweet bright person, always so kindly. Things are hard to understand. She suffered so – she who wouldn't have hurt anyone or anything.

In 1948, Jessie Holme was to figure prominently in Nella's diary. Her baby – a girl – was born on 21 January. 'Even allowing for Jessie's exhaustion,' Nella wrote the next day, 'she was indifferent to it. I asked if she had thought of a name and she shook her head and said, "We never thought of a girl coming."' Nella wrote of visiting the following day: 'I felt concern for her listless, languid look, all vitality and humour drained out of her smiling face. The baby is thriving but she doesn't take much notice of it.' On 26 January things were looking up. Nella was 'really delighted to see the change' in Jessie. 'She looked her old self, and quite happy with wee Katherine Ann, as they have decided to call the baby, and she seemed to have got over her deep disappointment.' On the 29th all seemed well. 'To hear Jessie talk now, she got her dearest wish when she had a baby girl! She is such a sweet person. I knew she would come round and love it.' (They finally settled on 'Kathleen' as her name.)

Friday, 20 February. I had a blazing fire of wood backed with coke and kept putting on more wood as it burned down, but it was cold if we moved far from the fire and the shrill wind had the sound of snow. My bones felt they creaked. I relaxed on the settee but could not find ease for long and moved to the fire. I've a restless, unsettled, nervy feeling on me, a 'don't-know-what-I-want, won't-be-happy-till-I-get-it', a feeling of foreboding, as if I was worried about something so deep I couldn't lift it into my thoughts. Nerves and cold probably. While I do get like this, I wonder if I'll ever see Cliff again. I wonder how he is, and knowing the dependence under the most forthright independence of men-things, I long to smooth out little household cares, do his mending, etc. A 'Martha' complex [*a woman devoted to domestic affairs*] is a mixed blessing! If I could hear he was married I'd feel different. Sometimes I think of his bad dreams, and wonder if he has them now, if in his work he can find release and peace from hidden terrors. I think of the stiff pompous way he walked when his leg tired and he would have limped, of his determination to put all thought of pain and illness away and not think about it, always my thoughts a montage of thankfulness and relief he has found his own path – God does answer mothers' prayers – and the deep sadness of never seeing him or hearing his voice. I look at Shan We and wonder if all Siamese have his intelligence, understanding and deep affections, as if Cliff whispered in his little brown ear, and told him he was going far away, and he must be a good cat and try and 'make up'.

In late February and March, Jessie Holme's fragile health was a big concern for her husband, George, whom Nella thought very well of – she said he was attentive and considerate. He 'is so worried', Nella wrote on 1 April, 'when Dr Miller says she is so bloodless, and needs meat, liver and kidneys. When doctors know well it's impossible for them to give permits for extra, they should be careful about giving orders. Poor George said, "I wish I knew where I could buy some" – and he is a railway detective!'

Monday, 5 April. I called at Jessie's but she was not back. George left word with Mrs Atkinson she was coming back this evening. She had been so ill on Sunday they had to bring in a Broughton doctor, the one she always had before coming to Barrow. It was a kind of fainting attack and George was badly frightened. The doctor confirmed Dr Miller's diagnosis but prescribed some kind of liver tablets as well, and said she was in very poor health and must relax and rest, feed up and have all the fresh air possible. George looks worried to death. I feel they are realising the difficulty of a big rent out of his wage. He is only a plain clothes railway policeman. I don't think he gets a big wage, and I can tell all extras for the baby and its arrival have been taken from savings.

Tuesday, 6 April. A cold wet morning. I didn't feel like going down town for ten o'clock, to meet Mrs Higham at Boots, to buy a few prizes for Thursday, and had to hurry and knead bread and tea cakes and leave them to rise. I'd packed Aunt Sarah's little fortnightly parcel of odds and ends, and when I missed the bus decided to walk. I wished I hadn't. Halfway down Abbey Road I heard such a dreadful cry not far away and on reaching a corner saw a man lying in a big pool of blood, and two workmates kneeling by him. I asked a man if they had phoned for the ambulance and he said someone was doing so. Nothing could be done by us standing staring – we walked down the road together. I felt sorry for this man. He had actually seen the poor fellow fall off a fifty-foot roof. In tonight's *Mail* it said he died two hours after admission to hospital …

This Easter I felt my mind go back so plainly to Easter spent at Spark Bridge. Oddly enough, Arthur spoke of the same memories, and on Easter Sunday Cliff wrote, 'Do you remember when we all used to stay at Spark and walk down the field to church on Easter Day?' Often a feeling of awe creeps over me, to hear little things I've said or done so long ago recalled by my grown men. It's rather a terrifying thought to realise how a child's mind can be influenced, but perfectly true. In my child-life, my mother seems a rather vague lonely shadow, my father very remote, till I was old enough to realise he was an unhappy man who had a magic key he was anxious to lend me, into a land of books. Odd vagrant thoughts of life and people. But Gran – my prim-lipped Quaker Gran – at fifty-eight I find my life shaped by her maxims, her faith and never failing kindness, and a goodness that was part of her very fibre. If Gran said a thing, you could steer by it. If she said a thing was 'not done', it lost any charm it promised. When you are young you don't realise this power, or else it would have more importance. I always try to impress young mothers with the power of love, the importance of seeing the good behind the naughty and, most of all, letting a child see good in a mother, never telling them untruths or breaking a promise.

I had to hurry round when I got home. I'd a nasty feeling of butterflies in my tummy – nerves affect me like that. I knew I'd best keep to cornflakes and milk and have a rest. Pity, it was a nice lunch, tinned tomato soup with onions grated in, bacon and egg, cauliflower and potatoes, and a steamed pudding, made from the surplus mutton fat at the weekend, which I cut out before cooking the bit of meat. My husband said, 'You don't look well. Why not go to bed for the afternoon?' I half agreed, but felt if I did I'd hear that dreadful cry echo and re-echo in my mind. So after I'd washed up and dusted I went as usual to the whist drive …

It was my day for shocks. I heard the Committee talking amongst themselves about Mr Jefferson, who went back to India last November – he is dead. He has left over £12,000 and has no near relatives. Speculation was rife as to whom it would be left, and hopes he had remembered the Club. It's a good thing he won't be unhappy any more. He was of so friendly and kindly a disposition, and when he was in England so lost and alone.

Wednesday, 17 April. Mrs Salisbury is a treasure. Her passionate love of a 'good turn-out' far outvies any little odd ways and slapdash methods of ordinary routine. We looked at gleaming walls and ceiling, and she asked anxiously if 'Everything was OK'. I said, 'Yes indeed, it's perfection.' She said, 'I said to my boss the other night, "I could take a job anywhere now. I know all the right things to use in cleaning, and the proper way to go about things. Mrs Last is very particular."' I said, 'Not thinking of leaving me though?' and she shook her untidy little head and reminded me again she had only left me before when little Billy was coming. She said, 'My boss said if ever you went to Australia we would sell up and go, even if we didn't live near you. We would feel we had someone, and he thinks with us both being workers and three lads and a girl growing up, we would stand a good chance of getting on.' I felt a family like the Salisburys was ideal for Australia. I'd lettuce in the fridge, and we had it to corned beef and toasted tea cakes, and there was wholemeal bread and butter, jam and cake. I felt very picky. I wished I'd had some of Cliff's lovely honey. I hope another tin comes soon.

I picked up the local *Mail* to glance through, and felt my blood chill with horror and pity. A lad I'd known from a baby had been 'found hanging' in his cabin on his ship at Chatham. The father was a grammar school master when both boys were there. Arthur was a favourite with him because of his interest and work in drama. The only son, he was their idol, and brilliantly clever. They wanted him to be a doctor, but gave way to his wish to go

as a cadet at Dartmouth. The mother went back to teaching so
there should be plenty of money for Kenneth's career, and now at
twenty-six he is dead by his own hand, after all the horror of war.
I felt sick with pity to think of the agony of mind and shattered
nerves that would make anyone of twenty-six, with the career he
loved before him, and all his life to enjoy, choosing to end it so
dreadfully.

Friday, 9 April. I had to go down to the hairdresser's, and did a
little shopping. I went out early so didn't go into Jessie's, for I
intended going out this afternoon and thought I could have done
any shopping then she needed. When I called in on my way back,
I found her brother had come from Broughton, in answer to a
phone call from George, who is distracted about Jessie's nerves.
She walks about all night and complains she cannot breathe if
she lies down. Her eyes looked so wild and furtive I felt alarmed,
and she wouldn't let either Mrs Atkinson or I do anything, or get
ready. Luckily George came in and I could see he was determined
she should go to her mother's again. I felt upset to see the change
in the poor thing. Mrs Atkinson and I have tried in every way
to be kind, but she didn't even say goodbye and wouldn't let us
offer to do anything about shopping or looking after George,
etc. She has suddenly developed a grudge against everything and
everybody, and George the most of all. I hope she stays till she is
thoroughly herself.

Saturday, 10 April. My little attack of acidosis flamed up into a
bad gastric attack. I felt feverish and ill when I came to bed, and
woke at one o'clock, to be sick and ill till after six o'clock. I felt so
shaky when I rose, but a cup of strong tea and bit of toast pulled
me together. Mrs Atkinson came in looking upset. Before she was

up, the phone had rung and Mr Atkinson answered. It was Mary Easton, Jessie's friend at Broughton, who said in an anxious tone, 'Could you contact George, please?' Mr Atkinson has off every Saturday and George had told him last night he too had a day off and intended 'pulling up a few neglected jobs in the garden' before going to Broughton by the teatime train. Mr Atkinson brought him to the phone and after a few minutes' talk George told Mr Atkinson, 'Mary thinks I'd better come at once', so we are wondering if Jessie is worse in some way. Her furtive eyes worried me. She seemed to let them glide vacantly over everything and everybody, with no interest or focus.

Sunday, 11 April. Such a lovely day. I didn't feel well and was glad of my usual Sunday rest, but I longed to be going to sit by Coniston Lake. I wrote two letters, read the *Sunday Express* and had a nap, rising to make lunch for 1.30. Soup, cold beef and salad, wholemeal bread and butter, cornflour mould with jam and a cup of tea. I dusted, packed the laundry, washed up and then sat on the edge of the rockery wall and gossiped to Margaret, who was sitting knitting. My neighbour on the other side gave me some yellow sunflower daisies – little roots – so I planted them. People sat or stood about in the surrounding gardens, glad to be in the sunshine. Children laughed and played happily. Sunshine does make a difference to us all, even to my happy little cat, who rolled on the lawn and stalked little insects in the grass. Arthur Procter comes home tonight, so Margaret will have someone to go out with. Her mother said the other day she 'Would never have thought our Margaret could be so dull in the house – I don't know what's the matter with her.' I often have thought Margaret should have been married and begun a family, at about twenty–twenty-one. Some girls mature early and if they have their family young seem to keep young and gay all their lives. If not, it's as if something goes sour or runs wild in them.

When Mrs Helm was giving me the sunflower roots she said, 'What did you think of Chislet?' – Mr Helm is a magistrate and often met him, as Clerk to the Magistrates.* She said, 'He has never been a happy man, and I think would have been off before, but he thought a lot of his old mother. She died last year and there was a lot of money in the family, so it looks as if he had waited to realise all before he went.' Mrs Helm is a very religious woman and said sadly, 'It's a great pity – and even more for the mud it has stirred up', and she named a string of prominent townsmen who were unfaithful to their wives, some just visiting different, rather shady women, two who travelled rather out of the town, where small children were growing up, suspicious like their wife's family. She said, 'There's no goodness or honour left anywhere. Clergy and doctors are so changed. They are no different to ourselves. There's no one to look up to' ...

As we strolled slowly up from the cinema, a big Wesleyan church door opened, and the congregation came out. I knew most, if only by sight, and suddenly Mrs Helm's rather whining voice came back to me as she said, 'You don't know who's who nowadays. Mud is everywhere, only waiting to be stirred up.' Amongst the ones coming out were two she had mentioned as well-known visitors to a 'doubtful' house. Two girls I well knew had been 'fast', to put it kindly, with both our own RAF and the Americans – I knew of two weekends spent at a quiet hotel near Spark Bridge – and could tell the girls knew most of the hotels of

---

* The well-paid magistrates' clerk for Barrow and Ulverston, a married man in his fifties, had recently left his wife in favour of a woman in her thirties, also married. The scandal was a major topic of conversation in Barrow.

the Lakeland. Now they are married and look settled. There was
a knot of men talking together. My husband said, 'There's three
of the "Forty Thieves"' – a name given to a few businessmen who
buy and sell houses, etc., and it is said force prices up. I thought,
'I suppose in every gathering of people a similar "bag" could have
been made nowadays.'

Monday, 12 April. To say I was amazed at my husband's remarks
as he sat down would be to put it mildly. He said, 'I'm taking the
car down to Kelly's in the morning to get a car radio fixed I've
ordered.' I said, 'But isn't there a big tax on them?' He said, 'Yes,
but isn't there on everything, and isn't life flying past with no
signs of much for people like us?' And he went on about 'Two big
wars in our married life' and 'Not having got much out of life'.
I'd to firmly check an impulse to lay my hand on his brow and
make him put out his tongue as I did when the boys were peevish
and upset! He said, 'Now when we are sitting by Coniston Lake
or on the seashore we won't be dull.' I wondered if I wanted any
noise when I sit by the lake. It has always been its beauty when
only the splash of water, buzz of insects and occasional coo of
wood pigeons from the wood, when the muted voices from a very
odd rowing boat sound eerie and disembodied, when the wind
blowing over the moors and through little gullies sounded like
a whisper, which, if you could only hear plainly, would tell you
all you ever wanted to know, but in its gentle soft rhythm was
always a blessing.

It's very kind of him. I felt, though, it was 'another green
umbrella', a phrase that is part of our family vocabulary. I always
wear brown, dull maroon, soft copper or blue, and once chose an
umbrella for a present when my husband asked what I needed. It
was before all nice things disappeared, though they were rapidly

being bought up. On Xmas morning I opened my parcel – obviously an umbrella – and speech completely left me. A really lovely and very expensive umbrella lay on the table – of harsh bright green, with a wreath of silver green leaves round. My husband looked at it complacently and said, 'The girl wanted to persuade me to buy a plain brown thing – just as much as this one, too.' Tactfully I worked on him in the holidays, and he agreed, 'Perhaps brown would go better with your clothes', but it was too late, the other was sold. My green umbrella has never been unfurled. I've stuck to my old brown one if carrying one 'in case it rains', and if I know I'm going out in the rain I dress accordingly, and as I like rain in my face, never carry an umbrella.

The older I get the more I shrink from imposing my will on people. I often wish I could convince Edith she has nothing to fear of any influence I might have over Arthur. She seems to want to show me always 'Arthur belongs to ME now', and after that first visit, when she was so sweet, she began to build up a queer little attitude. We see so little of each other, and her mood of silence whenever we are alone, her way of shortly saying 'yes' and 'no', makes it difficult. Perhaps she will understand when she has a baby. After all, you have to experience relationships before understanding them.

Tuesday, 13 April. I've felt wretchedly ill now for a week, nothing settling when I eat it, however simple. I was undecided whether to go to the whist drive, but finally decided I would, and spent a pleasant afternoon. I went into Mrs Atkinson's when I came in to see some curtain patterns she had got, and the phone rang. It was Mary Easton, Jessie's friend, who had been trying to get both of us in the afternoon. Her news shocked and distressed us. Poor Jessie is in a very bad way, though after last Wednesday, when

I'd seen the furtive, aloof stare in her eyes, her news didn't surprise me. Jessie's parents are old – seventy-four and seventy-six – and past worrying, and they don't like the idea Jessie may be like her two uncles, one of whom died in a home, and the other drowned himself in a nearby tarn. On Saturday night her father and brother took her for a walk, to try and make her sleep. She got away from them, and after a search they found her kneeling in church, sobbing bitterly. Mary took the law into her own hands and begged the family doctor, who knew poor Jessie from a child, to 'Do *something*.' He paid a casual friendly call, and has sent for George for a talk. George is one of those 'fine big' men who often are so negative. He doesn't seem to bother, not even when he woke suddenly and found Jessie dressed and going out. Jessie has turned against everyone, even her dear little baby. She won't even wash or feed it. I've a great sadness on me. She was the gayest, kindest and most gentle creature. She does need love and understanding …

My husband brought the car back. The Ekco radio is a small, neat thing, fitting on the shelf under the dashboard, and has a very good tone. He is so delighted I felt a worm I couldn't summon up a lot of enthusiasm. I felt how little it mattered somehow. I sat down to knit, but I will never make a knitter. Never have been either. I soon felt irritated and put it away, and as I felt sick, came to bed. I'll have a cup of milk food later. That Nestlé's dried milk food Cliff sends is so easily digested.

Wednesday, 14 April. I woke dull, after a broken night. I couldn't sleep for thinking of poor Jessie. I'd just finished breakfast when the postman came, and Cliff's letter made me hoot with laughter – he is growing a beard! I felt whatever else that one is or has been, there's never been a trace of dullness! Mrs Salisbury changed her day this week – she comes in the morning – so I did all my little odd jobs, and dusted and vacced. I was washed and changed by eleven o'clock, so I could go round to Jessie's aunt to see if she had heard what the doctor had said yesterday. She cried bitterly – she is seventy-three, a year younger than her sister, Jessie's mother. She said, 'Oh, Mrs Last, what can I say? We are all so stunned. The doctor says Jessie must be watched day and night, and the baby kept out of her way, and that the next move is up to George.' I thought of that wireless programme *Lamentable Brother*. I felt the doctor could have stressed the importance of the poor woman having the benefit of skilled attention and care as soon as possible and not merely thrown the discussion on poor George to have her put away. The doctor says it is 'nothing that will pass', and that it is too complete a breakdown for that. Her aunt said, 'I once had a bad breakdown after an operation and had to go for a month's holiday with my sister to Southport. Perhaps if it could be arranged, it would cure Jessie.' I could have wept as I came home, to think of the dreadful cloud on poor kind Jessie, and that dear little baby.

Thursday, 15 April. Mrs Salisbury came. Yesterday she had been to the Women's Clinic. She has rather a bad prolapse, and they want her to go into the hospital – book now, for July. It's a private ward, run by the Maternity Home doctor. The town pays part for all women patients, who only pay £2 a week, and I think another two guineas for the operation. Mrs Salisbury wonders if the Government will take over and she could come under the new scheme. It's so muddling, it's difficult to know these things.

George called with a big bundle of laundry, to send when the van man called. He looks nearly dead with worry and loss of sleep. He said Jessie had stood against the wall in the kitchen since Sunday, never moving or speaking, eating or drinking. The doctor says she must be taken to a brain specialist at Lancaster, but I can see that George is hoping that the few days' leave he has been given will see a change in the poor dear ...

My husband looked tired out. He has had a lot of worry lately with his work, and his mother takes all her troubles, real and imaginary, into the shop. Of all her family, she only turns to him, and when her ration books were lost again this week, it was an added worry for him. I've put my foot down. She shan't have them again. I took the bus down to see her after tea, and told her I insisted on doing all her shopping in future. I've offered many times and been refused, but when I took a firm stand tonight she said, 'I'd be very grateful.' I was so taken back by her gratitude I looked closely at her. I feel she is perhaps failing quicker, since Grandad had his accident. I'll go out in the morning and see her shopkeepers. She gets groceries from the shop where I deal, and shopkeepers are always kind and considerate to arrangements affecting old folks.

When I came back, my husband was writing in the front room. I decided I'd cut out the piece of brown silk I have in. I'd got a pattern and felt in the mood. It's a plain, well-cut pattern, relying on cut for any attraction. I detest drapes and bows here and bows there. It's a pattern, too, that won't date. It's a great surprise often when I see how little the new look is worn by ordinary people, beyond a longer skirt and a softer shoulder line. I don't see much change, even in visitors from larger towns. I suppose the fact of 'utility' with a more or less central control of fashion is the cause.

I walked down the garden path with my little cat. Such a heavenly sweet night, with the smell of growing things, spring flowers, budding trees. Jessie and I planned to do our sewing on the lawn this summer. She said, 'I'm going to live outdoors all summer. Perhaps that will be my best tonic.' I looked across Mrs Atkinson's lawn to the half-made rockery they had started, poor Jessie, and poor, poor George. I wondered who would look after the little baby. I listened to *ITMA*,[†] relaxed on the settee. I didn't feel very appreciative. I didn't feel in the humour for nonsense. I felt as if Jessie's illness had broken the little ring fence round me, that it showed clearer and more focused the strife and chaos all round. A real good cry would have done me good, but I felt beyond tears. I felt a blanket of futility smothered me, mentally and physically. I'll be very glad when Edith has had her baby and they are both well.

Friday, 16 April. Mrs Howson was so shocked about capital punishment being abolished. Somehow poor Jessie's illness has swung me for all time to the side of this decision. To see that gentle sweet woman so altered, to hear of the pitiful state she is in now, made me realise how little – none at all – 'badness' there is, only pitiful twists and warps, and that 'only by the Grace of God' do any of us escape. Bad people must be shut up safely. Doctors could study them, and perhaps help others afflicted, but punishment can only be revenge, which is evil. Mrs Howson said, 'You have some very queer ways of looking at things, but Steve says you are always sincere, and that word used by Steve often means "You've got something there."' But she feels murder will increase now that people will not think 'It's not worth swinging for.'

Saturday, 17 April. I was shaking my duster out of the stairs window, and I heard Mr Atkinson call, 'Will you come down a few minutes, Mrs Last' and found him talking to an elderly woman, the mother of a nearby confectioner. I felt my breath catch as I looked at her parcel, remembering suddenly today was Jessie's birthday and that she had taken some marg for a birthday cake to be made. Mrs Waugh knew poor Jessie was very ill, but not just how ill. I peeped in the folds of the paper at the attractive little brick-shaped cake, snowy iced, with a spray of violets at each end and 'Happy Birthday Wishes' written between. We talked it over. George and Jessie's brother are taking her to Lancaster on Monday – she is no better, and her physical health is failing rapidly. We decided the gay cake would only be another distress to poor George, and Mrs Waugh said her daughter could easily sell it and would credit the marg and make another cake when Jessie came home, if I could let them know when she was expected. As I resumed my dusting I felt I wished I knew ...

George called with the key. I don't quite know why – there won't be occasion to go in their house. He looked distraught. It's a dreadful thing for a man to have to take his loved wife and leave her in a mental home. I longed to ask who had the baby. He said Jessie hadn't spoken, cried or eaten for a week. When they coax her to sit or lie down she looks blank and vague and fights so desperately if they try and make her. The doctor gave her some kind of injection and they laid her down and took off her clothes, but in less than two hours she was up, had got some clothes on and was standing against the wall in the kitchen again. The doctor has stressed the fact he could do no more and wanted them to take Jessie to Lancaster for last Thursday. Now it has to be Monday to see this particular doctor. George seems incapable of thinking he will have to leave her. He seems to have a hazy idea of some magic which will bring back the Jessie he has always known. When I phoned to the laundry, I asked for the manageress and explained a man neighbour had left a huge pile of washing, and I'd be very obliged if a van man could make a detour off Abbey Road as our delivery and collection was over for this week, and added, 'It's a case of rather desperate illness. Will you please return it as soon as you can?' It was only lifted Friday morning – and returned before tea today. I thanked the van man and expressed surprise, but he said, 'We are human beings down there, you know, and try to please our customers.' Just a week tonight since Jessie was found in church, kneeling and sobbing wildly, as if she felt all human help was failing her.

Monday, 19 April. We went out in the car. My husband dropped me at his mother's home, while he made various calls. I looked round in desperation, wondering what will have to be done. My husband and I are the only ones to bother at all and beyond always paying them £2 10s each week tax clear, he doesn't really feel concerned. His quite understandable reply to anything I've said is, 'Surely the other four can take something on their shoulders.' Trouble is they don't want anybody round, and are happy in the dirt and disorder. In the dining room there was a little heap of coal in the corner – 'It was handiest there.' I said, 'You are not fit to do any housework at all, Mother. Let me come down with Mrs Salisbury, who will scrub through.' She said, 'I never do any housework. It never wants doing, and I won't have anyone in the house poking about, you or anyone else.' What worries me is what will be done soon – very soon if I'm not much mistaken. They are both failing fast. I've neither strength nor endurance now to tackle taking them over. As we came home I said, 'Would you agree to shutting up our house for a few weeks and moving down into your mother's house to take charge? I would do, if I could get a competent woman to come in every day.' He shook his head and said, 'No. You have done more than your share for my family. I've not been as blind as you think. One of the girls must take charge and we will do our share.' What puzzles me is where all their little private income goes, but wonder if my husband's remarks about money going where the clothes coupons go is correct. Flo was always a 'grab', though if she is getting them, she should do something in return. I can see we will all have a share in the big problem ahead.

We were back by nine o'clock. I don't know whether it was the peaches or the feeling of worry I came back with, but I was sick again. My husband actually said tonight, 'Why don't you go to the doctor's?' But as I pointed out, I had the stomach mixture he gives me, made up by my brother-in-law, and know well what he would say – 'You must stop worrying, lie down after every meal and cultivate that sense of humour you are in danger of losing.' I don't consciously worry, but it's times like these I realise how nice it would be to have a little social circle which didn't depend so on my own efforts. No one drops in. They come with that 'Where's Mr Last?' if they come in, and if he looks busy or quiet, they never stay. For one reason and another, I've fought rather shy about making a close friendship. Jessie was an exception. I felt as if I opened barriers, didn't care whether my husband would approve, and felt Jessie belonged with me. She used to say, 'Kathleen, we will have such a lot of kindness to repay, but we will, my darling, won't we?' and smile so sweetly over the wee thing's head, lovingly. The baby always seemed to know me, even when I'd not seen it for a day or two when they went to Broughton for weekends. Its wise dark eyes looked widely. Its wee hands clasped in a little gesture all her own. She had such pleading always in both eyes and gesture, as if begging to be loved. Poor George. It's so difficult to understand why this heavy blow has fallen on him.

Tuesday, 20 April. George called early. He had come down to tell

Jessie's aunt that he had left her in Lancaster, and was very cut up at the brief, not to say callous, reception they had got. A woman friend of the family went with them and Jessie was perfectly docile and allowed them to wash and dress her and get her ready, never speaking a word to anyone, but she took notice of the signposts on their journey. When they got to the mental asylum, Jessie was led into another room and they were asked to wait. A little later all her clothes from her vest to her coat were handed out, with every little toilet requisite, even her comb and toothbrush, and they were told they would be communicated with, by post ...

I had a pleasant afternoon at the cricket pavilion, and not a bad game of whist, and hurried home to make an early tea, for my husband had said he might come home early enough to go to the pictures. I wanted to see *Mrs Miniver* again. I only made a simple tea, peaches, new buttered tea cakes, wholemeal bread and butter and jam and sponge sandwich. I often get so out of patience, knowing so well we both need more gadding about, but he won't go to last house shows. He insists if he is not in bed before 10 o'clock and gets eight or eight and a half hours' sleep, he feels too tired in the day. I say, 'Well, I don't and never will see how you cannot plan one evening so we can go to a show.' Now the variety doesn't start till 6.30 – it's all right – but mainly owing I think to the stoppage of the last bus service before the old time of coming out, we stick to the wartime picture showing, 5.30 first house, and the second always starts before eight o'clock.

Last time I saw *Mrs Miniver* was in wartime, when we had worry and fear, but high hopes and courage – hopes of all the good we would do, the feeling we could do as much for peace as for war, never realising the queer frustration – frustrating everything – everybody would find when the ceasefire sounded in

Europe, and certainly never thinking of the flare-up in Palestine, or that Stalin would replace Hitler in his bid to rule the world. I loved every minute of the picture, wondering again just why futile silly pictures are made, crime and sex glorified, slime and mud flaunted, when a simple picture of nice people packs the cinema, as I'd not seen it for a long time – first house at that! My husband enjoyed it thoroughly and had that 'we must do this often' air. I bet if he could see a few comparable pictures he would! We have booked for the variety tomorrow night. The first week was a triumph for the promoters. The second, with the all-male cast and memories of the queer set-up of some of the leads when it was in Barrow once before, must have made them wonder if it would meet expenses. Yet the Five Smith Brothers and a goodish support packed both houses in that big place, and it looks as if Sid Millward's 'Nit Wits' is going to do even better, for those who went last night are saying, 'You mustn't miss this show, it's a yell.' Barrow is unique in many ways. If word goes round the Yard a thing is good, or bad, men seem to rely on their workmates' word, and a failure or success relies on the huge Yard crowd.

Mrs Howson brought in such a lovely little worn coat for Mrs Salisbury, who is always glad to give coupons if she can get good clothes without money. I looked at this non-utility coat – I recall the material was very expensive, and Mrs Howson insisted she 'must have silk lining, as she had always been used to it'. She went to Manchester in her search, and it's a coat little worn, and younger than either of mine, yet to hear Mrs Howson talk is 'quite unwearable'. She was in such a queer prickly mood tonight. I bet she will be difficult to live with. The jealous skitty way she always had in a pawky malicious manner, which once made us laugh at Canteen, is settling on her, and like a bag of pepper on a piece of meat, tends to utterly spoil any goodness or niceness. I saw my husband stare in blank amazement as she talked so shrewishly of anyone who had pinched and scraped to buy houses while their men folk had been at war. She said, 'I believe in enjoying life while I can. Doesn't it make you sick to think of the way women worked and saved every penny, and grew old before their time?' My husband rubbed the top of his head in perplexity. I know he was searching for words. He said, 'Well, I cannot say much. I know it's what Nell would have done. She was a grand manager in the last war and managed to save £100 for us to put on our house.' I felt the glare she gave us both. I could have giggled wildly. As long as I've not to work or live with her, I can see a funny side.

Someone of my own blood will die soon. I had Gran's old dream of carrying flowers for someone. As I didn't feel very sad, perhaps it will be one of the old ones. It's a long time since I had the flower dream. Poor Dad joked about it, when I told him, and said, 'For goodness sake, don't get the same silly ideas your mother had about dreaming of flowers', but he died very suddenly, and the daffodils I'd carried in my dream were in the wreaths heaped on his coffin. I've not been sick once today and had only faint butterflies. Perhaps my rest after meals is helping.

Wednesday, 21 April. Mrs Salisbury came, and we had a busy and unhindered morning, and I found time to slip round to Aunt Eliza's before lunch and took her a little bottle of damsons, some papers Cliff sent and a bunch of such lovely spring flowers out of the garden. She was looking bright, but felt neglected – nobody loves her. I said flippantly, 'What the heck, ducks, you've got your parrot', and to my horror she said, 'I've decided you must have Colchester when I die.' I said, 'Now you know darn well I detest birds in cages', but as she pointed out he rarely went in his cage. I said, 'He wouldn't have much fun with my two cats', but really meant my poor cats would have none at all if that wretched bird was round. He delights in biting their tails or tweaking their ears, and his raucous voice and really terrible laugh has always kept any of Aunt Eliza's cats well under his claws. I said firmly, 'Now don't wish that bird on me. You are worse than my mother-in-law. She wants me to promise to look after Granddad if she goes first, and no arguments made me falter. Have that nasty parrot – I WILL NOT.'

I had tinned soup to heat and sausages to fry and I did steamed fish for myself, cooked cabbage and potatoes and made a semolina sweet to go with bottled apples. Mrs Salisbury washed up and I got washed and changed, for I wanted to do some shopping before going to a big Social and Moral Welfare meeting in the Town Hall. Two bishops, Lady Fell and most of the clergy in Barrow and Ulverston, as well as a good number of subscribers, made the meeting a big success – and me feel like a fish out of water. I nearly disgraced myself by falling asleep, as the Bishop of Carlisle's sonorous voice boomed platitudes. To my embarrassment the Bishop of Penrith thought he recognised me and warmly shook me by the hand. I'm sure he mistook me for someone else. I've only seen him twice when he was at Hawkshead and we went to church there in wartime. I didn't feel at all interested somehow, good cause or no, and I looked round at the best workers and thought how dull, not to say sour, some of them looked. I'd a little game with myself, trying to pick out the ones I'd turn to if in trouble, plainly recognising that much as I like and respect Mrs Higham she wouldn't be amongst those I'd feel would understand passion and temptation.

'It's been such a lovely day – we longed to be off in the car,' Nella began on Sunday, 25 April. Often in the first half of 1948 she and her husband took car trips on Saturdays, for he could usually find some business-related excuse for these journeys on a Saturday but not on the Sabbath, when virtually no business could be done. 'I do long for the time petrol can be used,' she had written the previous day, after an outing to Ulverston. 'Even to go and sit by Coniston Lake would be good for him, and now there is the wireless in the car, he would settle happily.' Since the petrol ration was about to be restored, initially at a lower level, their Sunday motoring could soon be resumed. Petrol rationing was not entirely eliminated until mid 1950.

Sunday, 25 April. It was so warm and lovely I took a chair out and sat in the sun. I could see George and Jessie's cousin busy in the garden and later he came in, looking a little happier. He had a letter from Lancaster, saying Jessie had spoken to the nurse, and asking permission for some electrical treatment to be given. He gave me the address so I could write each week, saying letters were allowed but didn't know about flowers or papers. He said the baby was unbelievably good, and Jessie's mother was having no trouble at all looking after her, and he will travel from Broughton each day. He said sadly, 'Eight years married and I've only been able to look after her for less than a year, and a sorry job I've made of it.' I said, 'You may find that Jessie is better sooner than you expect. They said she was in such poor physical condition, you know, and she will get the very best of care for body and mind.' I prayed my words could be true.

Friday, 30 April. Early this week I heard the cuckoo, and the Howsons disputed it, but this morning both she and Steve had heard it. We talked of when the nightingales sang so sweetly from somewhere near. The gun batteries seemed to frighten them

away, and the last time I heard one round here was the night after
our heaviest raid. Cliff was home unexpectedly, and we had just
heard that little Kath Thompson had died in the hospital from
bomb injuries. It was the first death like that that had touched
us closely. I was standing listening to the liquid bird notes, in
the still, sweet evening dusk, and Cliff came out. Perhaps something in my attitude kept him from his cheery 'Come in for your
supper'. We stood quietly till the bird moved away from the
nearby tree, and he put his arm round me, kissed me lovingly
and we came indoors without a word. Both of them had such an
'understanding' way. We didn't need words.

I fried fillets of plaice for tea and they were delicious and my
husband was in at just the right time. He does look so tired and
worn out lately, and I know well how his parents worry him, his
mother especially. If I'd my way, I'd get a good daily help – a
rough and ready type, used to old people's odd ways. I'd not give
in to them in the spineless way all the family do. When I was
in town I took time to go and scare the pants off a woman who
occasionally visits. She was once kind when my mother-in-law
had a dizzy turn and took her home, and I know would get a good
return. Her story is that she is sorry for them and keeps calling
to see if she can do anything, but things have been missed out
of the home, and my husband said doubtfully, 'Mother might
have given them to her', though as I said, 'Old people have to be
protected.'

Nella confronted this Mrs Ellis, threatened to report her, and insisted she
not visit the elder Lasts again. Later, Margaret visited.

We talked of poor Jessie, and when she went I listened to *The
Clock*. I think the productions dealing with mental kinks and

illness the wisest, most worthwhile features ever put on by the BBC, *Lamentable Brother* especially. To unthinking or ignorant people, who have never come into contact with breakdowns, they give an insight and understanding. Years ago I had a very bad breakdown after a major operation and a lot of worry. I said to my doctor, 'Do you think I'm going mad? I feel I'm losing some kind of protecting sheath off my mind, and feel people's emotions, thoughts and fears, have queer clairvoyant dreams and can tell fortunes in a really odd way.' He said, 'No, lassie.' (He was a Scot.) 'You are not the type to have melancholia.' But it made me realise deeply how minds can change and grow perplexed. I once told him a dream I had, so queer and arresting it did me as much – perhaps more – good than the long sea voyage he said he would like to prescribe. I thought I was standing leaning over a low parapet, looking at a wide, strangely green river. As I looked closer I saw it was closely covered with leaves of every possible shape, colour, condition and variety. I stood dreamily gazing, growing more conscious of each separate leaf. Some were jostled by others, some sailed calmly and effortlessly, some were battered and bruised, carried in cross-currents, some actually seemed to be trying to flow upstream against the stream. For one I felt real contempt – it seemed to be so determined to be bruised and broken and to go any way but to glide serenely. Then I knew I was that leaf, broken at the edges, getting nowhere at all. I felt conscious of a pulsing Rhythm, of the countless leaves sweeping by me. I lifted my hands off the parapet where I had gripped so tightly and, not praying, not conscious of any plea, held them outstretched for help. So moved was my whole being, I felt strength flow into me. He was a nice doctor. He didn't laugh or make fun at all.

Jessie Holme, though absent, was often in people's thoughts and conversations. On 10 May George 'told Mrs Atkinson that Jessie was fretting badly to come home, that she looks perfectly normal, and worried about her house getting dirty and dusty, and the house being too much for her mother. I felt again that the poor girl should never have got to the beaten state she did. Most people I've heard visited for the first time in a mental home have either not known their visitors or bitterly reviled them for "shutting them up".' On 29 May Nella reported that 'Jessie is worrying and pining to come home, but the treatment is for three months. Someone told George that he had not to build up too high hopes on the sudden recovery Jessie had made – it could only be temporary. What cruel people there are. It took the light from poor George's face.'

Meanwhile, Mrs Higham raised the possibility that she and her husband might move to Ulverston, which led Nella to have, she wrote on 20 May, 'a queer feeling that I always had to "walk alone". I felt loneliness, as I rarely do.' She had lots of contact with old people, and on 26 May, after visiting troubled 80-year-old Mrs Waite, she 'wondered sadly how anyone could wish to be old. I'd a longing for the peace and beauty of old Jocelyn Forsyte in *The Man of Property*.' Nella's parents-in-law were increasingly a worry, partly because her mother-in-law was suffering from dementia. On 7 June she spent several hours dealing with her. 'By teatime I felt a wreck, a completely wrung-out rag. I'd answered simple questions – the same ones – dozens and dozens of times, things like when Cliff was likely to be in for tea, and if Arthur and he were both working now, when my fat old Murphy expected kittens, and so on … Her mind is like badly set jelly, with hard pieces of fruit in it.'

Wednesday, 9 June. Lucky it was I had tea ready early – tinned chopped ham and salad, wholemeal bread and butter, honey and sponge sandwich – for my husband came in so cranky tired, and nothing upsets him more than not to have a meal ready to sit down to. I couldn't but reflect that it's generally the most muddly person who insists on the peak of perfection in others. He ate his tea without one word of appreciation, as usual. I looked at the bowl of roses, my snowy lace and linen cloth, and wondered as often if women *did* dress or do things as much to please men as to satisfy some kink of their own. For what appreciation most of us get, we might as well serve food in a nose bag!

Friday, 11 June. I came in just before ten o'clock in the evening, wondering if there had been a phone call while I was out, wishing I could hear how Edith was before I went to bed. Just as I made supper, it rang, and Arthur's delighted voice told me they had a baby boy – their dearest hope. He is a strong, lively baby with a mop of black hair. Arthur is thrilled to the core. I don't think he has ever been very close to a new-born baby since Cliff was born. Edith is well and very happy. I breathed a sigh of relief. Perhaps it's with her having a miscarriage before that has made me feel so anxious. Cliff will be delighted. He never had the least interest in baby girls. I wish we could be nearer, to go straight away to see him. With the Barrow plane being forced down in the sea – three of the young fellows were known personally in the street – my husband won't go from Walney in the eight seater, so we will book from Liverpool and fly from Speke and I'll book and fix all up next week if I can, to go mid July.

CHAPTER NINE

CLOSE-UPS

June–December 1948

In the second half of 1948, there were holidays for the Lasts: a coach trip to Torquay in late June, a week in Belfast in July (they met grandson Peter), various outings in the North, and a day trip by coach to Scotland. There were also deaths – Aunt Eliza in July and Nella's father-in-law in early September. There were several meetings of the WVS and other social events, and some evenings at the theatre (Nella and Will still went to variety shows). There were also stresses and strains in the family, many of them relating to Nella's in-laws. Coming back from Coniston Water after a Sunday drive on 8 August, she and Will visited his parents, who 'don't and never did welcome callers'.

Sunday, 8 August. We didn't stay long. I longed to open windows and doors, pour disinfectant down drains and wash bowls, anything to sweeten that dreadful fetid air. I felt choking too with the utter unconcern and lack of interest in them both, beyond the weather and the price of coal. I couldn't raise a spark of interest. They were not concerned about Cliff, or little Peter, or anything. I felt that beyond breathing, they had died long ago! I felt little worry thoughts chase round in my head as I came home, wondering what will happen if they should need care and attention through any length of time. They so hate to be 'bothered', as they call any attempt to do anything for them.

Monday, 6 September. I got some nice filleted plaice and decided as I'd time to take my mother-in-law's groceries and the fish. I found all in an upset. Dad had fallen out of bed – he did on Saturday too – and my husband and one of the men were struggling to get him lifted and put back. I felt ill when I went in, and at the sight and smell of that room I felt something click in my head and one of my rare icy rages sweep over me. I felt as if I hated the whole family – hated them for their lack of common sense, decent feeling and all the little kindnesses and loyalties. I felt, 'Darn it all, they have less humanity than decent cats.' I walked downstairs and phoned for Harry, stressing the point he must come at once, and by the wee man they both got to hear a few things. It's years since I put the wind up the lads when they went too far, but my tongue rasped as sharp. Neither my husband nor his brother were left in doubt as to my opinion of their slackness in letting old people rule them and get into such a state. One thing made them sit up. I pointed out if anything happened to Dad, there would have to be an inquest and people would have to go in then, and if they didn't mind shaming, I damn well did, and from now on things were going to be different. I insisted on the doctor being sent for. Harry went for Flo, and we made up the bed in another room. I washed the window and Flo scrubbed the floor. I ruthlessly sprinkled disinfectant everywhere, not caring if it stained the carpets, and Dad was carried into the clean room, to wait for the doctor. I'd our bacon ration with me and cooked most of it for my husband, and Flo went for bread and cakes, and we had cheese. I left before the doctor came. It was my husband's and his brothers' and sisters' affair.

I felt so edgy and nervy, and it threatens rain again. I got the rest of the ramblers and climbers pruned, with the window open to hear the phone if it rang. Dad slept soundly, not waking even when the doctor came. He left tablets to help him sleep if needed, but he could always sleep well. My husband said, 'He cannot do anything – we needn't have sent for him.' I hung up. I felt I'd stood all I could without further argument. I thought of Harry's wife's words: 'You know, Nell, it would be God help us if we were ever very ill and it was left to these two saps to care for us.' It was only temper that kept me going. I suddenly felt as if I was going to pieces, and had to relax on the settee, and then was very sick. I'd some brandy, and laid on the bed and drifted off to sleep, waking just in time to make tea. I put cheese and tomatoes, wholemeal bread and butter, honey and cake on the table, with a come-and-get-it feeling, and went to lie down again. My husband brought me some hot tea, and it pulled me together, and I insisted he got the car out and we went down with clean pyjamas, sheets and some old sheets I'd meant to put 'sides to middle',* and Harry had brought the cotton wool I'd told him to get. No waterproof sheet. No attempt at 'pack'.† No wonder the place smells so, for the poor old man has had no control for weeks now.

I looked at my mother-in-law and realised how impossible it was she should come to live with us. She would drive me as batchy† as herself, for our ways – little fundamental ways – are so different. If she was bedfast, I could care for her and keep her clean, but not while she was about. Flo or Elsie must have her if she is left alone. I thought, 'If I'd past kindnesses to repay, memories of any occasions where I'd felt I owed a debt of gratitude, it would have been different.' Only a stern sense of duty would affect me now.

---

* Since sheets wore out towards the middle, where people slept on them, it was common to cut them down the middle and sew them so that the unworn edges were attached in the middle.

Not all days were this dispiriting, and the happiest incident this summer occurred on Tuesday, 24 August:

Margaret had sent to Hutton's of Larne for a catalogue and then a piece of linen for a big tea cloth – she likes the way I always lay a 'nice' table. Mrs Howson came to see what she had got and to see the catalogue, and we were sitting happily discussing linen, 'bottom drawers', etc., when there was a ring and I went to the door. A radiant, laughing-eyed woman seized me in a loving hug, saying, 'I've caught you in this time.' It was *Jessie*. I looked at her and couldn't speak. I felt tears brim and fall down my cheeks as I said, 'Jessie, my dear – I'd have passed you on the street and not known you.' George was with her. They came in for a few minutes. She had been to get her hair permed. She said, 'I'm going to try and repay all your kindness, though I shall never be able to tell you how much your letters and papers meant, even more than the flowers and "tit bits". The sister and doctor used to be interested in all the cuttings you sent and we all used to read them, and once the doctor said, "Well, it seems the papers *do* still have happy bits of news" – and he bought his wife a Siamese kitten because he said Shan We seemed such a pet.' Mrs Howson is very tender hearted, and Margaret too got weepy. George looked at us all and then at my husband and said in deep disgust, '*Wimmin*', and it made us all laugh. I said, 'It's all right for you. You remember this happy-eyed Jessie – we don't.' He shook his head and said, 'No, I never saw her like this. I think I'll keep this one instead of the Jessie I used to know. I feel we are going to have such lots of fun together.'

We seemed to laugh and talk nonsense, and a remark of Jessie's made us laugh out loud, as she said seriously, 'George said you gave him the most comfort and hope of anyone when one day you "snorted" at him and told him that the only thing wrong with me was that I was *buggered* and you laid down the law about one thing piled on top of another.' Mrs Howson looked a bit startled, but no one knew how worried poor George was that day, or that he had such a deep fear Jessie's mental trouble would mean she would have to be kept in Lancaster for a long time, perhaps years. I'd forgotten what I had said to comfort him, poor dear, but it was certainly an odd way to comfort a man, and I laughed with the rest. She said nothing about giving up her home, and I don't think she will do so. It would be a tragic error. Jessie begged us to go up and see them at Broughton if we can. I've hesitated to call. I don't know the mother so very well, and felt I might have intruded, but Jessie was shocked at such an idea. They hurried off to catch the 7.30 train, and soon Margaret and Mrs Howson went and I began to iron, a feeling of such deep happiness in my heart I'd not felt since my Cliff began to walk with only a slight limp.*

Much of Nella's activity this autumn revolved around the aftermath of her father-in-law's death on 9 September.

Friday, 10 September. I've felt baffled this week. I've cudgelled my tired head, trying to see a way out about Mother's future, getting no help, feeling it was left entirely to me to arrange something, others blandly believing 'something will turn up – it's no use upsetting ourselves'. It was such a fair sweet morning, and I persuaded Mother to go for the bread needed, so she would get out a little. I heard a step outside, and it was a very old acquaintance, known to the family for as long as I can remember. She and her

---

* Cliff had been wounded in the war.

husband kept the Church Institute, later the YMCA Hall. He died a little time ago and she is getting past great effort – she cannot be much under seventy, but is very active and clean as can be. She had called to offer condolences, and came in to wait for Mother. She talked of old times when we were young, and seemed so very down, and I learned she had got a month's notice, given very curtly after twenty-six years' good service. She said, 'And where I'll get a house or flat I don't know.' A thought sprang into my mind. I've prayed so hard that I could find someone, but I dared not broach the subject till the family knew. They don't mind 'bossing' if they don't know! My sister-in-law Nellie came in and spoke a few words, and Mrs Brown went out. We looked at each other. Neither wanted to speak first, and just then my husband came in and we both eagerly put forward our plans. He dashed off without delay, and with a further talk, we arranged everything. In return for two bedrooms, the bathroom and a large sitting room – all empty, which we will have freshly decorated – she will do odd jobs like steps and windows, stairs, back kitchen and washhouse, do any shopping and take bills and letters safely for the shop. Mother knows her so well she consented without further trouble and added that electricity for cooking and light and a share of the fire in the dining room if she cared, on winter evenings, would all be included. Flo and Elsie, Nellie and Harry were delighted and the latter said, 'Trust our Nell to find a way. I've never known a problem she couldn't solve.' I shook my head and said, 'Wrong this time, Harry. This is a direct answer to a prayer, believe me.' It made my endless task of tidying after Mother, trying to clear out drawers and cupboards, seem light.

The funeral was the following day. Then several days were consumed in cleaning the exceptionally filthy and slovenly house ('curtains in rags, not a decent cooking utensil of any kind') and disposing of quantities of rubbish, while contending with the erratic behaviour of the new widow. Nella spent much of the week at 73 Greengate toiling to bring some order out of chaos. 'It's been a day to set one wall climbing,' she wrote of Wednesday the 15th, before enumerating the day's frustrations. Disputes erupted, notably between Nella and Harry's wife, Nellie, which the two brothers were drawn into. 'We all parted on reasonable "friendly" terms,' Nella wrote on 16 September, 'but I took a solemn vow that after Mother's death, the whole lot could fry. I felt I would avoid them like plague patients. I felt as soiled mentally as I've done literally this week, by handling dirt and squalor I'd not let strangers see. I told my husband so, and to my surprise he said, "Nell, you've been an angel. You've stood too much already, one way and another. I wish we could clear off to Australia."'

Friday, 17 September. It was a real effort to rise this morning. Only the thought of the upset and Mother being on her own and wandering about got me up and out. The plumber put his head round the dining-room door and said, 'How are you feeling today, ma?' I said, 'Not too good', and he insisted on making the fire and suggested I lay down on the sofa, which was covered with a dustsheet. I did, and he soon made the fire and said that water would be on very soon. He said, 'If that woman comes upsetting you again, give me a call and I'll chuck her out.' I said, 'It's not as easy as that. She is my mother-in-law.' And he said 'She's barmy anyway' ...

Getting lunch ready was a task. What should have been half an hour's work was over one and a half, for she had to be watched constantly. She turned out the stove, or turned it up too high, and worried the workmen incessantly by hiding their tools away. How Mrs Brown will manage her I don't know. One thing, with her only having the old age pension – she is over sixty-five – and houses or flats being so difficult to get, she may find a free home, light and coal compensation. Me, I'd rather live in a hut on the seashore, and beach comb for fuel.

Tuesday, 21 September. The amazing strength of my 80-year-old mother-in-law has to be seen to be believed. She must rise about 7.30, for she has breakfast and nearly always walks the mile from Harry's, where she sleeps. She never sits down all day except at meal times, and she keeps jumping up often as her wandering mind impels her to see to one thing and another. Her energy is all so wasted. Not one positive thing does she do all day, beyond her fierce determination to pile chopped sticks in one corner of the dining room and coal in the other! By the time I've made lunch my back feels as tired as my ankles and knees. I crave to relax, but by four o'clock I'm exhausted, while she still scatters round with seemingly fresh energy! Today I fried them bacon and egg, and there was tinned soup added to Bovril and grated onion, potatoes, cauliflower and steamed suet pudding, heated in sauce. I felt better to stick to my light diet again, for my digestion seems to have gone back on me completely. Much of my time has been taken trying to keep Mother off the paint till it's dry. Today she leaned against a wall in the hall and brought off a patch, clean to the newly plastered base, where it had needed so much touching up ...

Mother cried a lot today, not the easy tears of old age, but deep sobs that shook her poor little frame. I think she is beginning to realise Dad has really gone. She lamented, 'No one wants me' and 'I don't know if I'll like Mrs Brown.' I tried to comfort her by saying Mrs Brown knew more stories about people and things than I did, and how cosy they would be sitting talking by the fire in the winter. But it's hard she should have to make a change at eighty.

Monday, 27 September. I'm so thankful tonight. Mrs Brown got part of her furniture moved, including beds, and made a bedroom ready to sleep tonight, so I won't have to go down each day again. It's been such a heavy, really hot day, with drenching showers of rain. I had a fire lit. I've had a quiet amusement, which today came to a climax, when I gently broke it to the two daughters that things were going to be different altogether in the future. Mother loses everything she touches – it worries her to distraction, and everyone else near her, when money and keys go. She would never relinquish the keys of the shop and yard, but I've got them off her. She thinks she has lost any extra ones, and there's only the ones my husband has. After real tear-ups to find her purse and £5 in paper money disappearing altogether, I told my husband it was best not to give her £2 10s housekeeping in notes on a Friday. She's not had any left on Monday for months and asked for 'Bank money', as she calls her own little income, out of the safe. As since Xmas she has got rid of £59 and not spent it on the bare decencies of life, I knew that had been given away, or lost ...

Flo said in her whining drone, and her lovely but vacant blue eyes widened, 'Elsie and I think it seems unnecessary to spend so much when Mother is eighty, and mightn't live long.' I said coldly, 'Mother has only been eighty since April, and by the look of things she hasn't renewed much since I left Greengate, which is twelve years ago. You know they would never have got into this state if I'd been living near and going in every day as I used to do.' Most normal daughters would have bitterly resented an in-law taking command and bossing round as I've done this last fortnight, but they have meekly scrubbed and cleaned while I've raged and sworn, as I scrapped soiled rubbish, and given opinions unasked about things in general. Instead, as we shook the hall runner, and folded it before the men began to carry furniture in, she said, 'This will be the last time we will be here together, but if you ever want any help or are ever ill, just send for me and I'll come.' I might have felt more grateful if an unjust thought hadn't popped into my head that as a 'limpet', she sought some place to cling, and to her advantage. I thanked her and said I'd remember, and she added, 'Being all together has made Elsie and I talk of when we were little and had to turn to you for any fun, like Xmas trees and fireworks and duck apples. Remember the fun of ducking for apples, and how you bought soft pears for Elsie because her teeth were so bad she couldn't bite into any hard apple?'

Nella was fond of babies, and Jessie's Kathleen, now eight months old and thriving, was a favourite. On Thursday, 30 September Jessie and her daughter were at Nella's for tea. 'I felt so dead tired, glad of the peace and the baby's happy content, and Jessie's quiet but merry voice. I looked at her and thought "What a lot has happened in a year", for she came about this time.' Nella was also claiming time and space for herself in the evenings. 'I was very firm the other evening and told my husband he must use the front room on Thursday and Friday evening, when he is busy writing. I'm not going to sit dumb and still, afraid to move lest he is disturbed. I'll have anyone in those nights, too, or listen to talks on the wireless.' Will objected to having the radio on when he was doing paperwork.

Tuesday, 5 October. I went down town early, with Mrs Howson. We wanted to choose patterns, she for a new coat and I wanted a dress pattern to make up one of my birthday dress lengths Cliff sent. It was such a good meeting – a speaker from London. I'd thought our big launch – the *Himalaya* – would have kept WVS members away, but on the contrary, those who had gone came on to the meeting. The speaker, Mrs Cresswick Atkinson, spoke of the WVS as a power of thought and service that would always be a part of life, taking the place of the Church, later feudal landlords and gentry in caring for those in need of help. She spoke of the need and value of leadership – those who could lead should – so moving us all. I found myself later promising to help organise a Hospital Visitors scheme, and was deeply touched to have most of our Hospital Supply members eagerly offering to help me, if I'd organise things. I suppose they got used to me in the war years. Vivid pictures of our war efforts were brought into our minds as the speaker mentioned canteens and servicemen. I saw tears in many eyes, and it wouldn't have taken much more to make me have a real howl!

Friday, 8 October. Mrs Brown looked so bewildered as she said, 'I'd no idea Mrs Last was like this. I planned to be so kind to her, but she won't let me be!' Mother scowled persuasively at me and began a long tirade about wanting things as she had always had them. She liked coal in the dining room and to chop sticks on the hearth and leave them piled, etc. Flo wouldn't let her have her old corsets, had made her put on her 'best' pair. Two such nice people had come, wanting money, and all she could give them was five shillings each, etc. Mrs Brown said in a worried way that she knows Mother gave the woman tea, jam and a bit of meat, and I wondered if it was the woman I'd had trouble with. Mother said, 'She said, "God bless you, Mrs Last – you are an angel."' I said, 'You're not, you know. You are so afraid of burglars, but are silly enough to encourage that woman who took your little mat and Dad's scarf and gloves', but I know how quickly she forgets. I listened as she went on and on. I felt such a sadness. Every little grudge had stayed in her mind, not one memory of kindness shown to her. All the latter had slipped through the meshes of her mind.

Saturday, 9 October. I felt so dead beat and was thinking of making a real strong cup of tea and having two yeast tablets, when my heart sank as I heard the scrabbling knock my mother-in-law gives. She knew I'd be cross. Her face showed it. I said, 'Mother, you shouldn't come out without your coat. Does Mrs Brown know you are out?' She said, 'I don't know and don't care. I'm tired of her living with me. I'd much rather you came down like you did.' I knew it was hopeless to reason. I said 'Ah, I've to stay at home with my two little cats – and look after the garden.' Her eyes narrowed cunningly as she said, 'I'm going to tell Mrs Brown to go away and I'll come and stay here.' I said, 'No, Mother. You wouldn't settle. We would both be unhappy. You must settle with Mrs Brown, who is so kind and willing to help you, and you must be kinder and more pleasant to her, or she will leave you, and then you might get a family billeted on you. The Council says that the squatters must be off the gun sites before winter, you know.' I didn't add that they were putting them top of the list for houses as they were completed. She looked horrified and I talked casually of crying babies, noisy wireless, rough noisy children and quarrelling women, hoping some remarks would stick in her poor muddled head.

She wouldn't hear of going back by bus – said she would walk – but I was firm, and phoned for a taxi – another 4s 6d. But my husband said the other day, 'Do whatever you think best, at any time. I'll gladly pay for anything.' Mrs Brown looked beaten. She said, 'Mrs Last is so unreasonable. There's no pleasing her.' I said loud enough for Mother to hear, 'Then you will have to put a fire in the other room and have your friends in, and go out all you can, and make yourself as happy as you can, remembering this is your home now.' Mother said, 'I don't think I'd like a fire in two places in the house.' I gave her a warning look and tried to remind her of our talk, but felt it beyond me. I came back in the taxi. I know the driver well. He said, 'Your old lady will get run over yet, or else cause an accident – she wanders so heedlessly', which remark did not lessen the feeling of worry I had.

Monday, 11 October. A letter from Cliff, to tell me his exhibition promised well, and in which he spoke of his regret none of us could be there, saying he realised we were really the 'only people who mattered', as if it had come as a surprise to him. A phrase he used set my rhythm for the day when he spoke so lovingly of the 'love and background' I'd given him. As I went down town there was a prayer in my heart that if I grizzled or indulged in self pity it should be my biggest sin, and prayed for the chance to show my deep and ever-growing gratitude for so much where Cliff was concerned. I went to the library and suddenly began to feel really ill, as if I was going over. The heating was on full blast because it was the 'date' to start it, yet on the street people looked flushed and over clad in the close heat of the morning.

In the afternoon baby Kathleen was left with Nella while Jessie took the bus to the town centre.

Jessie was glad of a cup of tea when she came in tired. She said, 'I feel half dead – don't know what I'd have felt walking all the way.' The blank in her mind seems permanent. I'm so glad I wrote her all the gossip of the street. Today she said, 'You know, I read your letters yet, going through to pick up little remarks about people's families, and then I can piece up remarks made after I came home, and today I could sympathise with dear old Mrs Thornborrow about the way her husband suffered and died. I'd have been so distressed if I'd not had some little inkling of what she talked about.' Dear Jessie, smiling and loving. I so pray her little mental illness will never recur. One thing – George adores her. She and the baby are the centre of his life, and with Kathleen being such a comical little scrap, there's always laughter in the house.

Wednesday, 20 October. I've had such an upsetting day. Everything has gone wrong and two things, at least, were really worrying. Mrs Salisbury was late. I put all rugs on the line and began to bake. The phone kept ringing. Three times I had to wash my hands, while I was kneading my bread. Mrs Higham rang to say she was not coming to Lancaster next Tuesday – her husband has bronchitis and the painters have come in. Another ring brought a curt announcement that an acquaintance was 'coming round as soon as convenient'. She is a spoilt, petted woman about my own age. She was a pampered child whose mother thought a sickly child brought some little distinction. Her husband was Mayor twice, and has been a councillor for years, quite a nice man, if somewhat pompous. Some little time ago I met them and they were in great distress. A very good maid suddenly grew tired of Mrs Jones' tantrums, after over eight years in which they steadily grew worse. Mrs Jones whined, 'I cannot get another maid, even to sleep out. Do try to see what you can do.' I said, 'As it happens, I do know someone who would perhaps suit you. She is very slow, in fact somewhat "mental", but someone who had her said she is very clean and trustworthy.'

I gave the Joneses her address. It seems they drove round straight away. I'd no more talk with them, but heard they had got

a maid at last who 'seemed a bit simple'. Mrs Jones swept in like
the wrath of God, and pointing a bony finger at me demanded
why I hadn't told her Elsie was a bad, immoral girl. I said, 'But
she isn't. She is a very kind silly creature.' Mrs Jones shrieked –
positively shrieked – 'Did you know she had had two children
and got them adopted?' I said, 'Yes, but that's her own affair.
Perhaps if you had had sons or boarders I might have hesitated to
tell you about her wanting a place, but you are only paying half
what most people are doing. You say your house is beautifully
kept, and that you can trust her with anything – your cousin told
me so. I cannot see why you should feel like this.'

She was so rude to me, and it made her angrier when I failed to
see her point of view. I had to tell her husband he must take her
home, that I'd stood all I intended at Hospital Supply, where she
used to often 'create'. I felt really shaken, but quite unrepentant.
She went down and engaged her, and had a long talk before she
did. I jolly well hope now she cannot even get a charwoman. I
could tell she had been beastly to Elsie. Even Mrs Higham, who is
very stern with girls in the Social and Moral Welfare home, liked
and pitied Elsie, as more sinned against than sinning.

It delayed me very much. I had to leave quite a lot of little
jobs undone, but managed to get my bread, an egg custard and
a sponge sandwich done, and my bits of brass and silver cleaned.
The butcher brought such good bones for my stock pot, a bit of
beef to stew, and sausage for lunch, so with tinned soup, mush-
room, turnip and potatoes, and sweet apple slices fried with
the sausage, and a sago pudding, lunch was soon ready. I'd sago
pudding, a beaker of dried Australian milk and three charcoal biscuits, and hoped for the best as I felt my tummy begin to develop
butterflies. I gave Mrs Salisbury my good but shabby tweed coat,
and she went off with the air of a duchess going slumming! She

looked nice though, and I'll give her a hat and gloves to match. She is such a good little thing and tries so hard to rear her family nicely, and for their sakes goes out day working. I'd shopping to do. I'd nothing for the cats, so in spite of the stormy day went down town. Fur coats and bootees were everywhere. It was like a January day. I met an old Hospital Supply member but it was too cold to stand talking and we went into a café for a cup of tea and a chat, and looking round it seemed as if most people sitting there had the same idea of getting out of the cold …

Tensions persisted concerning the care of Nella's mother-in-law and the perceived responsibilities of her various children (three sons, two daughters), and later that day Will and Nella mulled the matter over.

My husband said, 'Mother seemed to think she would have plenty of money to throw round, and has been promising fur coats to the girls, trips to London (dear knows why) to all around her.' I said, 'What has she promised you?', and as he smiled a bit wryly he said, 'Nothing. I'm the guy who has always paid their money, every Friday morning.' I said, 'Your fault and folly was to ever come back to Barrow when you escaped in the First World War. You lacked the courage to strike out for yourself in Southampton, where you would have done well. It looks as if you will go on paying for that folly.' But I said half jokingly, without malice, 'Things work out. Arthur and now Cliff are making their own way ahead. I only wanted money to help them.'

Thursday, 21 October. I'm tired out tonight, mentally more than physically. I got all the little jobs done I couldn't finish yesterday and was hindered by phone calls. One made me hopping mad. It was from Mr Jones, who apologised for his wife's temper, and attitude to Elsie. He said, 'Elsie was the nicest girl we have had, simple minded it's true, but she laughed at little jokes and, if slow, got done with no fuss. I really rang you to ask if you could find another girl for us. I know my wife offended you, but she needs understanding, you know.' I said, 'Perhaps I know her better than you do, Mr Jones. I've known her about twenty years longer, and she hadn't altered much, and I'm afraid I would hesitate to recommend anyone else. You say Elsie was simple minded. I doubt if a normal girl or woman would allow anyone to speak to her as Mrs Jones apparently did, or work for so little money.' I felt I could have been really rude. I made a little casserole of the beef and carrots, turnip, onion and potatoes. The bone stock was made into good tomato soup, and I'd enough sago pudding.

My husband rang up and sounded very worried. I could tell Mother was in one of her most aggravating fits, and Mrs Brown was going out this afternoon and evening. If Mother is so nasty with her, it's common sense for her to clear out. I went down after lunch, wondering what I could do. I couldn't help recalling the really dreadful life I had with her interfering, her malicious, tell-tale, fault-finding ways, and with my husband so tied to them with working for his father, there was no escape, for whatever I did was misconstrued and twisted. I scolded her soundly, and suggested she was more friendly with her neighbour next door, who would gladly keep her company any evening. It's dreadful to think of living to eighty, and no one even liking you, let alone loving you, beyond detached pity. I felt quite indifferent to her tantrums. I said firmly, 'You must never think you can come and live with Will and I. I couldn't stand things even as well as Mrs Brown. I know I'd go out when you got difficult, and then you would still be on your own.' I think she resents sleeping alone most of all. She said, 'I've never slept by myself.' Even if anyone said they would sleep with her, she has such a reluctance to simple cleanliness they couldn't share her bed for long. I coaxed and scolded, knowing how futile it was. She would forget rules she really wanted to remember ...

I felt baffled and helpless as I came home. I could have wept with misery, my prayer to outlive my husband more fervent. I made up the fire with wood logs. Their leaping flames and the cup of hot strong tea I made pulled me together. My head felt full of bits of broken glass. I cannot think what to do, and only my husband or I seem to realise the position, or care at all. I don't 'care'. I have no liking or respect, never mind love, for the difficult old thing. She is like a snapping turtle anyway. But she is old.

Saturday, 23 October. My husband wanted to be in Kendal by one o'clock, so we set off early, just after eleven o'clock, meaning to have lunch at a little café on the way that has always advertised chicken lunches and teas. Today, however, they had stopped making the lunch, and there was only sausage and chips, poached eggs on toast, with cakes, fruit, etc. My husband suggested we went on further. He was hungry, so we tried a place that has only been open a short time. On the main road just past Leven's Bridge a Georgian mansion, set in its own rolling parkland, has been opened as an unlicensed hotel. I'm often puzzled at my reactions to houses reared in late Victorian and fussy Edwardian 'pretty pretty' surroundings, where a space on wall or floor was hastily filled. Even the house where Gran ended her busy life was a cluttered horror, of far too big pieces of furniture, too much china, etc. she couldn't bear to part with when she left the farm. I crave space and wide surfaces. I felt I could have cried aloud in admiration as we stepped through the door into the most perfect black and white tiled hall, and then into a spacious yet gracious room that had evidently at one time been one large and one small room, with three fireplaces. The linen, silver, furniture and décor were perfection. The many long windows that would have been impossible to curtain in anything suitable in today's shortages have long Hessian curtains, the height making for graceful folds, the borders weighted with wonderfully worked herbaceous flowers in wool work. My serious love of perfection of simplicity crowed over the 'Pink Dawn' appointments of china, on snowy damask cloth, and napkins, the silver, and the simple but perfectly cooked meal of oxtail soup, beefsteak and kidney pie, potatoes and creamed turnip, baked apple and custard, as well cooked as we would have had at home. A little oblong silver tray with snow-white coffee pot, and cups and saucers, was set before me. There was about five and a half cups of perfect coffee in the pot! And the meal was only 10s 6d for the two of us.

During the following fortnight, Nella continued to be concerned about her mother-in-law; she spent much time making dollies; and she ensured that a suitably enthusiastic notice about Cliff's exhibition in Melbourne was placed in the *North-Western Evening Mail* on 3 November. This exhibition marked the start of Cliff's successful career as a sculptor.

Friday, 5 November. It's just three years tonight since Mrs Newall's husband 'nearly knocked her senseless' with the announcement that he had fallen in love desperately with a girl who went to the house. Mrs Newall is a woman I admire deeply – one of those often managing types but kind to the last degree, with a gift of friendship I've never seen excelled, if equalled. When the mother of her young hairdresser died suddenly, the father of the two girls nearly went insane with grief – he only lived two years after her death. Kath (the hairdresser) told Mrs Newall with tears that 'All life and sunshine had gone out of the house', and Mrs Newall began to invite the two girls round. What Mr Newall saw in Dorothy puzzled everyone. About thirty, untidy, with that lack of personal care that let dandruff from a badly permed head of unruly dark hair lie on her black dress, a sulky expression, scuffed shoes, generally down at heel, and a way of making you feel your tastes in library books were deplorable and she pitied you – she was a librarian and, it was reputed, very, very clever. After two years in which they spent weekends together – he often travelled as far afield as London and Bristol, where she held posts – they came to live together in Ulverston, where on the death of her father, when she divided all monies with her sister, she bought a house, giving up a post of over £600 a year. Mr Newall is head of all dredging operations in and round Barrow docks and, Mrs Newall thinks, 'hasn't come out of this nationalising stunt as well as some of the other bosses'. I can never quite see her point of view about divorcing him, for she is in no sense a vindictive woman like Mrs Chislet, who 'prays to live to be 100, that my husband and THAT woman have a family of bastards'. Today at the WVS office as Mrs Newall sipped her tea she said quietly, 'No – I've no intention of giving him a divorce. He would like me to give it to him for desertion now the three years are up, but I shan't, you know.'

I'd perched on a bale of 'Help for Britain' clothes – the chairs and desks were all full. I must have been looking thoughtful, for Mrs Newall slapped a 3d on the desk and said, 'Hey, Mrs Last, three pence for your thoughts – the price of everything seems to have trebled.' I didn't want to start anything. I could see the clock on the Town Hall through the window and it was time I was home. We all dearly love to chew things over and could have spent the afternoon giving advice, which Mrs Newall always listens to and blandly ignores! I said as I slithered down off the bale, heartily hoping I didn't smell of the queer pungent moth balls too badly, 'I wasn't thinking of anything really, but the thought ran through my mind that I could never bear withered flowers around me, and as for dead ones, their look and smell would so offend my soul and spirit I'd be ill. I throw them away when they droop, and remember their colour and fragrance.' Mrs Newall said, 'Here endeth the first lesson, and I can see a bus coming you can catch if you put a move on', so I dashed out. I cannot see any happiness either way for her, and she is such a worthwhile person.

One day the following spring (13 May 1949), Nella happened to encounter Mr Newall while she was waiting for a bus. He talked with her – and she was exposed to 'his Don Juan tactics'. 'He has an ingratiating, smarmy manner, and obviously thinks he is irresistible … How Molly Newall, so cultured, kindly, so quick to see round and through people and situations, could ever marry the toad in the first place, or spend futile longing and hope that he will come back to her, puzzles me.' Whatever Mrs Newall's reasons for being attracted to this man, some of her motives for not divorcing him were later revealed. On 19 October 1949, Mrs Howson, after a visit to the WVS office, reported that Mrs Newall 'had decided to get a court award from her husband and clarify the position of the income tax. He is furious, talks about his "position in the town", etc. Mrs Newall had said, "Perhaps, Dick, you would like me to go on a cruise and drop off the ship in mid ocean without comment – or any blame on you?" And she refused flatly to discuss divorce. She said to Mrs Howson, "Look at it from a business point of view. Dick's superannuation fund allows for a pension for his wife if anything happens to him. I'll not give up prospects like that so that Dorothy can throw up a job worth £500 or more a year and live idly the rest of her life, as she is doing now, while I've to keep on working all my days. Again, if I divorce Dick and anything happened to him, I'd not get a Widow's Pension. I'd only be divorced.'"

Sunday, 7 November. We went through the Lythe valley to Bowness. We haven't been recently, though I remembered it's a place for holly trees, and recalled their gorgeous appearance two years ago before such heavy snows. They are as colourful this year, and an old man who came past as we stood to look at two giants of trees with more berries than leaves said, 'That don't look so good, does it?' I said, 'Let's wait till after the last change of the moon in November and see if there's a sharp frost. Remember, "November ice to bear a duck, nothing follows but slush and muck".' He was delighted to chat about weather ways and signs. He was a gamekeeper, or rather had been. I felt I could have spent hours listening to him. He seemed like an echo of my childhood. We gave him a short lift, and parted reluctantly. He seemed to enjoy our meeting as much as I did. I wondered if he felt a little loneliness of spirit this stark November day. Coming down the lake, we didn't meet a car, and only a few people strolled along. At times I felt in the calm stillness we could have been the last two people left on earth.

Every little war memorial we passed had or was having a Remembrance service. At Ulverston the square was blocked and traffic had to make a detour. I looked at the rows of British Legion of both wars, and felt I could have wept. We used to feel a sad but proud 'Never again' feeling in the two minutes' silence. Now, God pity us, we feel a shrinking 'How long before another war?' creeps into our minds. It's so ghastly to think that people who fight, endure and suffer are not the ones to begin wars, and are so helpless to stop them. Only if people's minds and hearts could unite and change, only if we all could unite in a single purpose of personal responsibility to each other, to life in general, towards people we know exist but never see, to teach little children the beauty of peace and concord, how to agree with each other, share things – and laugh – can simple forthright peace come.

Such a lot of vicious circles. People are cold and hungry and resentful. They 'strike', literally or figuratively, and cause hunger and cold to others, and then it comes back full circle to them and makes the position worse. Maybe I've too literal a mind, and think too much of the importance of creature comforts, but I've seen so many cross, quarrelsome soldiers turned into happy, laughing lads and men with mugs of scalding hot tea, a plate of sausage and chips and a fire to lay by, even if most of them sprawled on the floor. I grew to feel those chipped mugs were in some way a symbol, that our Canteen work was a little dumb reaching out to help, some seed planted that could grow into a tree of some kind. But it all passed, all the good fellowship. I looked at the rows of faces as we waited for the signal from the traffic policeman, and realised why they liked the British Legion, and why soldiers spoke feelingly of their Army life.

We were home before five o'clock. I packed the laundry and made tea, bottled peaches, wholemeal bread and butter, cress sandwiches, chocolate biscuits and cake. I began to put hair on my dollies – only a tuft on the brow and over each ear, to show out of close-fitting felt bonnets with a flare to frame their faces. I got blonde, auburn and dark hair so crinkled it cuts into lovely natural-looking curls, and I'm really delighted with my dozen crinoline dollies. The combination of felt bonnets and curls is really amusing. Their faces take on a roguishness and coyness, with every one such an oddly different look. With enough resemblance to make my rag-bag children and 'family', they all have that little individual look of real people. They are a lot of work, and I realise all I 'could make for yourself', as Mrs Howson never tires of telling me, but when I took the four I'd finished tonight and put them under the sheet on the settee I felt as always the pleasure and company they had been making, beside the pleasure and fun they will give.

Tuesday, 9 November. There was an electric cut from 4.30 to 5.30 – a bad time for women who had to rely on electricity to cook a hot meal for husbands coming in from the Yard. People were rushing round trying to borrow candles. I'd been lucky enough to get two gay orange ones for my brass candlesticks, thinking when flowers were done they would be a gay note, so I lit them and my tea table looked like a party! There was baked apples and egg custard, toasted tea cakes, wholemeal bread and butter and honey and chocolate biscuits, but I wasn't hungry. I felt rather sick with bending over the wood stacking and the rush I'd had.

Now my dollies are all finished. I put the two last on the settee, under the cover to keep them from dust. All the smiling, pleasant little faces of the dollies and the kindly bear and rabbit and mousie faces, the cheerful grins of the gollywogs, seemed a very 'live' thing. My rag-bag children always seem so real to me. I will have a tidy dining room again – no carrier and bundles under the stairs to annoy me when I get my vac out – and I'll get down to the big pile of real sewing I have to do. Yet making dollies seems such company, so much more interesting than dressmaking.

Tuesday, 16 November. I called for Mrs Atkinson and we went to the cricket pavilion for the whist drive. It was warm and cosy and it's always so pleasant to meet people you know each week.*

---

* Nella had different feelings about the atmosphere at the weekly whist drive a few weeks later, on Tuesday, 14 December, when some squabbling broke out over

Thinking of Mrs Howson's words made me keener to notice what people said of the new Royal baby. [*Mrs Howson doubted that the birth of Prince Charles would cause much excitement.*] I thought, 'I'll not mention it first', and waited for Mrs Atkinson to mention it as we walked up the street – in vain. We were overtaken by two women going to the whist drive – their talk was a bitter complaint that dried fruit was in so short supply 'yet some people seem to have got hold of plenty'. I said, 'Perhaps they had a little sent from overseas, or saved it in summer', but my words only seemed to annoy them rather than comfort.

Several women come by very early bus service, from out of town, and two from Rampside had brought sandwiches and been in the pavilion since 1.30, and two groups had joined and were discussing something very animated. I went over and it was cold perms, which have reached Barrow in a flood. I was very cautious in my approach to the idea. I said, 'I've heard of a good many cold perms done by hairdressers that have been so unsuccessful. They have been "out" in a week. I should think a lot depends on different hair, and personally, I'd think twice at my age of experimenting, and leave it to those with young hair.' To hear many of them talk, it was as big a marvel as the atomic discovery, and I heard of hairdressers all being ruined in the States and Barrow ones 'trembling in their shoes', etc.

I had a good game – could have had second prize but three already were cutting for the 5s – the small attendance made prizes very small today. It poured as we came home and I realised I'd

alleged deficient play. 'I said to the one who had been so bitchy in her remarks about Mrs Atkinson's play, "You sound cranky today, Mabel. Don't begin your monkey-shines with me. If you begin passing personal remarks, you've had it." In a wordy battle she wouldn't stand a chance. I know too much about her.'

heard snatches of conversation of local gossip, Xmas preparations, the Australian holiday two townspeople were taking and their preparations, Mrs Horne's lovely new evening dress, prospects of snow after Xmas, coal shortages and fuel cuts, odd scraps of shopping gossip – but not one word of the Royal baby, though they are a kindly lot up there, and many are grandmothers!

The next morning, by contrast, 'Mrs Salisbury's first words were, "What did you think of Princess Elizabeth's baby boy? Won't they be proud?" I looked at her smiling face, feeling she was the first person to look as if she really cared about the new baby.'

On the evening of 16 November the phone rang at home, and it was Harry, Will's brother, calling to ask for Cliff's address so that he could write and congratulate him on his success.

To hear him talk of how glad he was Cliff – Arthur too – had made good, how he had always realised the frustrations and repressions of my life and admired the way I'd reared the boys, had given life to them, never 'cling', etc. etc., made me feel if I'd not been kneeling with one knee on the little hall chair I'd have fallen flat, but when he said, 'You're a grand little person, Nell old girl', I did squeak, 'WHAT?', wondering quite bitchily if there could possibly be a snag. He said, 'I've been sitting by the fire, thinking of bygone Xmas times and preparations, and suddenly thought, "I bet Nell is up to her neck in preparations already."'

Tears washed down my face as I thought suddenly of something I'd once said when my husband complained peevishly of all the fuss I made. I did used to be gallant and gay in those so far-away days. However my back ached, I put up paper decorations and let the boys do every room in their own thought-out décor. That year I'd not been well. It was just after I'd had a bad nervous breakdown that had taken the use from one foot and made it drag. I would see the strings of little blossom flowers I was making for festoons and hear myself say, 'When I don't make a fuss over Xmas, you can begin worrying, for I'll be dead.' I felt the words echo through the hall. The moon that we have seen so rarely flooded through the lead lights of the window, bleaching my hand as it held the phone. I felt my gay words so true. Some part of me is dead.

Nella often went to Walney on Wednesdays to visit Mrs Whittam, as she did on 17 November.

Wednesday, 17 November. The rain had stopped but it was so gloomy a day. Shops were lit up, and the flowers, piles of oranges, and gay-coloured Xmas oddments made a bright note. On the Channel, as the bus ran along its muddy side, flocks of seagulls looked for food left by the tide, and fished in the little pools on the sand. Their black backs looked in harmony with the dreary, mist-covered land and sea. I'd got Mrs Whittam's shoes, and some stockings she had liked and changed her mind about getting after reaching home. I thought I'd call at one of the girls' houses first – she will be sure to want company on a dreary day like this.

All was strangely quiet and when Olga opened the door, her face was strained and white, and I saw Mrs Whittam, whose fingers were flying over a gay-coloured rug, looked sad and worried. I said, 'Where's Ena?' and they said, 'Gone to the hospital to see Billy' (her husband). 'He was rushed to the hospital in the night, with tetanus – lockjaw, you know.' About a fortnight ago he took the end off a finger while chopping turnips. He has had it dressed and kept covered but they are a slap-happy family, and last week when I said Billy should go to the doctor when it didn't heal after a week, they pooh poohed the idea. Billy has worked like two men all summer. He wants to make this little farming venture a big success, and with not being too used to animals, has had to learn. He has gone in for stock feeding, bringing young animals to graze on the salt flats, bred pigs, looked after newly cultivated fields, and started a hawker's business for two days a week to sell his own produce, as well as going to market two mornings a week. He has had to rely on part-time workers all the time for any help too, and has looked so pulled down lately. He was all right last night and went to the pictures in Barrow, and jokingly began to help them when they got the rug frame out on their return – they have had a real turn-out of unwearable torn clothes that had been pushed in cupboards and a drawers, and wanted to finish the little gay woollen runner-rugs to put on the children's bedroom floors before winter came. Ena took the dog for a little run and when she came back Billy was a shaking, jerking wreck, unable to speak. When Ena phoned the doctor and gave his symptoms, he said, 'Little use my coming. He needs hospital at once. I'll have the ambulance there in a few minutes.' He is dreadfully ill. They cannot bring down the abnormal temperature, in spite of every injection and drug they are using.

Anyone can go in at any time. Ena was asked if she would like to stay all night and had come home while I was in to change her clothes and shoes into something more suitable than her best 'new look' clothes. I felt a slight shudder as I looked at the sombre black coat and hat she had chosen with only a blue ostrich feather to relieve the gloom. It hung over the brim, damp and lank, and added its little note of sorrow. How Billy hated that rig-out, and how he swore in his rage he has always seen Ena in gay colours, which suited her flamboyant bulk. I said impulsively, 'Don't go in that rig-out again, Ena', and added a bit weakly, 'You mustn't make it shabby going out in the rain and then sitting round in it if it pours.' She was going out in an old pale one, with a shabby rose-coloured dress under it, and I said, 'Put your coral earrings on, Ena. Sick people are fanciful, and you look so nice with them on' ...

I always chuckle at the appearance of Wilf, a policeman friend of Billy's who loves pottering round – at times he can be quite a good help. Dressed in his smart uniform as a mobile policeman, he looks like a film star. He has the features of a Greek statue, the poise of an aristocrat. Anyone would say, 'There goes a leader of MEN.' Tousle his hair, put him into an open-necked shirt, tattered jacket and pullover, baggy pants tucked into old rubber fishing boots – and hear his uncultured, boyish vocabulary – he is a different person.

Thursday, 18 November. I had a little rest after I'd washed up, but set off early for Mrs Higham's and walked slowly through Croslands Park. The sun shone so brightly, giving beauty unexpectedly to everything, even the wet, sodden leaves underfoot, where it touched highlights of lovely brown and sullen yellow in the soggy mess. It gave the fields a spring-like green, any berries on the trees a gayer scarlet. It was Mrs Higham's birthday. I looked at her presents and realised the suspicion that had sometimes crossed my mind that Mrs Higham, left strictly alone, had not very good taste became a certainty! She is fifty today, and growing very plump, yet her fancy had been taken by a vivid tomato-red twin set of thin, clinging woollen material, and she had asked her husband to buy it. She had chosen a bright, gaudy tartan umbrella and a harsh lime-green blouse, and a pair of most peculiar spotted fur gloves as presents from her sister and parents, and an apron of about the deadliest pink plastic I've seen. She has had two rooms decorated, and I politely admired them, but my taste doesn't lie in very panelled walls for small living rooms. I'd tire of their cut-up look, and prefer plainly papered effects …

We listened to the discussion 'Do we do enough for old age?' I'd got interested before my husband came through from the other room, where he had been putting up wages.[†] As usual, I felt a short wireless programme merely scratched the surface, and little allowance was made for individuals – or perhaps it's my lot to meet odd ones out of old ones. Someone once persuaded Aunt Eliza to go to a pensioners' club afternoon – there was a very good social effort in Barrow before 'Old Pals' and 'Over Seventy' afternoons began. The person who took her had extolled the pleasures of these afternoons, and I too said, 'You go, Aunt Eliza. I'm sure you will enjoy it.' She went – once – and when I asked how she had enjoyed it, she lifted her hands and then dropped them; she had curious expressive gestures and shook her head and said, 'Dearie, it was awful, a big room full of musty-smelling old people who SANG when they were TOLD to do, and beat time and tapped their feet, and a patronising fat woman with a silly hat put numbers in a hat – everyone had a number on the 'resister' – and drew out thirty-six numbers and gave them round, and they were tickets to go to a free picture matinee. She couldn't have been more "grand" in her manner if it had been bread tickets.' I said soothingly, 'Never mind, next time you go it might be different', and got a withering glance from her lovely grey eyes that said plainly there wouldn't be a next time.

Wednesday, 24 November. It's been so wild and cold, beyond the paths and front windows Mrs Salisbury and I didn't do any outside work. She brought a parcel with her and said, 'Phyllis's doll has come, so I brought it up straight away' – I'd promised to dress it. I opened the box. It was a very nice 'baby' doll, and I said, 'What a nice dollie. How much was it?' She flushed and looked a bit guilty as she said, 'Thirty-five shillings – but all the war I couldn't buy them toys and every Xmas I promised to buy Phyllis a nice dollie. She has never had one and she is nine. Our Mary says I'm crazy, but I've paid in a club every extra day's work I've had.' I thought of all the half hours each way she had walked to do the additional half days, for which she gets 6s each time. I looked at the tatty, untidy little thing, growing old at thirty-five. I said, 'Of course you are crazy, but you know, my dear, you are giving your children precious memories that will bind you all together when they are grown up.' And I told her I'd dress it to look like a £5 dollie, and make a carry cot if we could get a suitable box. Her eyes sparkled and she sang raucously all morning as she rubbed and scrubbed. I always feel it a privilege to help her in any way.

The butcher brought two little sausage pats. I grated onions and mixed them with cold mashed potato, bound with an egg, and made little pats and fried them brown, and there was tinned tomato soup, potatoes, turnip and apple sauce, and yesterday's remains of sago pudding.

When I phoned to the hospital yesterday, they told me that Ena's husband had gone home. I went out early and did a bit of shopping for her, when I did my own, and took it over. Billy has gone to a skeleton, and the doctor told him he was lucky to be living at all. Only modern science had saved him. He has been lucky in his pals. All his potatoes are in pies[†] earthed over, his field of turnips which he grew for winter growing is chopped and ready for the wintering ewes, fences are mended that the squatters in nearby Army huts tore down for fuel, and I felt the old man who had taken over the care of the glass houses had some magic not possessed by any of the Whittams. I never saw such lovely sturdy crysanths in any of their greenhouses, and he had taken notice of my remarks about the forget-me-nots and purple primroses.

Thursday, 2 December. I mused as I came home through the wet and dark how far-reaching and true the term 'new era' really was, how people's minds had 'surged and boiled', altering actions and behaviour. I felt if I thought hard enough I'd see my life in three distinct slices, though I cannot recall things very clearly before the South African war. I can remember country life best. There was a big country house near. Several girls I knew as children, daughters on farms near Gran's, went as parlour maids to people who stayed there, and I heard them talk. The owners of the house were relatives of the Cavendishes, not at all rich but exclusive to a degree. No Jews ever stayed and I remember the real amazement when an American was actually invited! I was such an intensely, not to say nosey, kid. I loved to keep quiet when elders were talking, knowing better than to advertise the fact I was there by asking questions. Day after day I prowled round the lanes like a tracker, hoping to catch sight of this American, complete with feathers, blanket and axe. I was lying on the grass one day, just listening to some grasshoppers whirring and hoping I could see if they did do it with their legs and not some mysterious instrument, when a tired kind voice said, 'Little girl, are you lost?' I said, 'Ah no. This is my gran's field.' He said, 'Then perhaps you can tell me how to get to Gawrith Field?' – the name of the Egeletons. I was up in a flash. Such luck. Why he might have seen the American! We walked slowly – it was one of my crutch days – and he asked about my accident and I politely answered all his questions, feeling I could ask mine in return, and then I blurted out, 'Have you seen the American? Has he come yet?' I was old enough to feel horror at my 'dropped kick' when he told me *he* was the American, and hadn't seen an American Indian till he was much older than I was!

It's difficult to believe nowadays the exclusiveness of the Edwardian era, or the rapidity the younger ones plunged into their 'brave new world', which no doubt felt as strange to the older ones as our atomic era. We lived in a big, well-built house – big for Barrow – and we moved into it from an outlying fishing village, where my parents lived for the first few years of their life. Mother was enchanted to find gas laid on, and a small room we could have made into a bathroom, yet never did for years, a sponge-down being considered quite enough each day! When Mother got a gas stove and a gas fire after a trip to Manchester, we felt very go ahead. And she lived long enough to see Dad's fears materialise – he was a great fan of Lord Roberts, who always feared trouble with Germany. I thought of all the wonders I'd seen – cars, planes, wireless, household use of electricity, amongst the everyday wonders. I felt the 'new era' had started some time ago – and only now is showing.*

I had to hurry to make my husband's tea, for I expected Mrs Newall from the office to choose a dollie for a friend's little girl. It was pouring down and she looked tired out. She has such a gift of friendship, as had her husband, before he left her to live with someone else. All his friends and relatives still visit her, and lately she has had her London evacuee and her little girl staying.

---

* Nella was well aware that not all this change was for the best. 'I get little sick feelings about atomic warfare,' she had written on 15 November 1948, 'not for the huge bangs that wreck buildings – they are a trifle and can be built again. It's for what radioactivity could do to precious soil and water that will be most devastating.'

She is not very old and has had a bad breakdown. Raids, flying bombs and two evacuations from bomb-damaged houses failed to break her spirit – it's been left to her husband's mother to do it. She is like my husband's mother but, in addition, dirty in her personal habits, never sleeps in the night and rouses the house several times by knocking them up; and one thing and another resulted in an illness for Mrs Hawkins and a longing for the peace she knew in Barrow. Mrs Newall is worried. She has been here three weeks and looks better but begins to shake and cry at the thought of going back to London. I pointed out to Mrs Newall it was most likely all her shocks and troubles had overtaken her – it was not only the fear of going back to 'old Grandma'. She wants to stay till after Xmas, and Mrs Newall wants to invite her sister and husband, and though there's room, she says they won't mix.

I always feel Mrs Newall cherishes the hope her husband will return. They used to quarrel so much, and he was often unfaithful; and she knew it, and took it for granted it was 'Bob's way – he's an old tomcat', which covered any heartache she felt privately. I see him with the person he now lives with when we pass sometimes through Ulverston. There's an old married look about them, as if their relationship has rooted. I cannot see him coming back. Life's a tangle.

Friday, 3 December. I had tea ready, salad with a hard-boiled egg and grated cheese, wholemeal bread and butter and jam, toasted fruit bread and cake. There was a leaping wood fire and warm slippers and the curtains drawn to shut out the cold and wet – rain was falling heavily. I saw my husband was very upset, and thought perhaps his mother had been revolting today, but he said, 'More trouble. I'm sure I'm the unluckiest man living with staff troubles. Alec has asked for his cards.'* He did once before, when his pal went into the Navy, and only his mother's persuasion [*changed his mind*] after I'd had a talk to her and told her how worried I'd been over Cliff not having a trade when he came out of the Army. I explained how Cliff had not finished his apprenticeship, and how he had had to strike out afresh – and off to Australia. Tonight I said, 'What's his idea now? He has over two years of his apprenticeship to serve.' My husband had told him he was a bound apprentice, and refused, but Alec is going to see if he cannot break it to go into the Army or Navy permanently.

I felt really sick with worry. I told my husband more strongly than kindly that 'If you have the same attitude at work as at home, you will soon have no one left.' I told him that it was only that streak in me which made it imperative I should feel satisfaction with anything I did, irrespective of how others felt, that kept me cooking, etc. I said, 'You never say a thing is nice or give a word of thanks for any effort, and you pounce on any little error or fault. It's insulting to say the least of it.' I told him he often frightened me by his growing resemblance to his mother, to her fault finding, dislike of every little social contact, her complete indifference to anyone's opinion, comfort or wishes. He looked blankly at me and said, 'I cannot help how I'm made, can I?' I said, 'Well, judging by results, you had better begin trying. You would be surprised if I asked for my cards, and went off to Cliff in Australia.' I could have laughed out loudly at his look of horror!

---

* 'Cards' were an employee's documents held by an employer. To ask for them meant to quit.

Will wound down his joinery business in 1950 and retired, and he and Nella spent the rest of their lives in Barrow. Nella never did get to Australia. Cliff enjoyed a successful career there as a sculptor; his work is documented in Geoffrey Edwards, *Clifford Last's Sculpture: A Retrospective Exhibition* (Melbourne: National Gallery of Victoria, 1989). Arthur and Edith had two more sons, Christopher and Jerry, and in time moved, first to London and later to north Somerset. Arthur, who occasionally acted on the BBC, became a skilled bookbinder and opened his own bookshop in the 1960s. Nella's adeptness at handicrafts and her feel for colour and form undoubtedly influenced the younger generation, notably her sons. Her mentorship on these matters is remembered fondly in 2008 by Margaret Atkinson Procter.

Nella continued to write her diary until February 1966. On the 17th of that month she was thinking of giving it up. 'I wonder if it's ever read or if the need for it is past now.' She died in 1968, and Will outlived her by little less than a year.

AFTERWORD

Family was not, perhaps, everything to Nella, but it was certainly central to her sense of the meaning of life. 'I'm a homebody really,' she wrote in response to MO's Directive in October 1942, 'and raising my boys and making a home for them was the happiest and most blessed part of my life.' She pitied women who had not had children – she would have liked to have had more herself – and she was pained by the tragedies that overtook and perhaps overwhelmed families she knew. She often reminisced about her own family, especially about the good times. These 'I remember' moments, as she called them on 10 December 1948, 'seem to cling round the boys and their happenings so much'. She was sensitive to how children grew up in families and experienced life and developed their own personalities. She was drawn, almost despite herself, to Mrs Whittam's buoyant, somewhat chaotic, slap-happy and gregarious family; and two of her favourite novelists, John Galsworthy and Hugh Walpole, were admired mainly for their family chronicles.

When Nella wrote about Arthur, she frequently mentioned his intelligence, aspirations and domestic life, and she worried about his health. When she thought about Cliff, she often had mixed feelings. She regretted that he was so far away after 1946 but was content that he had done the right thing by going to Australia. She was both distressed by and fond of his 'differentness'. But she never – at least up to 1950 – records any explicit acknowledgement that Cliff was gay, though a few passages

suggest that the thought had crossed her mind (for example, 27
October 1945 and 16 September 1946), and he had told her on
29 October 1946 that he 'never was the marrying type'. Perhaps
her son's homosexuality was simply too painful to contemplate.
Perhaps, too, she was reluctant to speak openly of sexual inclinations which, if acted upon, were at that time a criminal offence.
Christopher Last, Arthur's middle son (born in 1951), recalled
talking with Cliff in London around 1980, 'when he said – and
these would be almost his exact words – that his family had
always found it hard to accept his sexuality'. As for Cliff's own
feelings about his coming of age in Barrow in the 1930s, they
may not have been particularly happy, given what he apparently
told a writer in Australia many years later. Cliff was reported to
have found working with his father 'irksome and unfulfilling';
he 'derived no great pleasure from either the work of cabinet-
making or the Barrow environment with its industry and smoke
and cold coastal climate', and he disliked 'the established routines, the monotony, and the drabness of his working environment' – 'it was this that his whole sensitive being rejected'. Life
in Barrow, for Cliff, was said to have been 'unrewarding, unsat-
isfying, leaving him restless and searching for something; for a
personal fulfillment which he now realised he would not find in
his local environment'.* Nella, certainly, was aware of his need
to spread his wings.

As well as Cliff, Nella's in-laws were at times much on
her mind – usually painfully, sometimes passionately. On 16
November 1948, when speaking of Nellie, Harry's wife, she
virtually exploded in fury. 'It's one thing for one's husband's

---

* Max Dimmack, *Clifford Last* (Melbourne: Hawthorn Press, 1972), pp. 4–6.

relatives to have the idea you are slightly mad, a "fine lady" and at best "peculiar" in outlook and rearing children, etc., but for an in-law, and one for whom I've always had that little contempt I feel for narrow-minded boneheads, to reveal the depths of jealous spite as she did for my sons' "success" and "luck", in not costing a lot of money to "make them gentlemen", as well as the way she acted when Dad died, made me feel the barest politeness was all I could offer in the future.' Privately, as her diary for 31 January 1950 recorded, she saw this sister-in-law as 'one of those featherheads who open their mouths and let every passing thought out'. In most in-law disputes Will sided with Nella.

As for her marriage, readers of the diary are bound to wonder what drew Nella Lord to Will Last in the first place. In one brief passage, written on 30 January 1950, she sheds light on this question. She had known Will since he was nineteen, and 'I thought his extreme shyness so attractive – so different. I'd never known what it meant to feel shy or out of place. I was so gay and lively, so full of life and fun. That's what attracted him – and what to him was such an attraction. I could "stand up anywhere and recite or tell jokes". Odd he should so quickly think differently, should think I should keep all and any gaiety for him alone, and to show such boredom and aversion to going amongst people as soon as we were married. If I'd not been so young and inexperienced I could have seen the danger signals. If I'd been stronger minded and made a firm stand, perhaps then he would have grown to like company.' Clearly, Will was an anxious person, a worrier, preferring to keep himself to himself, and prone to nightmares that Nella thought stemmed from 'deep fears'. On 21 August 1947 she mentioned that he didn't like eating in public. Perhaps in a later generation he would have been diagnosed as having an anxiety disorder. There is little doubt that his temperament and hers were very, very different.*

On her own side of the family, Nella's mother was a rather limp presence. When, on 16 December 1947, Aunt Sarah was speaking of her short life and 'of her sadness and inability to take life as it came', Nella 'had a vision of the sadness and aloofness of my mother's face – Dad always said she should have been a nun'. Nella's kindest words were reserved for her father and, in particular, her grandmother Rawlinson. She wondered on 13 November 1948 if 'I measure people by my gran, and my father, who in their different ways were so wide in outlook. My father was an accountant, but had an interest in starting the first music hall in Barrow, and he also was a great reader and seemed to know every answer to a child's eager questioning, or would help me to find out for myself.' Nella valued curiosity, engagement and the imagination – she admired her deaf Aunt Sarah, who apparently read a book every couple of days and followed current events closely. 'Gran', too, had been a thoughtful, clear-thinking woman, whom Nella almost always wrote of with affection and respect. 'She as a Quaker learned to read and write, though far from town,' Nella recalled on 8 December 1948, 'and educated herself by reading, finding time and ways in her so busy life, and taught her family and servants who wanted book learning. I wondered how many rebel thoughts she had planted, teaching grown farm men to read.'

What can be said about Nella's own religious views? She denied being a Christian – 'I don't believe in Heaven or Hell, in

---

* In September 2007, both Norah Redhead and Margaret Procter – the Atkinson sisters – remembered 'Mr Last' as 'a lovely man', but quiet and reserved. Will had been a school friend of their father. Both were sons of joiners.

the resurrection of the body.' In November 1944 she mentioned
some reasons for her disbelief, including 'a father who showed
me an escape from pain and loneliness through reading and an
inability to take things for granted without conviction or proof'.
She did, however, believe in a supernatural power. She seemed to
hold the view that God was everywhere and in everything, and
she sometimes spoke of a 'Force' or 'Plan' or 'Rhythm' in life, as
if she felt that humans were in some sense under the firm direction of a higher being. She almost certainly held some belief in
the occult – she was not at all averse to having her fortune told,
and occasionally she told fortunes herself. She also had a Hindu-
like conviction that individual life continued after death. 'I've
always had a strong belief in life going on,' she wrote on 28 February 1950, 'not a Heaven where there is singing and walking
by green pastures, but somewhere where we got the chances we
threw away, or never had, to grow.'

While many people start to write a diary, few persist for very long
(only a small minority of Mass Observation's almost 500 diaries
continued for more than two years). Nella not only persisted, she
did so at extraordinary length, often producing at night an essay
on the happenings of the day. Why did she do it? What drove her
to produce a million words or so every two to three years, and to
post her writing each Friday to Mass Observation's headquarters?
No doubt her diary gave her satisfaction in various ways, some
of them therapeutic. However, it seems that the critical fact for
Nella was that she had always wanted to be a writer, and that
MO allowed her to become one. With time this writing became
a habit, a part of her way of life and her identity, and almost certainly a pleasure. Words flowed, images came to mind, vignettes
of ordinary life called out for description, smiles and laughter

were to be remembered, surprises and peculiarities caught her writer's eye, and crises concentrated the mind and needed to be grappled with by means of pencil or pen and paper. 'My childhood craving to be a writer has materialised,' she remarked on 20 November 1948, 'if not quite as I planned.'

So, from her suburban semi-detached home in an industrial town in north-west England, recording her life in semi-secrecy, Nella Last became a noteworthy writer. 'Of all gifts I crave,' she wrote on 7 September 1946, 'that of "expression" would be my dearest wish. I've met such interesting people, and always heard unbelievable stories about people's lives. If I could put all in written language and sequence, I could write books, I'm sure. Maybe I'll get my wish in some future reincarnation!'

GLOSSARY AND ABBREVIATIONS

Arab	someone wandering, unsettled
ARP	Air Raid Precautions
ATS	Auxiliary Territorial Service
bass bag	flat plaited bag
batchy	dotty
Bemax	vitamin supplement
book(s)	usually refers to ration book(s)
British Restaurant	cafeteria-style, non-profit restaurant, run mainly by volunteers
Canteen	operated by the WVS in Barrow
chara	charabanc – a large open bus, often used for sightseeing
clippies	women bus conductors
cob	a round loaf of bread; or a (baked apple) dumpling
dodged (up)	ingeniously improvised
doll-eyed	foolish, tasteless
dollies	stuffed dolls made from scraps of fabric; usually sold or raffled for charity
Fair Isle	a multi-coloured geometric design for knitting
Glaxo	a powdered milk product for babies
Inner Wheel	women's auxiliary of the Rotary Club
ITMA	*It's That Man Again* – a very popular comedy programme starring Tommy Handley

jerry (built)	insubstantial, of inferior materials
Judith Paris	a central character in Hugh Walpole's 'Herries Chronicle'
Mail	*North Western Daily Mail*
NAAFI	Navy, Army and Air Force Institutes – canteens and recreational facilities for the armed forces
pack	wrapping part of a body in a sheet
parkin	a kind of gingerbread or cake made with oatmeal and treacle
pie	a heap (of potatoes) covered with earth and/or straw for protection
points	credits used to buy controlled goods
put up wages	prepare employees' wage packets
rack rent	excessive or extortionate rent
Rawlinson	family name of Nella's mother; Nella recalled the family as the 'proud Rawlinsons'
Social and Moral Welfare	intended, according to the *Furness and District Yearbook for 1939*, 'to protect the tempted and restore the fallen' (p. 110)
soul case	the body, especially under stress
spiv	someone shady, unscrupulous
WAAF	Women's Auxiliary Air Force
wee man	fairy, spirit
whitening	chalk
WVS	Women's Voluntary Services

MONEY AND ITS VALUE

In the later 1940s, British currency was calculated in the following manner:

  12 pence = 1 shilling
  20 shillings = £1

One shilling was written as 'is', a penny as 'id'. A farthing
was a quarter of a penny. A guinea ('ign') was worth 21 shillings.
A sum of, say, three pounds and ten shillings was usually written
at that time as £3–10–0; this amount is presented in this book
as £3 10s.

Efforts to propose rough modern equivalents seem pointless.
Since the 1940s were years of widespread rationing, the price
of an item was sometimes less important than its availability.
Moreover, household economies were for most people simpler
and more spartan than they would become a few decades later.
Material expectations were generally modest, some produce was
home-generated, borrowing and bartering were often an alter-
native to buying, and recycling was customary. Nella was very
price-conscious, and she is constantly reporting the prices of
items in shops and elsewhere. One reference point worth keeping
in mind is the weekly wage: most full-time male wage-workers in
Barrow immediately after the war were probably earning between
£4 and £10 a week. Men were almost always paid considerably
more than women. In 1947 Nella was paying her cleaning lady
1s 6d an hour, plus a hot lunch; and in 1948 an older man who
was working for her as a gardener charged 'only' 2s an hour. Will
supported his parents with £2 10s every week from his joinery
business.

CHRONOLOGY

Detailed portraits of life in post-war Britain are presented in two highly informative books: David Kynaston, *Austerity Britain 1945–51* (London: Bloomsbury, 2007) and Ina Zweiniger-Bargielowska, *Austerity in Britain: Rationing, Controls, and Consumption 1939–1955* (Oxford: Oxford University Press, 2000). Andrew Marr, *A History of Modern Britain* (London: Macmillan, 2007), Part One, surveys the period admirably.

1945

July	General Election: Labour wins a landslide majority. Clément Attlee is Prime Minister, Winston Churchill Leader of the Opposition.
August	Atomic bombs dropped on Hiroshima and Nagasaki (6th and 9th). Japan surrenders to the Allies.
	Government announces a comprehensive programme of social reform.
	United States terminates Lend-Lease aid to Britain.
October	United Nations, to be headquartered in New York, formally comes into existence.
	Widespread dockers' strikes.
November	Labour makes major gains in municipal elections.
	Beginning of the Nuremberg Trials.
December	United States agrees to a loan of $3.75 billion to Britain.

1946

February	Bank of England nationalised.
March	Churchill warns of an 'iron curtain' in Europe.
June	Bread rationing announced.
	Television licences introduced.
July	Coal industry nationalised.
	US atomic bomb tests in the Marshall Islands.
	Zionist terrorist attack in Jerusalem kills ninety-one people.
August	National Insurance Act takes effect.
	Squatters throughout the country begin to occupy empty military camps.
	Civil aviation nationalised.
December	Beginning of serious coal shortages.

1947

January	Severe winter weather begins.
February	Significant reductions in supplies of electricity.
March	Truman Doctrine announced, to help Greece and Turkey resist Communism.
April	Britain refers the question of partitioning Palestine to the United Nations.
	School leaving age raised to fifteen.
June	European Recovery Program (the Marshall Plan) announced.
	A drain of US dollars from Britain begins.
August	Independence of India and Pakistan.
	Government announces a new austerity plan.
	Town and Country Planning Act.

Britain's first atomic reactor becomes operational.

November Conservative gains in municipal elections.

Marriage of Princess Elizabeth to Philip Mountbatten.

1948

January	Nationalisation of railways in force.
February	Communist takeover in Czechoslovakia.
April	Electricity industry nationalised.
	House of Commons votes to suspend the death penalty.
May	Declaration of Israel as an independent state.
June	Berlin blockade begins.
	End of bread rationing.
July	National Health Service inaugurated.
	Gas industry nationalised.
November	Harry Truman re-elected President of the United States.
	Prince Charles born.

EDITING NELLA LAST'S DIARY

Nella Last's handwriting is in some respects eccentric, and even after one gets used to the peculiarities of her ways of forming letters, from time to time individual words emerge that would challenge almost any reader. In some cases we have examined a word at least a dozen times before getting it right (we think). We believe that we have eventually solved almost all problems of legibility, but it may be that a few misreadings remain (we hope they are rare). We also exercised judgement in deciding what to insert in the diary in the way of editorial additions. These are mainly in two forms: brief italicised phrases in square brackets placed in the text of the diary; and occasional footnotes designed to identify or explain something that Nella wrote about.

We are responsible for several other interventions, of which the following are the most important. (1) Since Nella did not use paragraphs, wherever they now exist they are our creations. (2) Her punctuation was casual – this is not uncommon in diaries – whimsical, even bizarre at times. We have routinely re-punctuated her writing to make it as clear and smooth-flowing as possible. (3) Obvious errors – she almost certainly wrote in haste, and usually at night – have been silently corrected. These include misspellings (for example, she spelt 'even' as 'evan'), and phrases that lack a necessary word, such as a preposition, article or conjunction. (4) Occasionally an additional word or two is needed to convey the meaning of a sentence. In these cases we have silently supplied a suitable candidate. (5) We have standardised the usage of particular words in order to ensure, for example, that a word is always spelt the same, or that it is consistently capitalised or not

awhile or her return from the students and he increased and
his never bountiful — she is always thinking he will be going
nearer any time now. I got two new paper covered
books from the Library today — one called "The Way" by
J M Hartley — & the other "Playing to the Gods" by John Owen
novel. I chose them — primed or chose — he — because the
cause of their clean new-ness in their paper of a clear new —
they both looks readable.

Sunday. Nov 4

Last night I was kept awake by fire winds going
off as if these children who had been lucky enough
to get any had not the patience to wait till tuesday
day. I'd my mind next & before I had my bath &
slipped down in my dressing gown & popped a little
dish I'd prepared last night in the oven & put my soup
on to heat on a low heat. I'd sausage in a flan
dish & stewed apples & made apple sauce & put it in
the sausage & added a layer of mashed potatoes & it
made a very tasty of lunch. It was turned savory
with my cooking my meat but & added a little
thyme for flavour & extra goodness. We had a
cup of tea — pure of extra for a minute & & hastily
washed up — we were met by 1—45 expect it — but
such a lovely day & we planned to go to

capitalised, and that the prices of goods and services and other numerals are presented in a consistent form. (6) Nella was given to underlining words for emphasis and to putting a great many words and phrases in inverted commas. We have eliminated these practices except in cases where they are helpful or even essential to grasping her full meaning, such as when she is reporting words actually spoken by others. (7) Three dots are used to indicate omissions in a selection *other than* those omissions made before a selection starts and after it concludes. Omissions at the start and at the end of what she wrote on a given day are more the norm than the exception, for her first and last sentences are often less interesting than what comes in between. Many entire days of her writing – and she wrote almost every day during these years – have been omitted altogether.

This might seem like a rather long list of editorial interventions. The need to make them stems in part from the fact that Nella had no reason to think that she should edit her own work, to polish it or perhaps even to re-read what she had written. So her writing, while rich and robust, tends to be raw. The photograph opposite shows a page from her handwritten diary and gives a sense of the decisions that any editors would routinely have to make in converting her diary into pages suitable for a book.

MASS OBSERVATION

Mass Observation, the organisation for which Nella Last wrote her diary, was set up in 1937. It was created to meet a perceived need, which, in the eyes of its founders, was to overcome Britons' ignorance about themselves in their everyday lives. MO aimed to lay the foundations for a social anthropology of contemporary Britain. Given that so many basic facts of social life were then unknown – opinion polling was in its infancy, social surveys and field studies had just begun (with a few exceptions, such as those of Charles Booth in the late nineteenth century) – how, it was asked, could the nation's citizens adequately understand themselves? This ignorance was thought to be especially pronounced with regard to the beliefs and behaviour of the majority of Britons: that is, those who lacked social prominence, and who had little political or intellectual influence.

It was vital, according to MO's founders, to focus on routines, norms, customs and commonalities. The goal was to help bring about a 'science of ourselves', rooted in closely observed facts, methodically and laboriously collected. And in order to pursue this science of society, MO recruited hundreds of volunteer 'Observers', who were asked to describe, to question, to record sights and sounds and sometimes to count. Their efforts at observing were likened to those of an anthropologist working in the field.

Volunteers were crucial to MO. Without them it would not have been possible to acquire the facts on which a proper social science would have to be based. And it was accepted by MO's leaders that these Observers would not only be data-collectors; they could also function as 'subjective cameras' that captured their own experiences, feelings and attitudes, and circumstances of living. This acceptance of the legitimacy of subjectivity in social observation was a major reason why diary-keeping came to be promoted as a promising vehicle of both social and self-observation. A diary was another way of recording; and it was a way that inevitably tapped into the individuality and inner life of one personality. MO's pursuit of a better science, then, facilitated the production of a particularly personal form of writing; and from late August 1939, with another great war imminent, many people responded to MO's invitation to keep a diary and post their writing every week or fortnight to MO's headquarters. Nella Last was one of the dozens – eventually hundreds – who responded to this initiative. She was, though, one of the few who wrote regularly throughout the war, one of the few who wrote at length, and one of the very few who continued to write regularly after 1945. (James Hinton has written a summary of her life for the *Oxford Dictionary of National Biography* (2004), vol. 32, pp. 606–7.)

These diaries – some 480 of them – have been held since the 1970s in the Mass Observation Archive at the University of Sussex. Numerous books have drawn upon these riches. Sandra Koa Wing (ed.), *A People's History of the Second World War, By the writers of Mass Observation* (London: Profile Books, 2008) is an excellent anthology of extracts from MO's wartime diarists. Dorothy Sheridan's edited volume, *Wartime Women: An Anthology of Women's Wartime Writing for Mass Observation* (London: Heinemann, 1990), includes extracts from numerous diaries. Simon Garfield has edited three collections drawn from the MO Archive, each published by Ebury Press: *Our Hidden Lives: The Everyday Diaries of a Forgotten Britain 1945–1948* (2004); *We Are at War: The Diaries of Five Ordinary People in Extraordinary Times* (2005);

and *Private Battles: How the War Almost Defeated Us – Our Intimate Diaries* (2007).

Nella Last's wartime MO diary was the first to appear on its own as a book, in 1981, edited by Richard Broad and Suzie Fleming. (The 2006 edition published by Profile Books includes photographs, a new preface, and an afterword by Clifford Last.) A little later Dorothy Sheridan edited *Among You Taking Notes …: The Wartime Diary of Naomi Mitchison 1939–1945* (London: Victor Gollancz, 1985). Several other MO diarists have now been published in volumes of their own. These include *Wartime Norfolk: The Diary of Rachel Dhonau 1941–1942*, edited by Robert Malcolmson and Peter Searby (Norfolk Record Society, 2004); *Love and War in London: A Woman's Diary 1939–1942*, by Olivia Cockett, edited by Robert Malcolmson (Waterloo, Ontario: Wilfred Laurier University Press, 2005; 2nd edn, Stroud, Gloucestershire: The History Press, 2008); *A Woman In Wartime London: The Diary of Kathleen Tipper 1941–1945*, edited by Patricia and Robert Malcolmson (London Record Society, 2006); and *A Soldier in Bedfordshire 1941–1942: The Diary of Private Denis Argent, Royal Engineers*, edited by Patricia and Robert Malcolmson (Bedfordshire Historical Record Society, forthcoming 2009).

The collection is open to the public and visited by people from all over the world. In 2005 it was given Designated Status as one of the UK's Outstanding Collections by the Museums, Libraries and Archives Council. Much helpful information, including details of the Friends scheme that finances the Archive, which is a charitable trust, is available on its website: www.massobs.org.uk.

ACKNOWLEDGEMENTS

Several people who knew Nella Last or were connected with her in some way have given us valuable help in preparing this edition. We met and spent several hours with two of her grandsons, Peter Last and Jerry Last, the former in Cornwall, the latter in Bath, each of whom helped us better to understand the Lasts' family history. Peter also kindly allowed us to borrow a family photograph album from the 1940s and 1950s. Nella's third grandson, Christopher Last, who had spent some time with Cliff Last, replied informatively by mail to our enquiries. We are grateful to all three brothers for their assistance and support. During our visit to Barrow-in-Furness in September 2007 we took the liberty of knocking on the door of 9 Ilkley Road (without prior notice) and were warmly received by its present owners, John and Margaret Williams – they acquired the house from the Lasts in the late 1960s – who showed us around the property and led us to the two daughters of the Lasts' next-door neighbours in the 1940s, the Atkinsons. Norah (Atkinson) Redhead still lives in Barrow, her sister Margaret (Atkinson) Procter in Pickering, Yorkshire. We met them separately and both were exceptionally generous in giving us information and opinion, and in lending us photos from the mid 1940s. It is a pleasure to acknowledge the assistance they graciously provided.

A number of other people helped in various ways, notably Richard Broad, Jocelyn Fisher, James Hinton, David McGinn, Peter Searby, Aidan Jones of the Local Studies Library in Barrow and Camilla Hornby of Curtis Brown. Caroline Pretty, our copyeditor, offered sound advice and proposed numerous refinements to the text. We depended on Sue DeMille and Janice Wilson of Cobourg Digital Imaging & Printing for technical support and services at various times.

The Mass Observation Archive at the University of Sussex, where the original of Nella's diary can be read, is held in high esteem by researchers, and for good reason. Its head, Dorothy Sheridan, who has herself written widely about the MO's sources and the work of its Observers, is impressively knowledgeable and efficient and always helpful, and both of us have benefited from her advice on numerous occasions during the past decade. It was she who suggested our names to Profile Books as possible editors of Nella Last's post-war diary, and we are appreciative of this recommendation. Dorothy's leadership of the MO Archive is supported by the work of an excellent staff, and we are glad to be able to acknowledge the help given by Fiona Courage, Mell Davies, Jessica Scantlebury, Karen Watson and Adam Harwood.

Our final debt is the most substantial. Since early 2007 we have been in regular contact with our editor at Profile Books, Daniel Crewe, and these exchanges of opinion and information have had a major impact on the character of this book. Daniel posed sound questions, raised reasonable doubts, detected problems that we had not noticed, offered many constructive suggestions and was excellent both in sensing the overall shape of the book and in spotting details that needed our attention. As a result of his contributions, this book is much better than it would otherwise have been. We are very happy to have been associated with him in bringing to light more of the writing of a remarkable woman.

Cobourg, Ontario
June 2008